Teaching
Handicapped Children
Easily

Teaching Handicapped Children Easily

A Manual for the Average Classroom Teacher Without Specialized Training

By

HERBERT NEFF, M.A.

Associate Professor of Education
Director of Special Education
Tennessee Wesleyan College
Athens, Tennessee

and

JUDITH PILCH, M.Ed.

Special Education Specialist
Reservation Elementary School
Cherokee, North Carolina

CHARLES C THOMAS • PUBLISHER
Springfield • Illinois • U.S.A.

Published and Distributed Throughout the World by

CHARLES C THOMAS ● PUBLISHER

Bannerstone House

301-327 East Lawrence Avenue, Springfield, Illinois, U.S.A.

With THOMAS BOOKS *careful attention is given to all details of
manufacturing and design. It is the Publisher's desire to present books that are
satisfactory as to their physical qualities and artistic possibilities and
appropriate for their particular use.* THOMAS BOOKS *will be true to those
laws of quality that assure a good name and good will.*

Printed in the United States of America
R-1

Library of Congress Cataloging in Publication Data

Neff, Herbert B
  Teaching handicapped children easily.

  Bibliography: p.
  1. Exceptional children--Education.   I. Pilch,
Judith, joint author.   II. Title.
LC3965.N43   371.9   75-6989
ISBN 0-398-03439-7

PREFACE

THIS book is written primarily for the teacher or teacher trainee who has little or no formal professional training in teaching exceptional (sometimes called gifted and handicapped) children.

It has considerable value for parents of handicapped and gifted children in giving them not only some understanding of their children, but also some suggestions that can be used for helping their children at home. This would supplement what is being done in school. If nothing is being done in school, as is the case far too often, the parents' help would be of supreme value.

Every attempt has been made to write this book in an informal style with as little technical terminology and educational jargon as possible. It is written by teachers with long successful experience in teaching exceptional children and teaching teachers of exceptional children.

Teachers of exceptional children with mild and moderate handicaps will find this book extremely helpful. It is the contention of the authors that children with severe problems need the help of trained professionals.

But children with mild and moderate learning and behavior problems must usually be taught by the average, untrained classroom teacher, if they are taught at all, in a manner to meet their particular needs. There are not enough teachers trained for exceptional children; there are not enough classrooms even if there were enough trained teachers; and finally, and most significantly as far as the besieged taxpayer is concerned, school budgets and tax levies are already very large.

Exceptional children are more like the average child than different, and there is enough commonality among the various exceptional children to make it unnecessary to identify, label, and categorize the types of exceptionality. (Not all special educators will agree with this statement.) Use the checklist provided to determine the actual learning strengths and weaknesses of the children and then provide extra help for them in treating their weaknesses and using their strengths.

No *specific* methods or materials are suggested; each child would use what fits his own individual needs as indicated by teacher observation and use of the checklist. This will vary greatly from child to child. The teaching methods suggested in this book are therefore generalized. Intensive personal attention is then given by the teacher to the materials used regularly in the classroom at a level which challenges the child but with which he can succeed for the most part.

The commercial market place is flooded with expensive and attractive materials and gadgets, few if any of which work better than regular classroom materials adapted as suggested in this book to the individual exceptional child.

This handbook can help the average classroom teacher do easily what otherwise might not be done; whether by default of the local school system or whether by law, the teacher is required to teach children for whom she has little or no specialized training.

It is not the purpose of this book to argue a thesis, but merely to share methods of helping handicapped children. With these methods we have been remarkably and significantly successful. Older handicapped children who are considered by many special educators to be extremely difficult to remediate and who had been in special reading programs for years without gains in learning, *made in one month an average gain of 1.1 years in reading with our methods.*

Because we argue no hypothesis, we have not included in our bibliography every reference we used. We have included there only those which in our judgement were most important and typical. The curious scholar will be able to locate from the name and date of the reference the information he desires.

Herbert Neff
Judith Pilch

CONTENTS

Teaching
Handicapped Children
Easily

Chapter 1

INTRODUCTION

THOUSANDS of administrators and supervisors, more than a million teachers, and millions of exceptional children are drowning in mainstream. Slowly a flood has been building to engulf unprepared educators. Exceptional children (a term that implies a rarity that does not exist) have far too long been practically ignored, and now the dam has been dynamited open by court orders, federal governmental agencies, and public concern.

The Bureau of Education for the Handicapped of the Department of Health, Education and Welfare has set a goal of 85 percent of all exceptional children receiving special educational services by 1980. No attempt will be made directly in this book to support the need for such special education; the need has been established — implementation is the current problem.

Nearly every state (we know of only one at this writing that does not) requires that exceptional and handicapped children receive equal educational opportunities and, if necessary, special schooling and educational care. For years exceptional children have been neglected and made to fail by default because they were unable to keep up with average children. Few people seemed to care; or if they did care, they felt hopeless and helpless.

Here and there were states, isolated school systems, and teachers that provided special education, which meant literally anything from babysitting a class of mentally retarded children to a valid and sometimes successful attempt at true special education.

Now something meaningful and special has to be done; and if it is accomplished, it will be by the regular classroom teacher. She is unprepared, inundated, frightened and resentful, drowning with her children in mainstream.

Why?

Special education started on a small scale, but what there was was special. Special categories were established that labeled some children feebleminded or mentally retarded, blind or partially sighted, deaf or hard of hearing, emotionally disturbed, socially maladjusted, cerebral palsied, and physically handicapped.

Specialized methods and materials were designed to teach them. What was effective for one type of exceptionality was considered not applicable for other types of handicaps. Each category had its own special formula of methods and materials that would not function effectively for any other category of exceptionality.

Then a whole new set of problems was thrust upon the special education program called specific learning disabilities or minimally brain injured or perceptually handicapped or Strauss Syndrome children, and more recently just learning disabled children. There are numerous other terms also used for categorizing this new set of educationally handicapped children.

While the purpose was to identify more clearly and set apart a new homogeneous category of children that had puzzled teachers and special educators for a long time, the true effect served only to confuse and frustrate, for no more heterogeneous group of children with disparate learning problems could be imagined. While the best intentions were to set up a homogeneous group of special children, paradoxically a more complex and heterogeneous collection of children that were discovered could not be imagined. One of the most widely used diagnostic tests for learning disabled children stipulated twelve types of disabilities plus countless combinations!

There are also the culturally disadvantaged, socially deprived, or educationally handicapped, *ad infinitum* as far as labels go. Right now these and the learning disabled are the *in* children educationally. Federal funds are being poured out for demonstration projects and various "title" programs.

To further compound the issue, arguments are flying wide and far as to whether the socially disadvantaged should even be included among exceptional children, or whether they should be considered a part of the complex set of *specific* learning disabled. (A recent article in *Exceptional Children* [Sabatino, 1973] was devoted to a symposium on the conflicting viewpoints.)

But one thing is sure. All these children are being dumped into the already overloaded lap of the regular classroom teacher. There are many reasons for this move:

1. Recent research has established quite surely that special classes have not been as educationally effective as their proponents claim. Children in these special classes learn little if any better than those not so segregated. One cannot help but wonder whether this is due to the special classes or the fact that they were taught by teachers of whom less than 50 percent were trained — only patient and willing.

2. Labels, often mislabels, are neither desirable nor helpful and frequently stick with the children for life. Moreover, there are more children mislabeled than most people realize. It is not easy to distinguish between a mentally retarded child and a learning disabled child or a culturally disadvantaged one or a socially maladjusted "pain in the neck"; or even a gifted underachiever, or unmotivated average child.

3. There are not enough trained and qualified special education teachers to do what some say is needed. James Gallagher, a leading special education authority, estimating the present rate of training, increase in children population, and normal teacher attrition rate, states that it will take until some time in the year 2008 to staff all the special education classes we need if we retain the traditional system of special education.

4. There are not enough classrooms to house all the exceptional children whom we now recognize as such. There are far more than most educators realize who are undetected save for the fact they are now labeled as lazy, unmotivated, or worse.

5. Other benefits are claimed for the education of children in regular classes, such as better social adjustment, learning to live in the real world, learning from other children, better self-image, and emotional adjustment, to mention a few of the most obvious reasons.

6. Then there is the final clincher, at least in the minds of the belabored taxpayer, *money*. At the present time and in the forseeable future, it is economically unfeasible to provide special education in special education settings. What is to be done since it is mandatory to help every exceptional child? *If it is to be done at all, it must be done in the regular classroom*

by the regular teacher.

She doesn't know how. We know a great many teachers. This writer has been a teacher, a principal, and for many years a teacher of teachers. We talk and write to teachers from all over the country, and they are frightened, frustrated, and resentful. Administrators are just as confused and frustrated, and most of the exceptional children are right where they have always been, in the regular classroom. Consequently supervisors, teachers, and students are drowning in mainstream. But there is a way out.

Traditional special education has categorized exceptional children under these labels:

Slow Learners
Educable Mentally Retarded
Trainable Mentally Retarded
Emotionally Disturbed
Socially Maladjusted
Learning Disabled
Sight Handicapped
Hearing Handicapped
Culturally Disadvantaged
Gifted
Gifted Underachievers

Traditional special education has said, in addition, that each type had to be educated homogeneously in its own way. Each category learns differently; therefore, it is necessary to label them clearly and differently and provide special classes, teachers, methds, and materials.

Furthermore, identification is laborious, complicated, and not very reliable. *It is extremely difficult even after exhaustive tests to determine for sure* whether a child is mentally retarded, learning disabled, culturally disadvantaged, emotionally disturbed, a gifted underachiever, or just poorly taught. We know! We have been in a special demonstration project for two years testing hundreds of children using the best test instruments available and the best consultants obtainable; and when it was all said and done, no one could say for sure that we had identified what we thought we had identified. This is not unusual in any sense; valid identification is next to impossible. But, it is relatively simple and actually easy and far more reliable to be able to discover and say, for instance:

Johnny cannot recognize words.

Jane cannot sound out her letters phonetically.

Larry has not the ability to remember sounds sequentially.

Susie cannot add or subtract or carry numbers.

Jack cannot get along with other children.

Elsie pouts most of the time.

Jerry cannot sit still.

Timmy cannot tie his shoelaces.

Ray is distractible and cannot attend to what he is supposed to do.

These behaviors are seeable and hearable. Some call them objective behaviors, and they do not constitute a new idea. What we are suggesting is that one forget the exceptional child categories and concentrate on what the children can and cannot do. There is no confusion here. The teacher can see the problems and count them. Why not start special education with a list of the things a child can or cannot do? A checklist will be provided (Chap. 5) that any teacher can use. Why does it make no difference whether a child is mentally retarded or learning disabled or a gifted underachiever? The simple reason is that within any labeled homogeneous category of exceptionality one will find as many or more individual differences as there are in the heterogeneous group of children.

If any therapy or remediation is to be accomplished, it must be done individually if it is to be done at all. This is true even for those so-called *normal* children, whoever they are. Why worry about what kind of special child you have to teach? Instead, work with his weaknesses and/or strengths — teach him to do what he needs to do in order to learn. Behavior modification strategy has taught us a great deal about this, and it works frighteningly well.

Also, teachers have long discovered that materials that have been prepared for, let us say, the mentally retarded work effectively for the learning disabled, and vice versa. The idea of special materials for a special child only has been exploded for all time. What works for one type of child works for other types of exceptionality when properly used. The one possible exception is the gifted, but he can be easily helped to help himself develop his great ability to the fullest. But he does need help; he cannot help himself to adequately develop his unusual abilities.

Now you ask, "How can I teach each child as an individual?" Our experience has shown that only a few minutes per day, or a few minutes per day three days a week, work wonders. Concrete, down-to-earth methods are suggested in later chapters that can make special education easy for you.

Nothing we have said so far or anything we will say later removes the need for really special classes or special education in the traditional sense by trained specialists for the severely handicapped children. The teacher can help the moderates and milds in her regular classroom far easier than she imagines, but the severely handicapped need the assistance of specialists who work with those the teacher cannot help in the time and space she has.

This book will not be concerned with the severely handicapped children, only with those whose learning and behavior problems are mild to moderate and who can easily and reasonably be helped in the regular classroom.

Nor will we be concerned with the entire set of categories of exceptional children such as those with orthopedic handicaps, sight and/or hearing difficulties, or speech problems. Only the more common general or specific learning disabilities will be considered.

To make special education easy for the regular classroom teacher, she starts with the student who is not learning as she thinks he should be learning. She then determines with the help of a checklist just exactly what it is he should be learning (doing). The teacher is her own diagnostician and her own learning therapeutician. With the help of this book she can accomplish these objectives easily.

Every effort has been made to keep the book from becoming threateningly technical, yet at the same time it must be authentic, and above all practical.

No single chapter, or several chapters, alone will function to make special education easy. Each chapter plays an essential part and should neither be taken alone nor skipped. This book was written to be used as a whole.

For instance, Chapter 6 describes the *techniques* used to teach exceptional children, and while they may function to some extent when pulled out of the context of the whole manual, they will not work nearly as effectively without some real consideration and practice of the concepts discussed in the other chapters.

JUST WHAT ARE THE PROBLEMS?

Labeling and Categorizing

The Child Who Wasn't Retarded*

WE knew that our son, Ray, was having difficulty in school, but we didn't understand the serious nature of his problem. We were totally unprepared for the note he brought home from his teacher. Simple and to the point, the note said that Ray was mentally retarded.

We couldn't believe it at first. The boy had shown no behavior to us to indicate that he had any mental deficiency. At the time, my wife and I were both teaching in a public school, and Ray didn't act at home like the children we knew who were retarded.

We knew Ray was unhappy in school, but we didn't know why. We didn't know, either, how he managed to "adapt" to his frustrations. But we were determined to find out. We didn't realize, however, that it would take us five years to do so.

We discovered, finally, that the feelings and frustrations experienced by Ray were similar to those suffered by the more than five million children in America who have learning disorders of one kind or another. Ray's methods of adapting, however, turned out to be unique.

That he was able to salvage at all some measure of self-respect and emotional stability was due, probably, to our support and belief in him, as well as to his own imaginative, creative, and sometimes humorous methods of coping with what might have been an experience of defeat for another child.

We learned, as we began to look into Ray's problem, that our son protected himself from teachers who labeled him retarded

---

*Reprinted from Herbert Neff, "The Child Who Wasn't Retarded," *PTA Magazine,* 67:20 (May, 1973) with permission from the publisher. The article won "The Distinguished Achievement Award" of the Educational Press Association of America 1974 All America Awards Program.

and students who jeered his apparent stupidity by constructing an imaginary world of his own. Whenever he was unable to perform as he was expected to, he slipped into that world to rest. While there, he sometimes imagined himself to be a midget secret agent, at other times a train locomotive.

Both roles helped him withstand the feelings of frustration and failure that the demands of school created in him. As a train — although no one was aware that he was a train — he knew that he should not be expected to spell, read, write, or do arithmetic.

Ray later explained the attitude he had as a train toward the schoolwork he found impossible: Ordinary arithmetic is one of a train's weakest subjects. Trains aren't skilled in addition or subtraction, multiplication or division. Trains are interested in things like schedules, times for departures and arrivals, so that is what Ray did with his arithmetic — he computed train schedules. His teacher didn't understand that the figures weren't wrong, just different.

And, of course, secret agents don't write the way normal people do. They write in codes so spies can't read their messages. It was unfortunate, of course, that Ray's teacher couldn't understand his codes any more than his train schedules, but that could not be helped.

Because Ray understood, in his own way, that he should not have to do the same things that ordinary children do — such as perform at the blackboard — he wasn't utterly defeated by the derision he received for his inability to do so.

He remembers now that he wanted to learn, but that no matter how hard he tried he just couldn't. He felt, of course, the emotional pains of failure: In fact, he was hurt a great deal by teachers who scolded him and children who laughed at his shortcomings. His imagination couldn't shield him entirely from the cruelty that reality had brought into his life.

How Ray made it through first grade without major problems being brought to our attention is difficult to understand. But he made it.

It wasn't until he began second grade that we became desperately aware that Ray had a severe learning problem. He couldn't read or write. He could do arithmetic, though, if it didn't depend on reading, and he found science difficult only when reading or writing was involved. Soon, however, he fell behind in these subjects, too.

Ray's second-grade teacher sent the note home about Ray's being mentally retarded and suggested that the school psychologist examine him. The psychologist did, and his diagnosis confirmed part of our own conviction that Ray was not mentally deficient. In fact, the examination disclosed that he was quite bright.

In the psychologist's opinion, Ray's problem developed out of a conflict created by the two different reading methods to which he had been subjected. His first-grade teacher did not depart from the phonics system. His second-grade teacher, however, had abandoned phonics and was teaching reading by a word-recognition method.

The diagnosis made sense to us, and since the psychologist and the teacher both recommended that we enroll our son in a reading clinic, we did so. Ray didn't seem to mind missing school.

Over a period of time, however, we found that any improvement in Ray was minimal. The director of the clinic told us that he had made little progress in reading. She suggested that we take him to a psychiatrist. Perhaps, she said, Ray had emotional problems that blocked his ability to read.

We took Ray to the psychiatrist. His diagnosis: a few little problems, but nothing that explained the difficulty he had learning. Perhaps Ray was socially maladjusted, the psychiatrist said. "Take him to the Akron Child Study Center."

Off we went, Ray, my wife, and I, to the Akron Center. There all three of us were studied. Again, the diagnosis stated that no problem could be found to explain the learning disability. "Take him to a neurologist," the center advised.

The neurologist found Ray's coordination laterality and neurological responses all within normal limits.

We were now becoming desperate. How could it be that an intelligent child with no discoverable disorder was unable to learn?

About that time I became associated with Kent State University as a research fellow in special education. One day, quite by chance, I discussed Ray's problem with Dr. Walter Barbe, then head of our department.

He said that the University Child Study Center might be able to help, since the specialists there approached problems like

Ray's from an educational rather than a physiological point of view. He arranged an interview with Dr. Stanley Krippner, the center's director at the time.

Dr. Krippner needed one short session with Ray to discover his problem: Ray was a perceptually handicapped child whose difficulty probably was caused by a minimal brain insult or dysfunction. He had a specific learning disability.

The U. S. Department of Health, Education, and Welfare's Bureau of Education for the Handicapped describes such children as having:

A disorder in one or more of the basic psychological processes involved in understanding or in using language, spoken or written, which disorder may manifest itself in imperfect ability to listen, think, speak, read, write, spell, or do mathematical calculations. Such disorders include such conditions as perceptual handicaps, brain injury, minimal brain dysfunction, dyslexia, and developmental aphasia. Such terms do not include children who have learning problems which are primarily the result of visual, hearing, or motor handicaps, or mental retardation, or emotional disturbance, or of environmental disadvantage.

In other words, if a child possesses average or above intelligence, and can see and hear adequately, but does not (cannot) learn, he is probably handicapped by a learning disability.

No one knows exactly what causes learning disabilities. In some cases, minimal brain injury is discovered. In many other cases, no injury to the brain or central nervous system can be detected. It's hypothesized, however, that in cases like these there is always some minimal brain injury of dysfunction of the central nervous system.

In all cases, though, there are perceptual problems: These affect the visual, aural, tactile, and/or kinesthetic ability to synthesize various stimuli into a meaningful whole.

Most frequently, children with learning disabilities cannot read, or they read poorly. In other cases, they do not understand what they hear. In fewer cases, they misinterpret or are confused by what they touch. Sometimes their coordination is very poor. In rare cases all sensory perception is distorted and confused.

Because of a general lack of understanding of learning disabilities, many learning disabled children are wrongly labeled mentally retarded (they score poorly on group intelligence tests), lazy, disinterested, or as nonmotivated underachievers. They have a history of failure in school, and usually they develop a poor self-image because they are made to feel worthless and dumb. Such destructive ego development often hinders them for life.

Some learning disabled children require the most sophisticated methods of identification and diagnosis before the precise nature of their disability can be determined. None should be classified, however, without being tested by professionals.

Many learning disabled children exhibit to the knowledgeable parent or teacher a syndrome of symptoms that point to their learning problem. One such symptom, hyperactivity, has attracted a great deal of publicity.

Some hyperactive children move constantly, using the large muscles to run and jump endlessly. Others are always active with finer movements, especially of the hands, which they use, for example, to manipulate buttons until they fall off or to make small rents in clothing until the tears are no longer small. Any object they begin to handle they might continue to handle until it breaks or wears out.

One must be careful to avoid false, amateur diagnoses: All healthy children are active; but the hyperactive, learning disabled child is excessively and compulsively superactive. He is always on the move.

Many of these children are also distracted by visual or aural stimuli that the average child screens out. Even though the learning disabled child has trouble making sense out of letters and words, he often pays too much attention to other sights and sounds.

And, although he may forget things that he should remember, he sometimes remembers other things too well and too long. We call this phenomenon "perseveration." Everyone perseverates at times by humming or repeating a tune, phrase, or word without meaning to do so. The handicapped child does it much more often than the normal child.

There are advantages and disadvantages in perseveration for the disabled child. If he hears, sees, says, or learns something correctly the first time, the "right way" might stick with him almost forever. On the other hand, if he does something incorrectly the first time, the wrong way might be "his way" forever, instead.

Another symptom is the "catastrophic reaction." Since the learning disabled child usually has a low frustration tolerance, he might have what appears to be a temper tantrum. However, very little real emotion might be involved, and the attack might pass almost as quickly as it started. It might seem as though the child had an electrical storm strike in his mind, and the mental equivalent of that might very well have struck.

Impulsiveness, word-reversals, mirror-writing, and figure-ground confusion are other symptoms of a possible learning disability. But it might happen that the learning disabled child exhibits none of these: He just doesn't learn as he should, and he demonstrates one or more different perceptual problems.

No label should be applied to a child, or diagnosis made, on the basis of the symptoms discussed here. Careful testing by a trained professional psychologist or educator is a *must* before one can say with certainty that a child has a specific learning disability.

Ray spent two summer sessions at the Kent Center in intensive prescriptive training to develop his perceptual abilities. After the first summer he showed definite improvement in learning. The next year, in seventh grade, he made the honor roll. He had come quite a distance since the day that note came home from the teacher.

It took Ray a little longer than the average student to graduate from college, but he did, with above-average grades. He is in graduate school now, studying ecology as the first step to a degree in environmental law.

Some residual problems persist: Ray's reading speed is below average; he is still a poor writer and speller; and when confronted with a mass of stimuli (such as words from a rapid lecturer or a maze of textual information), he tends to become confused. However, when he can break the stimuli down into small steps, and take them one at a time, his ability to learn is astonishing.

My wife and I and Ray have been very fortunate. Only a few of the estimated five to six million learning disabled children in American schools are able to obtain the kind of help that we were able to find for Ray.

No one knows exactly how many learning disabled children

sit undiagnosed in our classrooms. The U. S. Bureau of Education for the Handicapped estimates a maximum of 3 percent. The Association for Children with Learning Disabilities (2200 Brownsville Road, Pittsburgh, Pennsylvania 15210) triples that figure in estimating a minimum number.

Drs. James and Joan McCarthy, of the University of Wisconsin, are authorities in the field of learning disabilities. They estimate that 15 to 20 percent of all children are learning disabled. On the basis of my own observation — and I have had reason to be observant — I conservatively estimate the figure to be about 10 percent.

At any rate there are several million learning disabled children in our schools, and only a few of them are recognized for what they are and receive even nominal help. The sad thing is that a number of these children, with proper diagnosis and treatment, might eventually enjoy the kind of progress that our son has made.

Our experience with Ray began about twelve years ago. Perhaps you think that our schools have changed, that they are different now, quick to discover and help the learning disabled child. I wish I could report this to be so. But the truth is that, today, no more than a half million of the millions of learning disabled children in America are receiving even nominal help.

I personally know of hundreds of children with learning disabilities in our local schools. They need special help, but are not receiving it for lack of trained teachers and knowledgeable school personnel. Unfortunately, most of them will never be helped.

Part of this lack is caused by other lacks: Relatively few teacher-training institutions prepare teachers to handle learning disabled children. And few parents can afford to send their learning disabled child to a private school designed to meet his special needs.

Today, most learning disabled children live in our society undiscovered and frustrated. They're still being mislabeled — still being called "retarded," "disinterested," "unmotivated," or "lazy." They're still said to be "learning far below their ability level." Sometimes they're called "troublemakers," "mischief-makers," and worse.

True, we haven't found answers for all the questions we have about learning disabled children. But we do know enough now to identify them and diagnose their problems, and we could help most of them if more parents and school personnel understood these children and their special needs.

Case Not Unusual

Millions of learning handicapped children are being labeled and placed in out-of-the-way educational closets to daydream their school hours away and to learn to hate themselves and school.

Children with learning disabilities can be helped. Ray could have been helped years sooner than he was if he had not been carelessly labeled retarded, another way of saying hopeless, and treated as if he were something less than what was wanted in school.

True, exceptional children are difficult to identify and diagnose, and there are not enough specialists to treat them even if they are identified and diagnosed. Labeling may not be all bad if it is carefully and accurately done *and if* proper treatment is then prescribed. But most exceptional children can be taught by the regular classroom teacher.

Accurate Labeling Is Difficult

The difficulty of accurate labeling is part of the problem. As we will propose shortly, it is not even necessary unless the child is severely handicapped. Most children do not need identification as exceptional children of one category or another. What really matters for the mild and moderately handicapped (and why not throw *that* label out, too?) is the recognition that the child is not learning certain behaviors, knowledge, and/or skills.

Without going into great detail, let us illustrate the difficulty of diagnosis. One of the latest and broadest categories of handicaps or exceptionality in school is what has come to be usually called (there are literally dozens of other labels, too) specific learning disabilities, thought to be caused by some malfunction of some part of the central nervous system.

We have worked with hundreds of these children (or those who were thought to be). We and our teachers administered a dozen or more of the best diagnostic tests available. One, the Illinois Test of Psycholinguistic Abilities (ITPA), has twelve subtests and is probably as thorough as one can devise a test to be. After carefully considering all of the test evidence and calling in several outstanding consultants, we still were not at all certain what kind of special-need children we had except for 2 or 3 percent who were quite severely handicapped.

In spite of the diagnostic precision which some special education authorities claim, it is extremely difficult to distinguish between mental retardation, cultural or educational deprivation, gifted underachievement, emotional disturbances, lack of motivation and interest, or just simply not having learned how to learn. The only conclusion of which one can be sure is that the child is not learning within reasonable expectations.

We finally disregarded these specialized test results and worked with the children individually, observing carefully *what* they could do as well as *how* they did it. In other words we devised the checklist found in Chapter 5 of this manual.

Now We Had Something Concrete to Work With

It is one thing to be able to say that Johnny has a visual reception problem or that he just cannot read, but it is quite another matter to know that Johnny cannot tell a "p" from a "g" or a "d" from a "b." This or any other concrete problem we can work with. Here is something specific to get one's hands on.

What difference, really, does it make whether Johnny is a learning disabled child or mentally retarded or just a poorly taught child? The specific learning problem remains the same, and the remedial approaches, as we will show later, are relatively easy and similar.

How Many Exceptional Children Are There?

No one really knows.

The term *exceptionality* implies a rarity that does not exist. By reading the reference literature suggested in our Bibliography, in our Suggested Reading list or in other special education writings, one will find figures that range from about 10 percent of the approximately 51,000,000 school age children to 70 percent. How does one account for such a wide range of numbers? This is how:

1. *Purely by definition.* Take mental retardation for instance. If one defines as retarded those below one standard deviation from the mean (those below 85 IQ), we come up with about 16 percent; but if we decide to include only those two standard deviations below the mean (those below 70 IQ), we come up with less than 3 percent. Quite a difference!

   The same holds for giftedness. Where do we start, or how do we define giftedness? Is cultural deprivation based on the family income or the color of one's skin or the kind of housing one lives in in the poorest part of town?

2. *By economics.* When special educators were trying to obtain federal grants for research and demonstration projects for children with specific learning disabilities, they quoted figures of 10 to 15 percent. Officials of the Bureau of the Handicapped of HEW said, "We cannot afford that many. Get your figures down to less than 3 percent and perhaps we can talk business."

   They did by setting severity limits or the degree of variability on the diagnostic tests used. Dr. Samuel Kirk, an outstanding authority in special education once said, "Tell us how many you want and can afford and we will find them by definition and degree of severity."

3. *By performance.* Ask any teacher how many children she has that are not learning as she thinks they should, and she will quote a figure that ranges anywhere from 10 percent to the 70 percent we mentioned previously. Ask her why they do not perform, and she will no doubt explain that they are nonmotivated, socially disadvantaged, emotionally disturbed, mentally retarded, or learning disabled. In other words, exceptional in some manner.

4. *By estimation.* By authorities in special education. Our own estimate, as authentic as anyone's, would place the figure somewhere near 50 percent. Let us carefully estimate that 10 percent of school age children are mentally retarded, another 10 percent are gifted. We have good reason to believe that 15

to 20 percent are specifically learning disabled. Add about 6 percent with speech problems and 1 or 2 percent with sight and hearing problems.

The American Psychiatric Association estimates that 10 percent are emotionally disturbed, and at least 10 percent are socially disadvantaged. This adds up to 68 percent. Since some children have two or more handicaps we could cut this to our 50 percent easily.

If we add several million normal children who are not profiting from their school experience, our figures are even more conservative if we define by the generally accepted definition as exceptional any child who is not profiting as he could and should from his school experience.

In any event there are far more special-need children in school than most people believe. So when you say to average teachers, "You must do something to help them," they are frightened, confused, and frustrated. Instinctively they know their task is enormous for this and several other reasons.

Most Teachers Are Not Trained
to Teach Exceptional Children

State boards of education have specified extensive training for special education that includes at least eighteen quarter hours of specialized study. Teacher training institutions have done the same thing. Very few, we know of only one, require a course in exceptionality as a part of the teacher training program.

Therefore, the average teacher feels untrained, inadequate, frustrated. She therefore does little, all the while wanting to do something worthwhile to help. She feels concerned and anxious, not only about her lack of training or the numbers of nonlearning children, but about the conditions necessary for learning to take place.

Learning Takes Place If and Only If

1. *The students have the ability to learn what is presented to them for learning.* Most classrooms contain students with a

wide range of abilities. The average teacher finds various degrees of mental retardation, an assortment of average students, and a complexity of bright and gifted children. In addition, some of these children have specific learning disabilities, others are culturally disadvantaged, some are emotionally disturbed and socially maladjusted. Still others have the physical handicaps of poor hearing or seeing, medical problems, and central nervous system disorders.

To assume that these children can learn the same things, or even approximating the same, is like assuming that every bottle made will hold the same amount of any selected material. If the teacher attempts to teach the average child as she was trained to do, the low ability child will soon be frustrated, failing, and lost. The bright child will become bored and probably indolent. The handicapped children will become impeded. Even some of the average children will not be able to learn everything expected.

2. *The children learn at the rate the subject matter is presented.* While the rate of learning depends to some degree upon ability, this is not always the case. Some mentally retarded children can learn some things at a rapid rate. Some gifted children are slow learners. The handicapped are invariably hampered. Some students are meticulous and take time-consuming care in their work, while others dash through their tasks hurriedly. It is no accident that the most valid and reliable tests of intelligence are individualized power tests geared to the testee's own rate of response rather than timed or speeded.

The average classroom was designed for groups to learn as groups at a more or less uniform and predetermined rate. No assumption could be more unrealistic for the average classroom.

3. *The children have the necessary background to build upon with what is taught.* One cannot build a learning sequence without a good foundation any more than one can build a house or skyscraper without an adequate foundation. Nor would one build upon a foundation that is too tall. The textbook and subject matter structure found in most

classrooms assume similar backgrounds in its learners.

This cannot be, for background depends upon many variables: ability, home, culture, handicaps, motivation, previous learning, and what is remembered. Furthermore, the common practice of social promotion or assignment to a higher grade precludes an adequate background.

4. *The material is presented according to the children's style of learning.* Children do not all learn in the same manner. Some learn best by what they *hear,* others learn best by what they *see,* others by what they *do manually.* Some children learn best by abstract thinking, and still others by a combination of methods.

It is therefore patently absurd to believe that mass-produced uniform material presented by a book, lecture, or teacher-made handouts will teach, or even interest, all children more or less equally well.

It is for these reasons that individualization becomes fundamentally essential. (Individualization will be considered at greater length in Chap. 7).

The Stigma of Exceptionality

Every teacher of exceptional children must deal with the stigma that still in this "enlightened space age" attaches itself to exceptionality. The person who is different in some manner, especially mentally, is somewhat less than human.

Yet deviation is normal, not abnormal. Children are different. Special education teachers are considered by many as inferior teachers, and many regular teachers, we are sorry to say, feel as one teacher we know who expressed herself, "I don't want to teach those dumb apes."

The Report from Closer Look published by the National Special Education Information Center of the U. S. Office of Education, Bureau of Education for the Handicapped, Summer 1974, issue, contains excerpts from a number of letters which illustrate our point.

Ronny is a borderline case — not quite normal, but not terribly handicapped. He has no friends. His favorite activities are reading the paper and watching TV seven hours a day. His behavior becomes more uncooperative and antisocial every day. He no longer attempts to do things the right way — only "in Ronny's way." He has been told he's a dummy so much that he's begun to believe it himself and just doesn't care anymore. Something must be done to help Ronny salvage a decent, productive life for himself. . . .

Our daughter has a congenital visual handicap . . . In spite of her problem, she attended public schools, made National Honor Society in high school, and graduated from college with honors. She graduated from the state teachers college with a teaching certificate on the high school level. As of the present time, she has been unable to obtain a teaching job — or any other kind of a job. . . .

The judgment of uselessness belongs to the old view that handicapped people are less than human, not real people whom one expects to exert effort, make choices, achieve independence. The idea of uselessness goes back to the decades when the handicapped were abandoned to a limbo of boredom into which hardly anybody felt it necessary to intrude.

Teachers who work successfully with handicapped children, even mild cases, must understand, love, and accept these special-need children and clear away any outdated stigmatized attitudes harking back to days when people believed that deviation was a curse from God. They must also help the child to accept and like himself, as well as help the parents to deal with their guilt-laden overprotection or rejection of their exceptional child.

Involve the Parents

George Neill (1974), reporting on the success and failure of the new Right-to-Read program, makes this observation: "In any situation where Right-to-Read has achieved success, parents have been involved in the planning, as volunteers, as advisors, as enthusiasts, as reinforcers, as good-will ambassadors who involved other members of the community in the reading effort."

Some Special Classes Needed

Now that most states require special education of some sort for all exceptional or handicapped children, some special educators are clamoring for the abolition of all special classes, as all exceptional children are absorbed into the regular classroom.

We agree with James O. Smith and Joan R. Arkans (1974) who say, "Now more than ever: A case for the special class." What about the more severely handicapped? Is he suddenly to be integrated into the mainstream to drown quickly?

Our case for making special education easier for the regular classroom teacher is based upon the assumption and conviction that severely handicapped children need the services of specialists and the time attainable in a special class.

Education for all according to the needs of all requires intensive care for those who need it. Some do need it. The great majority of special-need children, however, can be taught by the classroom teacher in the regular class easily. Besides, we cannot afford special classes for all handicapped children.

Chapter 3

WHO ARE EXCEPTIONAL CHILDREN?

IT should be useful to the teacher to have a brief but clear knowledge of the children we call exceptional. She should be better able to recognize, understand, and accept them. She should also be able to make more applicable and valid referrals for children who are more severely affected and who therefore need specialized help.

In no case should these brief descriptions of exceptional children be used to label or stigmatize children that are educationally, and sometimes physically and psychologically, different.

Who Are Exceptional Children?

Exceptional children are usually defined or described as children who differ from the average child to such an extent that their differences require some unique type of special school adjustment either within the regular classroom or in a self-contained classroom or resource room. In other words, an exceptional child is any child who differs to such an extent from the normal child that he needs some special education intervention to profit optimally from his school experience. To put it still another way, he is the child who differs sufficiently from the norm that he does not learn as he should in the average class and therefore requires some special teaching or attention for some of his time in school.

It includes those whose differences make them unable to perform up to the level of the average, as well as those whose differences enable them to perform above the average. The differences can be physical, mental (psychological), social, emotional, or some combination of these.

How Different Are Exceptional Children?

As soon as one begins to discuss the problems of exceptionality and differences, the question arises, "How different must he be before he is an exceptional child?"

This is not easily answered for any area of exceptionality and is certainly controversial at the present time. Federal law decides the degree of sightedness and the decible loss for hearing handicaps. State laws set the limits for various other types of exceptionality, and various professional associations set their own limits.

However, within the local school or classroom, the determining criteria should be whether or not the child is able to profit to the limit of his ability within the experiences of the regular existing classroom situation.

The Exceptional Child Is More Like Other Children Than Unlike Them

A fundamental belief in educational thinking is that the difference of exceptional children is only one of degree: they are more like the normal or average child than they are different from him. They must be treated first of all and above all as children who need to express and develop their individuality to the fullest. The label *exceptional* is used only to obtain a better understanding of the child and his needs. Too frequently the label has become more important than the child. The purpose of any label should be to identify in order to help the *child*.

The way in which exceptional children think, learn, and behave is not a different kind of thinking or learning or behaving; it is only one of degree. However, even the degree of difference is not so great that it makes the child unusually different from other children. It is the degree of difference that establishes the matter as to whether a child is exceptional or not.

What we have said above holds true for 99 percent or more of exceptional children. There are a very few who do differ sufficiently from the normal that they are very different, such as the most severely afflicted of the so-called clinical types of mental retardation, the extremely physically handicapped, or the immoderately psychotic individuals. These are rare, extremely so. One would not usually see them in school.

For the purposes of this book the entire range of exceptionality will not be discussed. Only those who are most commonly found in the average classroom and those who do not need the services of highly trained specialists. These include the gifted, the mentally retarded, the socially disadvantaged, the specific learning disabled, and the emotionally disturbed. Some consideration will be made of those who have mild common speech problems.

We will not consider here the orthopedically handicapped, those with moderate and severe hearing and sight problems, epileptics and spastic paralytics, those with moderate and severe speech handicaps, or the clinical types of mental retardation.

The Gifted: The Most Neglected Exceptional Children

One of the most common and yet the most neglected of all of the various types of exceptional children is the gifted. They were once called *geniuses*, a term that is fortunately now used but rarely in educational circles. It connotes unfortunate and erroneous considerations such as the strange neurotic working in a stuffy attic trying to change lead into gold of the medieval tales of bygone days, or the bizarre antisocial book-worm who was portrayed as a skinny little fellow with an oversized head who rarely engaged in physical activities. The term also denoted a rarity that does not exist; at least 10 percent of all children in school constitute the bright and gifted who, a recent study by the U.S. Office of Education in 1972 indicates, are among the most promising and yet most neglected of all our exceptional children. According to this study by a congressional committee, more than 54 percent are underachievers. That is, they perform in school and in later years far below their great potential. (The gifted will be described and discussed at length in Chap. 13 of this book.)

The Mentally Retarded: The Most Common Type of Exceptionality

When we say it is the most common we do not mean to infer

that there are more mentally retarded children than any other type of exceptionality. Such is not the case. Children with other kinds of exceptionalities are more numerous, as we shall shortly show.

The mentally retarded child is the best known and at the present time is receiving the most special education attention in the public schools. Teachers and the general public seem to know more about them than any others, however inaccurate and erroneous that information may be.

If intelligence is more or less evenly distributed, as most authorities contend, it, if graphed, would form a bell-shaped curve with the greatest number near the center depicting the average group of about 68 percent of the population with measurable IQ's from 85 to 115 on most standardized tests of intelligence. One standard deviation (the common unit of measure of variability) above and below would add about 26 percent more (about 13% on either side) with IQ's of 70 to 85, and 115 to 130. Another standard deviation would add about only another 4 percent (two on either side with IQ's of 55 to 70 and 130 to 145). As one moves farther from the average, the numbers become fewer.

This means, for our practical purpose, that there are about as many people above the average as there are below the absolute average of about 100, although there is very little difference between the general average of 85 to 115. Nevertheless, some uninformed persons will claim a significant difference in this range.

Who Are the Mentally Retarded Exceptional Children?

There is a great variety of opinion as to what we mean by mental retardation. The problems of identification, classification, definition, and cause have become extensive due to the fact that so many disciplines work with retarded children, and each looks at the children from its own perspective. You can find dozens of definitions and descriptions.

However, for the purposes of this manual, we will use the definitions and classifications most commonly used in educational circles, and that used by the American Association of Mental Deficiency: "Mental retardation refers to the subaverage general intellectual functioning which originates during the developmental period and is associated with impairment in adaptive behavior." Subaverage intellectual functioning refers to one standard deviation below the general population mean on a standard intelligence test. Impairment in adaptive behavior refers to the inability to cope adequately with the common demands of our society and includes maturation, learning, and social and economic adjustment.

Once mental retardates were classified as morons, imbiciles, and idiots. These terms are no longer in general use (except for the most part as expletives). Terms that have some meaning educationally are now used and include:

SLOW LEARNERS — IQ's *about* 85 to 70

EDUCABLE MENTALLY RETARDED (EMR's) — IQ's of *about* 70 to 55

TRAINABLE MENTALLY RETARDED (TMR's) OR SEVERELY MENTALLY RETARDED (SMR's)— IQ's of *about* 55 to 30

PROFOUNDLY RETARDED — IQ's of *about* 30 to unmeasurable

We have italized *about* because absolute limits are not functional and are unrealistic. No test has yet been devised that will measure within a standard error of measurement of about five or six points, plus the fact that individual performance on a test will vary as much as ten to fifteen points from time to time. Many factors can interfere such as fatigue, emotional upset, motivation, illness, comfort, cultural factors. Of all the factors that can interfere with or depress a score, there is no known factor that can cause a child to do better than he is able. Therefore, when confronted with several scores that vary, the highest is always the most valid and accurate.

The Cultural Factor in Mental Retardation

Amid the furor that currently is raging over the factor of social and racial factors in intelligence, no evidence has yet been discovered that conclusively proves that there is a basic difference in the intelligence of various races.

We can say, however, that environment does play a significant part in the development of intelligence. That intelligence is the *product* of *both* heredity and environment has been established beyond controversy (yet controversy rages). Seventy percent of almost all mental retardation is found in the poverty areas of society (and is called *familial* retardation). Giftedness seems to appear most frequently among the middle and upper classes of our "classless" society.

How much of intelligence is due to heredity and how much is due to environment has not yet been incontrovertibly established. That both play an important part is unquestionable, but no 80-20 or 50-50 is acceptable as yet. We have not established that much about intelligence at this time.

Other Causes of Mental Retardation

While some 70 percent of mental retardation is due to some combination of heredity and poor environment, over 200 known causes of mental retardation are responsible for the other 30 percent. Accidents, illnesses, difficult births, anoxia, poisonings, Rh blood factor, malnutrition, genetic defects, etc., either occurring before, during, or after birth, account for the most severe (usually) types of mental retardation.

The most common type of severe mental retardation is mongolism (Down's Syndrome) due to an extra chromosome. The incidence is highest among children born to older mothers. No one knows for sure what causes mongolism, although there are several hypotheses proposed to explain the phenomenon.

Characteristics of Children with Mental Retardation

There is no such person as a typical mentally retarded child who exhibits all of the characteristics associated with mental retardation. They will vary greatly from child to child in kind and degree. But generally speaking mental retardates:

    1. Function at a lower intellectual, physical, and social level generally. The idea that since they may not reason well or learn academics adequately, they will excel on the football

field or basketball court, for instance, is a myth. As a rule they do better at physical activity than intellectual achievement but they do not as a rule excel in physical skills over more intellectually able children.

2. Find it difficult or impossible to reason or think in the abstract and use abstract symbols. They handle concrete experiences far better.

3. Are unable to plan well or manipulate plans made for them. (Family planning to limit offspring is exceedingly difficult and haphazard. One can see the problem implicit here.)

4. Have a shorter attention span than their more able peers.

5. Lack judgment and foresight.

6. Are more rigid, less adaptable in most activities. Can handle simple routine adequately in most cases, but adequate adjustment is not characteristic.

7. Have a limited power of association and understanding of cause and effect.

8. Lack the ability to assess their own skills and performance. They often tend to overestimate their ability.

9. Have a distorted attitude toward society and themselves. They believe strongly that luck and fate play an important part in their lives.

10. Tend to possess a large set of frustrating and failure experiences which control to a large extent what they attempt to do.

11. Have a strong overlay of emotional problems. Some authorities state that *all* mentally retarded persons are emotionally disturbed to some degree due not as an integral part of their limited intellectual functioning but as a result of their long series of failure experiences.

12. Are more visible in school than before going to school or after getting out of school where they tend, unless severely retarded, to blend into the background.

13. Are unable to work well independently.

14. Are easily confused by ordinary situations.

15. Break rules in the conduct of games, often without being aware of doing so.

16. Lack what we usually call *common sense*.

17. Are slow in all areas of normal activities: academic, social, psychological, and physical.

Nevertheless, the mentally retarded child:

1. Can learn academics far better than most teachers believe. The EMR (Educable Mentally Retarded) child can attain to a fifth or sixth grade level of school *if* he has the proper help and training, while most slow learners could graduate from high school *if* they had the proper courses and training.
2. Can learn to use leisure time.
3. Can learn to take care of his personal needs.
4. Can learn to communicate adequately with others.
5. Eighty percent could become self-supporting with proper special education.
6. Could learn to get along with others and understand them.
7. Could learn to enjoy the better things of life such as art, music, theatre, and hobbies.
8. Can learn to manage his own economics.
9. Can master a manual skill such as carpentry, bricklaying, truckdriving, auto repair, electrical work, lab technician.
10. Can learn to like school if he is taught so as to succeed in tasks that are meaningful.
11. Needs not be a discipline problem.
12. Can make a worthwhile contribution to society, rather than being a ward of society.

The Specifically Learning Disabled; One of the Newest and Most Mysterious Categories of Exceptional Children

(Although children with specific learning disabilities were discussed briefly in Chap. 2, we feel that some further consideration of this mysterious group of children is desirable.)

Specifically learning disabled children are mysterious because no one knows what causes the disabilities. Many hypotheses have been proposed to explain the cause of their learning problems. At the same time philosophies and techniques abound to provide therapy for their learning disorders.

One of the best-known diagnostic tools, the *Illinois Test of Psycholinguistic Abilities,* consists of no less than twelve subtests which supposedly can identify at least twelve learning problems, and perhaps many combinations of problems, which adds to the confusion and mystery because not all learning disabled children fall into neat categories.

Teachers have recognized for many years that there are some children who do not fall into any one of the classifications of exceptionality known. They are not retarded, although they often behave as if they were. They do not have sight or hearing losses or impairments. They are not emotionally disturbed or culturally disadvantaged nor do they seem to be gifted underachievers. But they cannot learn to read or learn arithmetic, etc.

A New Category of Exceptionality Develops

Many learning disabled children were labeled retarded because they did poorly on the usual *group* IQ test. (They scored much better on an individualized IQ test.) Others were called unmotivated or disinterested, and some were categorized as emotionally disturbed.

In the late 1940's and 1950's, Strauss and Lehtinen described children they called "minimally brain injured" and described a set of behaviors that seemed to characterize most of them, such as hyperactivity, distractability, perseveration, perceptual (visual, auditory, or kinesthetic) abberations, impulsivity, and poor conceptualization among other problems that had been observed in children and adults with brain damage. They came to be called the "Strauss Syndrome" children or "Minimally Brain Injured." Some insult had happened to the brain before or during birth that accounted for the problem.

The primary difficulty that developed from this explanation was due to the fact that many children who could not learn to read and who had behavior symptoms described by Strauss had no detectable brain injury. Even the use of the sensitive electroencephalograph detected no lesion, but they did all seem to have some type of perceptual problem. For a time they were called the "perceptually handicapped." Gradually through the efforts of Kirk, McCarthy, and others, these mysterious problem children came to be called "children with specific learning disabilities."

Two Classifications of Learning Disabilities

The children under discussion are called children with *specific* learning disabilities to distinguish them from children who have *general* learning disabilities, such as mental retardation, emotional disturbances, sight or hearing problems, cultural disadvantages: problems which affect *all* of learning. Specific disabilities affect some perceptual area of sight or auditory or kinesthetic senses or some combination of these areas.

How Many Specific Learning Disabled Children Are There?

Any review of the literature will discover about any figure you want to find. The Bureau of the Office of the Handicapped estimates 1 to 3 percent of all school age children. Kirk (1972) estimates about 7 percent, McCarthy and McCarthy (1971) estimate from 15 to 20 percent, and we have seen estimates as high as 79 percent.

Why the difference? Some of it is due to definition by severity, some is expedited by economics (how many we can afford), some by acceptable characteristics. Our own experience in working with hundreds of children diagnosed as children with specific learning disabilities puts the figure at about 20 percent, if one includes those who would profit from a special program and who are not learning as well as their potential predicts. In any event there are more than most educators are aware.

Many Schools of Thought Confuse the Picture

When it comes to the matter of the causes and cures for children with specific learning disabilities, one almost comes to the conclusion that there are about as many hypotheses and methods as there are children who need them.

Most authorities seem to agree that there is some malfunction of some part of the central nervous system which prevents or confuses the input of auditory, visual, and/or kinesthetic stimuli and prevents their being integrated into meaningful patterns or wholes.

The following are some of the theories and practices concerning children with specific learning disabilities:

THE PERCEPTUAL-MOTOR FUNCTION: The learning disorder is due to some discoordination, or malfunction of the perceptual motor system. Motor discoordination, lack of cerebral dominance, and confused laterality are the chief culprits. Motoric training and perceptual neurological organization are the prescribed therapy. Kephart (1964) is the primary proponent with Doman and Delacato (1964) popularizing it to its extreme form.

LANGUAGE DEVELOPMENT SYSTEMS: These systems are concerned primarily with the language development characteristics. Although they conclude that there is some underlying brain pathology, they nevertheless believe that conclusive evidence of brain impairment need not be demonstrated in affected children. The observable presence of inadequate language ability is sufficient to suggest the possible utility of these systems. Myklebust (1968), Barry (1955), and McGinnis (1963) are the best-known proponents, each with his own differentiation, however.

THE PHONIC SYSTEMS: These are termed phonic with the emphasis placed on the auditory teaching of sound letter associations. This does not mean no other sensory channels are used; but the primary reliance is upon the auditory input mode which characterizes the methods in contrast to the language development system, particularly that of McGinnis (1963) which incorporates visual meaningful clues at all times.

Gillimhann (1965), Spalding (1957), and Orton (1937) are the chief proponents, yet with differences in their approaches.

THE HIGHLY STRUCTURED SYSTEMS: Since those in these systems feel that insufficient practice is the basis for most language problems, the use of structured meaningful drill is suggested as an essential means for teaching the language arts. However, one should not jump to the conclusion that they believe in any unnatural or purely mechanical approach to language development. Drill is a part of the method, but purely memorized mechanical methods should be avoided.

Cruickshank and Lehtinen (1961) believe that all steps should be taken to avoid distracting stimuli from the extent of stripping the classroom walls of unneeded objects that may distract to the use of small cubicals to isolate the child from a distracting environment.

Fitzgerald (1966) should not be omitted from this category of methods. Though several scores of years (1918) old, they still are widely used or still significantly affect teaching methods. While designed primarily for deaf children, they have been adapted to learning disabled children's teaching methods because of their highly structured visual grammatic methods.

THOSE SYSTEMS RELATED TO TESTS: The most widely known and used of the test-related systems is that of Marianne Frostig, founder of the Marianne Frostig Center of Educational Therapy in Los Angeles, California. She developed a test of visual motor perception and has prepared a structured training program to accompany this measuring device.

The program, however, does not center exclusively on visual perception but emphasizes perceptual skills of all sorts and is based on a wide set of tests in addition to her own.

Next to her, and a widely used work, is Kirk and Kirk (1973) and McCarthy's ITPA (Illinois Test of Psycholinguistic Abilities). It provides diagnosis of twelve characteristics and suggests methods of remediation. Others have modified its application, but Kirk and Kirk remain the outstanding proponents.

AN ECLECTIC MULTISENSORY APPROACH: Instead of using an approach that is strongly visual-motor or language centered or neurological or highly structured, there are those who emphasize no particular modality, channel, or single method. Unlike most of the systems reviewed so far, the proponents of a therapeutic method for children with specific learning disabilities emphasize an eclectic multisensory system. The idea is to stimulate as thoroughly and involve as many senses as possible: the visual, auditory, tactile, kinesthetic senses in as many ways as possible.

Grace Fernald was one of the first of these concerned educators of learning disabled children (1943) long before we knew there was a group of children we call learning disabled. She has been followed by many successful eclectic educators. Although Lehtinen and Cruickshank have been included among the highly structured system group, they would not be out of place among the eclectic multisensory practitioners.

While there seems to be mystery and confusion in the area of children with specific learning disabilities, many children are helped dramatically to learn to read and do school work. We have seen the sometimes startling results when given a teacher who cares enough and who expects results with individualized therapy. Chapter 6 will indicate the approach preferred by the writers of this book.

Children Who Are Socially and Emotionally Maladjusted: Children Who are Most Troubled and Troublesome

Strictly speaking, the socially maladjusted child is in trouble with his relationships with others while the emotionally disturbed child is in trouble in his relationship with himself. More often than not where one finds one type of maladjustment, one finds the other also. Nevertheless the reason for making a distinction between the two is that they are not necessarily nor always associated together in one child. But both types of children are usually in trouble with their learning.

Children with Behavior Disorders are Increasing

There is no question but that the numbers of children who are maladjusted are increasing precentage-wise. Whether it should be 2, 5, 10, or 20 percent or even higher is purely a matter of conjecture, for while law enforcement agencies keep records of criminal offenses and juvenile delinquency statistics, no one keeps a record of maladjustment in the classrooms of the nation.

Yet almost any teacher will confirm that she has more and more troubled and troublesome youngsters in school each year, and our observation confirms the estimates. More and more teachers are leaving the classroom because of discipline problems.

Why Are Maladjusted Children Increasing?

There are no easy or sure answers, but here are some reasons that contribute to the problem:

1. Television violence.
2. Deterioration of the family as a stabilizing influence.
3. Moving families — no social roots.
4. Inconsistent discipline and increasing permissiveness.
5. Boredom — lack of meaningful work or hobbies.
6. Loss of values that make for meaningful purposes in life.
7. The desire for instant solutions to problems which is promoted by TV advertising.
8. Drugs, whether alcohol or hard drugs.
9. Consistent failure in school by the large number of exceptional children whose learning needs are not met. (This latter reason is far more significant than many realize.)

Some Common Symptoms of Maladjustment

What the watchful teacher may observe are:
1. Constant lying.
2. Hostility toward the teacher and/or other students.
3. Destructive acts of violence rather frequently.
4. Cheating at every opportunity — most children will cheat occasionally when pressures are high.
5. Stealing.
6. Cruelty to other children or animals.
7. Sarcasm, arrogance, and defiance.
8. Bullying.
9. Frequent temper tantrums.
10. Frequent attempts to get attention, whether by interruptions or being the class clown.

Other even more serious problems that occur frequently and are easily overlooked are:
11. Frequent daydreams and fantasy.
12. Undue quietness or retirement.
13. Trying too hard to please — being too good.
14. Anxiety and fearfulness.
15. Excessive selfishness.

Some physical manifestations of maladjustment are also significant:

16. Facial or other constant body twitching (tics).
17. Nail biting.
18. Enuresis or lack of elimination control.
19. Twisting hair constantly.
20. Chewing clothing.
21. Rocking of body front-to-front or side-to-side.
22. Weak, high-pitched voice.
23. Overly self-conscious.
24. Stuttering.
25. Rapid nervous speech.

Obviously no child will have all or most of these characteristics, but anyone with an extreme form or forms calls for the therapy of a professional.

Success Is Therapeutic

The milder cases can be handled in the classroom. F.M. Hewett (1968) describes a method that works well for even more severe cases. Glasser (1965, 1968), among others, also suggests that eliminating failure in the classrooms acts in a remarkable therapeutic manner for most children who have social and emotional disorders.

Whatever the factors outside the school, the classroom teacher can aggravate or remediate the problem(s) by how well she provides successful experiences for the troubled or troublesome child.

The Culturally Disadvantaged Children: Our Largest Group of Exceptional Children

As a frontispiece of A. Harry Passow's (1967), Julios Srebber in a cartoon depicts an old man sitting in an old chair. He is saying, "I used to think I was poor. Then they told me I wasn't poor, I was needy. Then they told me it was self-defeating to think of myself as needy, I was deprived. Then they told me deprived was a bad image, I was underprivileged. Then they told me underprivileged was overused, I was disadvantaged. I still don't have a dime, but I have a great vocabulary."

Take your pick: poor, needy, or disadvantaged, the words depict the same group of people and their children. They constitute one of the most controversial groups of children in school and one of the most difficult to deal with educationally. Dr. Banfield (1970) quotes Benjamin Bloom to the effect that after a child from a disadvantaged environment has reached school age, little can be done to reduce his handicap; it has become too firmly fixed. This is a controversial and biased statement.

So far, various interventions have been tried from Head Start to Higher Horizons to very early intervention in the home. From the wide observations of this writer, the Engleman-Becker *Distar* program sometimes called "Follow Through" has been the most effective.

It is our experience and contention that any child can be taught if his learning deficiency (see our checklist in Chap. 5) can be identified, its cause pinpointed, and the teaching to some degree individualized.

The Disadvantaged Have Many Sources

Due to newspaper and television publicity, one may come to the conclusion that disadvantaged children are primarily products of the inner city or slums of the large metropolitan areas, and some come from the hills, knobs, and hollows of Appalachia. Some are so produced, but not all of them by any means.

The disadvantaged child can be found anywhere the educational conditions are impoverished. Some children from poor homes could never be considered disadvantaged, while some children from affluent homes could be so classified. It depends upon the family attitude and concern for education. The notorious James Coleman Report indicated some homes as well as some schools. But generally speaking, the culturally disadvantaged and educationally deprived come mostly from:

The slums of the inner city with minority groups predominating.

The hills and hollows of Appalachia and Cumberlands.

Remote rural areas.

Migrant workers.

American Indians.
Various socially isolated religious groups.

Characteristics of Culturally Disadvantaged Children

While the characteristics of children from disadvantaged homes vary from place to place, nevertheless most children from disadvantaged homes have some general characteristics that seem to be shared in common. Predominent among these are the following:

1. Lack of development of the skills of attending, either visual or vocal or both, due to the parents' failure to enforce demands except under certain circumstances felt to be important.
2. An anti-education attitude. "Head knowledge" is far less important than practical "common sense" information and skills. This in itself stultifies in their minds the role of the teacher *and is difficult to change.*
3. Reluctance to move to better one's schooling or job. Home and family (clan) is far more important, although many of the younger generation no longer hold to this tradition.
4. Belief that one's destiny is controlled more by luck or fate or even God than by one's own efforts. One gets ahead or stays behind because of the star configuration in one's horoscope. Planting, harvesting, and other activities are determined by the phases of the moon.
5. A home situation which discourages conversation and discussion, and the asking and answering of "Why?". It obtains to such a degree that children from such homes rarely ask "Why?" in order to learn.
6. Suspicion of outsiders. Jack Weller (1965) discusses this at some length. It is not easy to gain the trust and confidence of foreigners or gangs from another part of the city.
7. Little reading material of any sort.
8. Poor understanding and little use of prepositions and basic concepts usually taken for granted among school age children.
9. Rigid and limited use of adjectives and adverbs.

10. Simple and repetetive use of conjunctions: so, because, then, but, and, etc.
11. Short, grammatically simple, and often uncompleted sentences frequently ending unfinished with a verb.
12. Frequent use of sympathetic circularity; these are statements which seem to require an assent such as "You see? Wouldn't it? You know? Hear now?"
13. Great stress on personal relationships. Jack Weller (1965) tells several stories that illustrate this point well. One anecdote concerned two people who were running for postmaster in a small town. They both used petitions. Later when the petitions were compared, practically everyone had signed both. No one wanted to offend anyone else, and it often is carried to extreme lengths.
14. Incessant use of idiomatic phrases and colloquialistic jargon and word use. The teacher may believe at times she is listening to a foreign language.

The Multiple Handicapped: Exceptional Children with Several Handicaps

Many exceptional children are afflicted with two or more handicaps. The most common are the culturally disadvantaged who are mildly to moderately retarded mentally. The most pathetic is probably the blind, deaf, and speechless child. Hutt and Gibby (1958) state that every mentally retarded child is also emotionally disturbed to some degree.

The fact that some children have several handicaps increases the difficulty of identification and supports our contention that categorization is not only unnecessary but often impossible.

Chapter 4

SOME COMMON PROBLEMS OF EXCEPTIONAL CHILDREN

IN spite of the fact that there are a number of different categories of exceptional children and in spite of the fact that in addition there is a great variety of differences within each category, most exceptional children have many areas of commonality insofar as their educational and/or behavior problems are concerned. In other works, exceptional children are more alike than they are dissimilar, particularly concerning their educational problems.

Furthermore, exceptional children are more like average children than they are unlike the so-called normal children. Their learning problems are basically the same although more extreme or severe and more resistive to change or remediation.

However, *they do respond favorably to proper educational intervention and treatment.* The basic problem of the teacher is to identify the problems or lacks and then to pinpoint the cause. Educational therapy then depends upon prescriptively working on the problem and its cause.

How This Manual Differs from Most Methods of Teaching Exceptional Children

Special education began with the careful identification of several categories of exceptional children who were then labeled in order to more easily differentiate their teaching techniques and methods. Unfortunately, the labels were many times wrong, but in any case they stuck as a devastating stigma (almost) forever.

Special education believed, and still believes for the most part, that every category of exceptionality had its own special treatment and specific methods. One taught one way for mentally retarded children and still another way for learning disabled children who were suspected by minimal brain injury. Teacher certification departments specified specialized training and certification endorsements, and the teacher training institutions faithfully complied in producing teachers for the mentally retarded and teachers for the learning disabled, and so on.

It is the experience and contention of the writers of this book that most exceptional children, expecially the mildly and moderately exceptional and handicapped, have basic common problems that can be taught the same way (fundamentally) adapting and using the same basic materials. This does not mean that they are not still taught as individuals using a personalized approach. What it does mean is that one does not need to spend weeks or months trying to identify and label the children so as to be able to prescribe precisely colored educational pills at prescribed intervals.

One major problem lies in the fact that although using the best tests and diagnostic instruments available, it is still practically impossible to validly and reliably identify a learning disabled child from a culturally disadvantaged child, from an emotionally disturbed child, from a gifted underachiever, or from a mildly mentally retarded child.

What we propose recommends that one discover the child's deficiency(ies). Using the information given below and the checklist of Chapter 6, the teacher can do this easily, validly, and reliably. It is practical, objective, and down-to-earth. One can see what the child can or cannot do, discover the cause(s), and tackle the specific problem(s).

In attempting to remediate a child's learning problems by spending, among other things suggested by this manual, ten or fifteen minutes a day on as nearly a one-to-one basis with a child as possible, no attempt should be made to teach all the required subjects.

It must be assumed that poor reading (or no reading) will be the most common and important problem. Therefore, reading should receive the most intensive therapy in the time allowed. If the problem is of another sort, such as a problem in attending, this should receive the priority therapy.

Does the Child Pay Attention?

At the top of the list and most important to learning is the ability or skill of attending. Most teachers assume and take it for granted that most, if not all, children in school have developed this most important of learning readiness skills. Yet, carelessness in paying attention is a very common problem and cause of nonreading and nonlearning. Directions cannot be followed; learning cannot take place unless the child is listening or watching *carefully* what the teacher is doing or saying.

Nevertheless, a thorough and careful study of learning literature and how-to-teach texts reveals an unfortunate lack of consideration of this problem. In the minds of most educators it exists, apparently, mostly in the learning disabled children as distractability, and in other exceptional children as a short attention span that will be outgrown developmentally.

If it has its roots in the learning disabled as distractability, it apparently is assumed that it is either incurable or falls within the responsibility of special educators.

Mostly, however, the skill of attending is taken for granted, and the child soon learns how to cover it up and act as if he is paying attention. If he is not, it is blamed on lack of interest and motivation or distractability when the real cause lies in the hard fact that the child simply has not learned how to pay attention and concentrate.

Children from Culturally Disadvantaged Homes Have Nonattending as a Common Problem

Jack Weller (1965), Banfield (1970), Reisman (1966), and other writers and authorities in the field state that the children from the mountains of Appalachia or the slums of our big cities are taught not to pay auditory (listening) attention by the fact that their parents make requests or demands or issue instructions that are not enforced. The child soon learns that his parents do not seem to mean or care what they say, unless it is in a particular tone of voice or reinforced with certain expletives or sure punishment. This attitude is carried to school.

Some teachers reinforce this lack of attention by repetitions of assignments or directions.

The middle-class child learns to pay attention from parents who act as though they mean what they say, plus reading to them and telling stories, providing reading materials and picture books. Printed material is scarce or nonexistent in the culturally disadvantaged homes of poverty.

Attention a Result of Set or Startle Response

The attention most teachers want is that of a set, or preparedness to receive wanted stimuli. The child pays attention to what the teacher says or does because he is more or less set or on edge to receive the information about to be imparted. The set continues as long as the child wants to receive the information (or has the skill to attend).

SOME PARENTS AND TEACHERS USE THE STARTLE METHOD OF GAINING ATTENTION: A loud shout or noise or unusual action can be used to gain attention (for a short time, usually). Threats of punishment or promise of a desired reward both fall into the category of startle methods of gaining attention. But they eventually lose their effectiveness.

Robert Travers (1972) states that paying attention is the result of a startle response or an orienting response, but they are very different in their psychological reaction. What is desirable in school for most instances is the orienting response.

Strong stimuli (startle responses), whatever their source, cannot be blocked from entering the perceptual system. *One can become so habituated, however, that strong stimuli are the only ones that enter as one develops an immunity system* to other stimuli. Startle responses seem to take over so that orienting responses are blocked out. In other words, in the culturally disadvantaged homes the training actually prepares the child not to pay attention of the sort usually needed in school.

Travers goes on to say that an attention posture is highly dependent on the amount of relevant information received (relevant as perceived by the person), the level of motivation, and the disposition related to maintaining an attending response.

Mildren Berry (1969), in studying, language disorders and their bases, found that attention plays a very significant part. She discovered that the brain wave patterns as shown by the electroencephalograph potential vary as the response of attention. When all systems are set to go, the electrical potential is high.

She concluded that the *ability to exclude irrelevant stimuli from the field of attention is basic to learning,* and the higher the EEG potential, the less distracting are external stimuli (italics the author's). Furthermore, too much distraction causes one to react to an unimportant signal, or he freezes into a position of inactivity.

Attention is basic to any learning, but too many distracting stimuli can cause confusion and negate the beneficial effects of attention.

Some teachers use various gimmicks to gain or hold attention. B.F. Skinner (1968) has discovered that instead of the gimmick's (game, device, audio visual aid, etc.), gaining attention to, for instance reading, and reinforcing reading, it actually gains attention to the gimmick and reinforces it. Reading must be its own attention getter and reinforcer to be an effective developer of interest and attention.

The idea that one can use a gimmick to start with, and then after a time, wean to the intrinsic task is asking for trouble. Weaning is a psychologically traumatic and difficult process that is not worth the effort. Intrinsic interest is a better method any way it is viewed.

Failure and Its Products Are of Paramount Importance

Failure breeds discouragement, and discouragement produces apathy or hostile behavior or a combination of apathy and hostility; apathy may affect part of a child's life and hostility another.

This syndrome constitutes the most frequent and deleterious configuration of behavior affecting exceptional children who do not receive proper educational experiences at home or in school.

All children fail at times, but the failure of the exceptional child tends in almost all cases to become habitual and incessant. The handicapped exceptional child lives in a world of failure while he is in school and often outside of school.

Failure is not the same thing to all children. Failure is not accomplishing what one expects himself to be able to accomplish or what someone he respects expects him to accomplish. It is the result of not coming up to standards set by the child or a respected adult.

For this reason failure can be real, or arbitrary, or imagined, but the results to the individual are the same as long as they are held to be attainable.

Failure is not destructive nor harmful unless it involves a strongly coverted goal, or, as in most cases involving handicapped children, it becomes the consistent pattern.

What Failure Does to a Child

Not all children react to failure in the same manner, and the reactions vary both in kind and intensity. Some of the most common reactions are as follows:

1. The child who fails consistently may lower his expectations or goals so that he is able to attain them. Some teachers use grades as motivators. For the successful they may motivate, but for the chronically unsuccessful they tend only to lower expectations and goals. Sears (1940), in her classic research on failure, exposed this behavior for all time. Instead of trying harder to reach a higher goal they tried less; they lowered their goals. Paradoxically, the ones getting good grades tried to better their marks.

2. Some children faced with constant failure will set their expectations and goals so high that they cannot be blamed if they miss their mark. As in the classic ring toss, they will set it at such a distance that blame cannot be attributed to them if they miss.

3. Other children will just quit trying at all. They could attain their goals if they tried, but since they no longer try they cannot be blamed for failure. This aspect of apathy is most discouraging and frustrating to parents and teachers. Lack

of interest and motivation are hard to deal with, and no amount of the usual type of encouragement and motivation will accomplish anything. Apathy is a most difficult mountain to move.

4. Still other children take their feelings of frustration for failure out in hostile behavior. They become bullies, destructive of property, thieves, or just sassy and sarcastic. It can be directed toward property, other children, adults, or society in general. It is significant that in a comprehensive study made in Texas several years ago, delinquency *decreased* two-thirds (66%) *after* the youngsters *dropped out* of school.

5. Some failing children escape into the world of fantasy. There anything is possible and success a common experience.

6. One might conclude that the fortunate failures in school are those who develop successful activities and hobbies outside of school. Schooling is made to become unimportant and the substitute actually important — and sometimes it is. Dr. Banfield (1970) makes an excellent case for letting school failures drop out after eight grades of schooling (pp.148-157).

William Glasser (1969) comments on his experience as a psychiatrist and concludes that after viewing the pains and struggles of people who fail and fail, he has discovered an important fact: regardless of how many failures and struggles a person may have had in his past, *"He will not succeed in general until he can in some way experience success in one important part of his life."* (italics his).

Success or failure, either one, over an extended period of time produces an image of one's self — how one thinks about himself. *Fortunately or unfortunately one tends to produce or act as he thinks or perceives himself to be.*

This self-image tends to be extremely stable and persistent. It is most difficult to change. No amount of persuasion or external evidence will convince a person he is other than what he believes himself to be.

This writer has presented evidence such as test scores, IQ

profiles, testimony to children who perceive themselves to be "dumb"; and it does no good. They merely reply, "I'm not that smart." Or, "The tests are wrong." Or, "No matter what they think I can't do it."

That is why Dr. Glasser and others say, *"They must experience success in some important way."* We wish every teacher could see the expression of astonishment and ecstacy on the face of a child who just succeeded in doing something he had not been able to do until then.

The Rewards of Teaching Exceptional Children

Dr. Glasser's experience and discovery explains why some teachers get such satisfaction from teaching exceptional children. Given that first success, the children almost literally explode with satisfaction as they go from success to success, and so do the teachers.

Most teachers scarcely realize the omnipotence of their presence in the classroom as they mete out success or failure to the child. Many excuse themselves by repeating the often stated aphorism, "I don't give grades (or success or failure) I merely record them." Yet, the teacher holds the key to success or failure. As we stated in Chapter 2, learning takes place if, and only if, four conditions are met. Satisfy those conditions and a child will learn, and learn easily, provided, of course, the term of failure has not been too long and thoroughly ingrained. The rewards for success are immeasurable, and they are possible.

Anxiety and Feelings of Rejection

It is generally agreed that some small feelings of anxiety enhance performance, as they provide motivation. Anxiety that exceeds that level, and it differs for different persons, acts as a block to successful performance.

Handicapped Exceptional Children Experience
Too Much Anxiety

Handicapped exceptional children are overwhelmed with

anxiety as they fail and fumble their way through school. Added to their feelings of failure are feelings of failure compounded by anxiety.

Rejection Has Many Sources

Not only do they feel rejection as a result of their feelings of failure, but the very acts and tone of voice of their teachers, parents, and classmates serve to confirm their self-estimation.

Add to these labels special classes where they are jailed and isolated from their peers, who can guess their feeling of rejection. (Reread Ray's story in Chap. 2; his feelings are quite typical.) Failure breeds isolation, isolation breeds fear, and fear breeds isolation; a vicious circle of anxiety imprisons the exceptional child who cannot succeed in his schoolwork.

Parents Often Contribute to the Anxiety

If the only environment that feeds anxiety and rejection were the school, it would be bad enough, but parents (paradoxically those who care) scold and compare their children with others down the street or perhaps even in their own family. This explains why parents need to be a part of any remedial program for handicapped children. Their support (or at least neutrality) is an essential part of teaching handicapped children easily.

Problems with Abstract Thinking and Symbolization

Two types of handicapped children have real difficulty in abstract thinking and symbolization. These are the mentally retarded and the culturally disadvantaged. Some types of the learning disabled have trouble in conceptualization, but they are relatively rare.

There is general agreement among educators that abstract thinking and symbolization tend to go together, that symbols are a type of abstraction. Words, letters, numbers, time, maps, grafts, and charts are all symbols.

The retarded child has trouble with all abstractions and

symbols and needs a great amount of drill and use of concrete practical applications. At the same time one should not be discouraged if there are some abstractions and symbols that are never understood. The degree of retardation determines to a great extent the amount of abstractions and use of symbols that can be learned. Specific concrete examples help his understanding.

The Culturally Disadvantaged Child Has a Different Style of Thinking

The cognitive style of the culturally disadvantaged tends to be slow, careful, and patient, as contrasted to being clever (in distinction from sly), easy, and flexible. One could, and many do, thereby jump to the conclusion that they are stupid. They want to think things through carefully, and they are in no rush.

The impatient teacher is his school's worst enemy. It is true that the teacher has a lot to do, but why cut the student off, make him feel like a stupid failure when a little patience would have helped him to arrive at a probably wise and able solution or conclusion? Hurry him up, and teacher and student may both be defeated.

Give him time and patience. The type of competition that cries, "Who will be first?" is exactly the wrong approach for the culturally disadvantaged child. Competition can be equivalent to cognitive murder.

Learning How to Learn

Learning psychologists have presented to hungry monkeys and other animals in cages little traps in which there were three geometric objects, usually two triangles and a circle. If the animal lifted or pushed off the circle, the one that was different, he found food underneath the circle. Then they used two squares and a triangle. Each time two were alike and one was different. Each time the one that was different covered the food.

Is this not what we do with the first-grader in reading readiness, and later? Which is the one that is different? The child can be told, but he is often frustrated by his trial and error pattern of learning to read.

The monkey cannot be told, but with sufficient trials and errors he will eventually learn that hefood is always under the one that is different. It takes a tremendous amount of time. Psychologists are patient people and eventually the monkey learns ty trick; he finds the food after solving the problem hundreds of times.

If one gives the monkey other problems of a similar nature, but different constituents, it will take him a long time to solve the problem, but not as long as it did for the first problem. Eventually he will do it ratherquickly. *He has learned how to learn.*

That is exactly what handicapped children do not know how to do because of lacks in their experience, lowered intelligence, or specific learning handicaps.

Learning How to Learn Outside the Classroom

Handicapped children learn other things outside the classroom. They learn to hunt and fish, get around through the inner city jungle and learn its jargon and ethics; they learn to play games within their skill limits and learn many other things — some of which we wish they did not learn.

Then we put them into a cage, a classroom. Here with their handicaps they have to learn to concentrate, deal with symbols, how to listen, see what they are supposed to see, how to narrow attention and abstract generalities from situations in science or English or history. But before they do that, they have to learn to read. No reading; no learning.

Each thing that is taught is not as important in itself as it is a preparation for learning more. They have to learn how to learn.

All of this is difficult enough for the bright and nonhandicapped children, but for the handicapped, it is practically impossible. We rarely teach children how to learn.

Therefore the handicapped exceptional child needs to learn how to learn.

Learning How to Learn Is a Complex Skill Often Missed by Exceptional Children

Learning almost always involves four processes. Sometimes

they are approximately simultaneous and sometimes it seems as if they occur over a considerable span of time.

First there is the *acquisition of new information*. Frequently it is information that runs counter to what is already known, and sometimes it replaces what the learner has explicitly or implicitly accepted as information. At the very least it refines what the learner already knows.

A second art of learning is *memorization*. Unless the new knowledge is assimilated, learning new knowledge is valueless. This does not mean memorization as mere rote learning; this may be no more valuable than no knowledge or forgetting. By memorization we mean not only the ability to recognize and recall information which in some instances may be enough, but far more often and more important it means that the new facts or behavior models take on meaning and become a lasting part of the thinking and behavior patterns of the learner.

The third aspect of learning is often called *transfer of training or transformation*. This is the process by which new information is manipulated so as to be used to fit new tasks and situations. In other words it involves the ability to analyze or unmask the information learned in one situation and then being able to apply it to another situation or process. It not only makes information valuable but also useful beyond the immediate reason for learning it. It goes beyond the now to the future — the here to the there.

A fourth aspect of learning is *evaluation*. This is the ability to check the manner in which we have used or manipulated the new skill or information. The normal person constantly does this more or less automatically. Is the skill or fact adequate for the task, did it work, and how well? Is the generalization adequate or fitting? Are we operating and manipulating the new learning properly?

Sometimes teachers unwittingly teach as if learning consisted of only the first, second, and fourth steps. The fourth, evaluation, is far too often an artificial step made in the form of various kinds of tests to be graded so as to evaluate learning. Again, far too often they evaluate only the first two aspects of learning — knowledge and memory.

To be valuable learning *must* include *transformation,* the ability to use in various situations the information gained. By use, we mean such things as appreciation as well as a skill; personality modification as well as recognition of a new aquaintance. Here handicapped children have trouble in all departments, depending on the type of handicap. Perceptually handicapped children may have trouble in acquiring — seeing or hearing perceptually so as to make sense out of what it taught. Retarded children will have trouble memorizing and making the transformation as well as evaluating their use of the new information or skill once they have acquired it. (The chapter on diagnosis should be invaluable here.)

Teacher-Made Problems: So Easily Overlooked

Not all the problems involving exceptional children (or normal children, for that matter) have their cause in the child. The teacher can cause a host of trouble, and since in many cases the handicapped child is more sensitive and even perceptive, he is more easily disturbed by teacher-made problems.

It is impossible for the teacher to be an effective agent in the learning process if by some means or another or by unpleasant personality traits, she constricts or destroys the *rapport that must exist* for effective teaching. If she is able to establish rapport and an atmosphere of acceptance and understanding, genuine learning can be effective under her leadership. If on the other hand, she manages to erect barriers of any sort she will be working at cross-purposes with her pupils all pulling in different directions and all frustrated.

Some of the more common teacher-made problems are:

1. *Lack of genuine love and respect for children.* This cannot be feigned; children are exceedingly perceptive. It is as if they have antennae sensitive to this trait. Little nonverbal kinds of communication give it all away: love and acceptance or the lack of it. On the other hand, however, there must be more than love to be an effective teacher. Although the Good Book says, "Love covers a multitude of sins," it actually covers only some.

2. *Lack of personal security.* Children can sense this,

too, far more accurately than teachers realize. The teacher who is anxious, defensive, unsure of herself, afraid, is usually recognized as such by her pupils and they will take unfair advantage of such behavior. We have known of such teachers being literally driven out of the classroom into mental institutions.

Not only this possibility looms as a problem-maker, but insecurity tends to replicate itself in the children. They tend to become more insecure and frightened, too.

3. *Rigidity in leadership in any form.* Rigidity shows itself in many ways. Most often it is seen in unreasonable expectations with little leeway for extenuating circumstances. It can be seen in grading, discipline, neatness, long sets of arbitrary rules, strict repression of physical activity, insistence that the children work rapidly and at the same rate as the rest of the class, and the list is endless. It varies in degree, but it always does cause more problems than it solves. It does not allow for individual differences, and exceptional children suffer most.

4. *Vacillating leadership.* Students are confused by inconsistency in teacher leadership. As in the nation and the home, so in school, there must be a visible plausible and generally consistent set of rules and limits understood by all. If the teacher is vacillating and capricious from time to time or child to child, the pupils are continually groping for clues as to what is to be expected.

Neither will the student be able to find a consistent way to relate to her. She may be warm one day and cold the next, friendly and then unfriendly, patient one time and impatient another. Frustration and confusion reign.

5. *Vacillating or unreasonable purposes for the class.* Expectations may be too low — they frequently are too low for handicapped children — or too high.

All of this affects discipline, but it affects learning as well, with the exceptional children hurt the most.

The Problem of Reading

We have saved the problem of reading until last because it is all important, and *because it grows out of the other problems. Solve them and you solve the problem of reading.* Chapter 6 deals with their solution.

Chapter 5

THE TEACHER AS
HER OWN DIAGNOSTICIAN

As a classroom teacher with a group of children representing a variety of abilities and problems, it is important to realize that some children have learning problems, *but they are all instructional problems* and must be handled as instructional problems if learning is to take place effectively.

The child's disabilities may be permanent, but as instructional problems they can and must be dealt with. This is not an impossible situation. It can be accomplished by using all the means available and the *talents every good teacher possesses.*

This chapter will present some suggestions for classroom teachers to use which do not require special talents or training. The only requirements are the willingness to try and a minimum of extra time.

Evaluation: A Continuous Process

When we think of obtaining or conducting an evaluation, we think of an accumulation of results. Hopefully, these results not only add insight about the child's difficulties, but include suggestions for approaches to remediation. Frequently, we forget the most important evaluation of all.

The most important evaluation a teacher makes will be that which results from her day-to-day teaching experience. This is not only true in discovering problems but is even more true in the monitoring of what is taught and how it is taught. Unless day-to-day evaluation is a planned part of each instructional activity, it is impossible to be sure which skills have been taught or to know what kinds of changes should be made.

It cannot be assumed that because children are exposed to material that all of the children in the group or class will achieve mastery. The only sure way to know that any skill has been successfully mastered is to teach, test, reteach, and then test again. Children should be given many individual turns in order to evaluate performance. Many times the opportunities are built into teaching methods, but we do not make full use of the responses and results we get. These are the results which should dictate the changes we make from day-to-day.

Diagnosis as Task Analysis

The success of remediation is dependent upon proper identification of the specific educational *tasks* which a child can or cannot perform successfully. It is impossible to teach effectively without knowing specifically what the child's strengths and weaknesses are. While we tend to be always on the lookout for these things a child cannot do, we sometimes do not attach enough significance to what he can do. After all, this defines our starting point.

The Teacher as Diagnostician

Why should the classroom teacher accept the additional role of diagnostician? In all too many areas, the services of trained diagnosticians are nonexistent, or the case loads are so heavy it takes months to obtain the services.

If the tests are administered and an evaluation completed, the results often do not yield the type of information most useful to the teacher. The information must be translated into meaningful descriptions of the child's behavior, abilities, and disabilities.

Many teachers have felt insecure in their own abilities to function as diagnosticians. Yet they are the ones who daily spend great periods of time working with and observing the children as they learn. This is the evaluator the child is most accustomed to. Who has a better observation post than the one person that is exposed to a child's efforts, successes, and failures? An artificial testing situation is at best unreliable. Consequently, the time and place to evaluate and observe is in the classrooms.

The very terms *evaluation* and *diagnosis* sometimes have

frightening overtones. Yet it is impossible to know where we are or where we are going without evaluation. According to Wallace and Kauffman (1973), "Evaluation is an on-going teaching procedure, one in which the teacher has the responsible role." Not only does the teacher have the responsible role, but perhaps the most valuable information available is that which is obtained as a result of day-to-day teaching.

The authors' purpose is not to minimize the importance of formal diagnosis but to encourage classroom teachers to use their many talents and every means at their disposal to better meet the needs of all children, and in particular to be more effective in their teaching of children with special needs. Certainly, when a more extensive formal evaluation is necessary, a teacher with some basic skills and enough practice can provide more accurate information and be a more active member of the diagnostic team.

TEACHER OBSERVATION IMPORTANT. As teachers, we frequently underestimate the value of our own observation. Many of the most valuable clues about a child can be obtained by careful observation of daily performance. For example, what kind of behavior does the child exhibit when reading? What kind of approach does he attempt to use when he comes to a new or troublesome word? Does he frequently lose his place?

It is possible to ask questions of this type about any of the tasks and subjects we teach. What specific skills does he appear to have trouble with? If the child has difficulty with story problems, is it because he does not understand the language or cannot read the problem? Does he have the necessary computational skills? Has he developed the necessary reasoning and analysis skills?

It is helpful to add some structure to the observation before starting. The question approach as described is very helpful. Decide first just what purpose this observation is to serve and then what behaviors you will want to look at. If at all possible make notes during the observation so that important details will not be forgotten. The details can be filled in at the end of the period or later in the day. Some record should be available to be considered with other information obtained from work samples, etc.

It is also advisable to make more than one observation to see if similar results are obtained if the situation during the observation periods varies to some degree. These observations can be made during the instructional activity or any other time which suits the particular situation. Again, what is it you really want to know? Under what circumstances and when can you best observe the behaviors you are concerned about?

The information obtained by observation will represent the first step in determining how a child functions, what he can do, and what he cannot do. It is an important part of the teacher's evaluation. Other steps will be needed before any specific conclusions can be reached.

Many times, close observation over a period of time will make obvious certain behaviors which interfere with learning. For example, a fifth-grade girl had been diagnosed as having a learning disability with problems in the auditory channel. Several months of remedial training did not appear to be making much difference. Close observation revealed that the girl demonstrated several behaviors that indicated that she had not developed many of the prerequisite skills for learning. Actually, she did not know how to learn.

When faced with a new task or one she perceived as difficult, she would sink down in the chair, engage in irrelevant conversation, and resort to speech and behavior that was immature and offensive to her teacher. She had also learned that if enough approaches of a trial-and-error type were tried, she just might hit the right one.

Her listening habits did indeed resemble those of a child with auditory reception and memory problems. However, when the interfering behaviors were identified, rules for acceptable behavior during instruction were set, and a reinforcement system was put into effect to strengthen the desired attending and responding behaviors, her performance showed marked improvement when these factors were reinforced and activities used to practice these skills. When she was allowed to fall back into the old behavior pattern, her performance dropped.

Training in the skills of attending and responding similar to those used with younger children were instituted and carried out in conjunction with academic remediation. While remediation will continue, she has made enough progress that the teachers have seen a marked improvement in her classroom work.

The point is that progress did not begin until those certain behaviors were identified and dealt with. While these behaviors were of the kind commonly associated with learning disabilities, we cannot help but wonder if this particular problem should not be called a *learned* disability. Once again, the label is unimportant; the result is what is important. She knows she can and will learn. Without close observation this could not have been detected.

Informal Tests and Work Samples

Many of the programs and materials in use in the classroom have informal tests included. These tests can be used effectively when and if the results are carefully evaluated.

Other informal tests are teacher-made which consist of samples of one specific task. There tests may include seat-work exercises, orally administered exercises, informal teaching lessons, and individualized written assignments (Wallace and Kauffman [1973]). In constructing the instrument, be sure it samples one task. For example, if you suspect that a child may be having difficulty discriminating between short vowel sounds, a simple way to check it would be to have the child sit with his back to you. This eliminates visual clues he might get watching your lips. Present a list of short, one-syllable words containing all the short vowel sounds. They should be in mixed order and contain samples of all the sounds. Ask the child to identify the short vowel sound he hears. On your list, check off the correct responses and note his errors. His performance will tell you which sounds he can recognize and which sounds he is confusing.

It is most important to be sure that the exercise you use really samples the one specific skill you are testing. If you want to check auditory discrimination, make sure there are no visual clues present.

Many teachers have found it helpful to use a form of task analysis as both a guide to the identification of the specific problem or breakdown in skill and to the correction.

This is perhaps a more organized approach to obtaining work

samples. This involves deciding exactly and specifically what is to be taught or what is being taught that the child is having trouble with. The next step involves breaking that skill down into all its component parts and arranging them in a logical sequence for learning. Most often it is possible to determine at this point how many of those steps a child can successfully perform.

Testing for Particular Skills

If there is any doubt, that particular skill must be tested. Once it is determined at what level in the sequence of the steps the breakdown occurs, it is possible to see where to start teaching. The child can then be taught and tested on each step and finally on the complete task. On the final test, if the child cannot perform successfully, it is possible to reevaluate which steps must be retaught.

For example, if a child has been taught to attack words by sounding them out and yet does not seem to be able to use that skill as effectively as he should, an attempt must be made to determine why he is unsuccessful. What is involved in blending sounds together to decode or identify a new word? What skills must be mastered and what is the logical sequence for learning? Using the word "man" as an example, a child must:

1. Visually recognize each symbol.
2. Know the correct sound for each symbol.
3. Be able to blend the sounds together.
4. Be able to synthesize those sounds or parts into a meaningful whole — "man."

Usually, once a task is broken down into its component parts, it becomes much more manageable. We begin to see what we are really asking of this child. It is possible now to quickly check each skill. We know where to begin to teach. We know we can easily check back if a breakdown occurs and we find that the total skill has not been taught successfully and learned. We know where to teach and reteach. If the child cannot attach the appropriate sound to each symbol, then you must begin to teach at that point. Whatever sounds and symbols have been taught must be retaught until the child can perform successfully.

Use a work sample to check on the ones he knows and those he does not know. Reteach the ones he has not mastered. Use the ones he has learned to give practice in steps 3 and 4. Make up real words and nonsense words using those sounds.

Once you feel he has learned the "trouble sounds," do a check and proceed through the sequence of steps or go back and reteach. Short periods of concentrated practice will help. Try using the sounds and symbols as passwords to get in line for lunch or recess or to gain special privileges.

The real value of this approach is that it can easily be worked into the normal routine, and while it is a diagnostic tool it also leads into the corrective procedure. There is no question about where to start or where to go and it is really mastered.

Observation and Diagnosis Actually Saves Time

The use of observation, task analysis, and work samples as tools for teacher diagnosis does mean extra thought and time. However, when we consider the amount of time spent making no headway or teaching things a child already knows or trying to find "a place to begin," it begins to look more and more like a time-saving device. Certainly, from the child's point of view it is a frustration-saving device, and also from the teacher's point of view.

Usually, as you begin to investigate the problem one child is having, you begin to see that other children also need some parts of the same skill. This means that those children can be taught that skill at the same time.

Teachers have said that once they become accustomed to thinking through tasks, they have found themselves doing it without much conscious effort. It became a means of anticipating possible trouble spots before they became a problem as well as a problem-solving device.

Formal Tests Can Be Helpful

Many teachers shy away from the use of formal diagnostic tests either because they are not readily available, too time consuming, do not yield the type of information that can readily be turned into useful teaching strategies, or have never been taught to use them.

There are, however, several educational diagnostic tests which can be effectively used by classroom teachers. (See the Appendix for a list of such tests.) Many of these tests can be used in their entirety, or subtests can be given separately.

When making a decision about whether or not to use formal tests, remember that giving any test is worthwhile only *if the results yield information you do not already have.* Also, there is no value in giving any test if you do not use the information to modify your teaching and curriculum.

Formal testing instruments also involve the expenditure of funds which may be difficult to find. Ask yourself again, "Can I find the information using some informal device of my own?" If your answer is, "No," then try every way possible to get what you need of the formal test instruments.

Many states and school systems have access to Instructional Materials Resource Centers where some of these diagnostic tools may be located. A local guidance office or psychological services center may also be a possible source.

Formal tests, carefully administered and thoughtfully analyzed, can provide a wealth of good information.

Be sure you are well prepared to administer the test according to the guidelines and directions suggested. Also, be sure you know why you are using a particular test and what you hope to gain from it. Most important, make the results work for you and for the child. (The list of tests in the Appendix is not complete, but it does provide samples of various diagnostic instruments available that most teachers can use themselves.)

Perhaps the most important thing to remember is that a teacher need not feel helpless in the area of pinpointing children's problems. True, all of the desired services are not always readily available, but there are options open to every teacher which do not require specialized skill and training.

Formal tests should be used in conjunction with an increased awareness of the problems experienced by different children and the need for change and modification as indicated by the results.

However, a teacher's own evaluation can result in more effective teaching and a less frustrating situation for all.

A diagnostic checklist is provided which can be very helpful in a teacher's diagnosis, and used subsequentially as a starting point for remedial teaching no matter what the child's exceptionality category may be.

TEACHER'S DIAGNOSTIC CHECKLIST

	NEVER	SOMETIMES	MOST of the TIME	ALWAYS
ATTENTION				
1. Stares into space or appears to daydream.				
2. Lets eyes wander away from stimulus as it is presented.				
3. Acts as if he is attending but does not make the appropriate response.				
4. Requires several repetitions of directions.				
RESPONSE				
1. Begins tasks but does not complete tasks.				
2. Has difficulty working independently.				
3. Is slow getting started on assigned tasks.				
4. Does not know how to start working.				
FOLLOWING DIRECTIONS				
1. Does not listen to directions.				
2. Does not attempt to read directions.				
3. Does not appear to understand.				
4. Is unable to initiate the required responses.				

WORK HABITS

	NEVER	SOMETIMES	MOST of the TIME	ALWAYS
1. Demonstrates poor organization of work.				
2. Does not know how to begin or fails to begin work.				
3. Does not work carefully.				
4. Works inaccurately.				
5. Is inconsistent in quality of work.				

BEHAVIOR

	NEVER	SOMETIMES	MOST of the TIME	ALWAYS
1. Is very restless or hyperactive. a. Plays with things continuously.				
b. Pesters or bothers other children.				
c. Destroys property.				
d. Gets out of seat.				
e. Wiggles or squirms in seat.				
2. Lies.				
3. Cheats.				
4. Steals.				
5. Tattles on other children.				
6. Fights or bullies other children.				
7. Is truant.				
8. Is not punctual (tardy).				
9. Is frequently moody.				
10. Is withdrawn.				
11. Pouts.				
12. Is fearful or overly anxious.				

READING

	NEVER	SOMETIMES	MOST of the TIME	ALWAYS
1. Has reading ability inconsistent with potential.				
2. Reverses letters.				
3. Reverses words.				
4. Confuses letters which look alike.				
5. Confuses words with similar appearance.				
6. Loses place frequently.				
7. Guesses on word identification.				
8. Recognizes words in isolation but not in the context of a sentence.				
9. Gets only first part of word right.				
10. Gets only last part of word right.				
11. Does not associate sounds with symbols.				
12. Cannot blend sounds.				
13. Cannot say the word after blending sounds.				
14. Reads too slowly for developmental stage.				
15. Has limited vocabulary.				
16. Cannot pick out the main idea.				
17. Cannot isolate and remember specific detail.				

	NEVER	SOMETIMES	MOST of the TIME	ALWAYS
SPELLING				
1. Cannot hear a word and break it into separate parts.				
2. Mixes up the sequence of letters in a word.				
3. Uses poor handwriting to disguise errors.				
4. Can spell orally but cannot write the words accurately.				
WRITING				
1. Does not hold pencil properly.				
2. Becomes quickly fatigued and quality of writing deteriorates.				
3. Does not form letters appropriately.				
4. Spaces letters and words poorly.				
5. Is unusually slow in recalling how to form individual letters.				
6. Makes jerky and uneven movements.				
7. Forms letters irregular in size.				

	NEVER	SOMETIMES	MOST of the TIME	ALWAYS

ARITHMETIC

1. Does not understand the basic language of arithmetic.

2. Does not have a firm understanding of basic concepts such as seriation, classification, combinations, and conservation.

3. Makes errors due to poor reasoning skills.

4. Makes counting errors.

5. Cannot remember numbers and facts.

6. Makes computation errors due to inadequate knowledge of procedures in operationism.

Chapter 6

TEACHING HANDICAPPED
CHILDREN EASILY

THIS chapter will deal with basic teaching methods for handicapped children. They do not differ greatly from good teaching methods for all children. This chapter also continues with the assumptions that to teach handicapped children easily and effectively:

1. One does not need to identify, label, or categorize children.
2. One does, however, need to discover and diagnose their *learning problems*. The checklist will be a helpful aid and tool.
3. One must concentrate individually, at least some part of the day, on the problem areas. Tackle one problem at a time.
4. One should have the children's attention — each one's.

In previous chapters, the practice of assigning labels to children with special handicaps has been discussed. It is the opinion of the authors of this book that these labels have little or no value when dealing with the mildly or moderately handicapped child. Labels do not tell us how or what to teach regardless of how impressive they may sound.

Often there is great difficulty in trying to apply the various segments of a handicap definition since children themselves cannot be separated into segments. We are presented with a whole child who must be taught because of his right to learn and his potential, in spite of his limitations.

Most children in today's classrooms who happen to have special problems are very much like other so-called normal children. They have the same feelings, needs, *and most of all, they will learn when taught properly*.

The obvious question is, "How can this learning best be facilitated within the limits imposed upon most classroom

72

situations?" In general, there are some basic considerations to keep in mind. The same principles hold true if we talk about a normal child experiencing a temporary difficulty or a handicapped child with some more permanent limitations.

Be Kind but Firm and Consistent

Many children who encounter difficulty in the classroom cannot set their own limits or function satisfactorily in an unstructured setting. They need to know what is acceptable and what is not acceptable. The rules must be clearly stated and consistently enforced.

One older teacher summed it up very nicely when she spoke to her class early in the school year. She said, "There is time to work and time to play. When we work, we will work hard. When we play, we will play just as hard as we work."

A few clear-cut rules for acceptable behavior which are consistently enforced with kind firmness rather than out of anger will do a great deal to help all children know what the limits are. It is best to concentrate on a few rules at a time. As it becomes necessary, rules may be modified.

We should not expect that because a rule is stated, every child will immediately be able to function within that framework. Some will require shaping and training before they can satisfactorily comply.

Perhaps the most important factor is consistency. Behaviors that are acceptable today and unacceptable tomorrow serve only to create frustration and confusion. Be kind but firm and consistent.

One Step at a Time

Most children, when experiencing difficulty, have trouble remembering and following series of directions. Initially, best results will be obtained when one direction is given at a time. We know this, but how often do we inundate children with a flood of directions? We are then surprised when confusion, inattention, and chaos result. For example, can you hear yourself saying,

"Open your books to page 42, find the third exercise, and answer the questions?"

We are assuming they know which book, where it is, will find the page, locate the correct section, and proceed. Many will not, especially those with poor listening skills or those who become easily confused or have inadequate memory for details. It is just as easy to start out by giving one direction, allowing an adequate amount of time to complete that direction, giving the next direction, etc. Most often it will save time by minimizing confusion.

It is also possible to train individuals and classes to respond appropriately. Once they know what you expect and can follow the one direction at a time easily, start working on two at a time. "Pick up your red crayon and color the largest ball."

The best time to initiate this training is the first day of school, but it is never too late to begin. This is one activity that will not only be helpful to the handicapped child, but benefits every child in a class, even the brightest.

Use a Minimum of Language; Be Direct

We as teachers tend to get carried away with our own voices. Children with learning problems (and some without) tend to "turn us off."

For example, if a child keeps popping out of his chair, be direct and positive, "Sit in your chair." Explanations of why he should and what will happen if he does not often will act as reinforcement. Instead of stopping the behavior, it will very likely increase the frequency.

In instructional activities, the same principle holds true. The language of instruction must be clear, simple, and concise. "Put your name on the line at the top of the paper."

When a child shows signs of being easily confused or simply refuses a task, make sure you do not overload him with unnecessary descriptions or directions. Too many words tend to confuse some children. They do not have the ability to pick out the necessary information. Consequently, they begin to rely on your saying it many times or getting visual clues by watching what the other children do. The result is often the development of a trial and error approach to tasks.

Work from the Concrete to the Abstract

Depending on the severity of the problem as well as the type of problem, most children with learning problems find dealing with abstractions very difficult. For this reason, it is often necessary to provide many opportunities for the manipulation of objects (concrete) before a child can be reasonably expected to deal with numerical operations (abstract).

The understanding of fractions is a good example. Before fractions can be understood, a child must have an understanding of what we mean when we talk about "part" and "whole." He must also understand the relationship of the numerals in a fraction to that part and whole. In learning ½, he may have to see one-half of many things — an apple, an orange, or pieces of paper in various shapes. He may have to cut many circles into the desired number of pieces before it makes sense to him.

Once the basic understanding is developed, he may have to color segments of circles to assist in the addition of fractions with like denominators.

The original objective may have been to add correctly fractions with like denominators of halves, thirds, and fourths. The point is that some older children, as well as younger ones, cannot deal with abstractions without going through concrete, semiconcrete, and semiabstract experiences.

Provide Many Short but Frequent Repetitions

Handicapped children frequently require many more repetitions to learn than do other children. Overlearning is generally the rule. Many short repetitions of a task scattered throughout the day are better than long periods of repetition given less frequently.

If a child has trouble discriminating between the letters *b* and *d*, provide many opportunities each day until the skill is mastered. This can usually be done at odd moments during the day. When everyone is getting ready for lunch, call the child to the board and try to fool him. Put several samples of the letters on the board for him to identify. Other good times would be before and after play periods or when activities change. Difficult sight words or number facts can be used as "passwords" to enter or leave the room or to take part in a favorite activity. The point is that the practice does not have to be elaborate or time-consuming. Frequent opportunities provide more practice and aid in retention. Using these times prevents the teacher from feeling that she is depriving other children in order to provide the extra practice.

Expect Ups and Downs

Learning does not usually proceed in an orderly, uphill direction. There are peaks and valleys marked by spurts and plateaus. This is even more true of children with special problems. Not only are there problems directly related to learning, but these are frequently *set off* by outside factors which most often do not affect normal children to such a degree.

As you work with a child and experience periods which resemble "disaster areas," try to identify the events which may have sparked the problem. Look at the events which directly preceded the onset. Also consider the task and your presentation.

Sometimes you will begin to see a pattern evolve. In this case, once the cause is defined, the problem can be avoided by planning ahead. For example, one class' going from one area to another frequently resulted in a jumble of pushes and shoves which resulted in arguments usually instigated by one disturbed child. Half of the time designated for the next activity was spent restoring order and getting ready to work.

The problem was easily solved by making a rule that before the class moved, all people with pockets put their hands in their pockets. Those without pockets folded their arms Indian style. The group did not move until all were ready. When someone forgot, it was easy to remind him by *complimenting* those "who remembered what to do with their hands."

Once you accept and expect that there will be good times and frustrating times, you will feel more confident and less frustrated dealing with them. Learning to anticipate potential problems and planning ahead makes it easier.

In the example given before, the problem was set off when the group was required to move. By putting their hands into their pockets, the children were silently reminded not to touch other children. Once the group got off to an orderly start, it was easier to manage the movement and begin the next activity.

Control the Quantity of Work and Length of Work Periods

The fact that the length of time children can work and the quantity of work they can handle varies is not news as such. The fact that children with various kinds of handicapping conditions can work for very, very short periods of time compared to their peers does create a classroom problem. Frequently a full page of arithmetic examples may lead some of these children to throw up their hands and quit. Try only a few problems and gradually increase.

One of the most frequent complaints of teachers is that these children cannot work independently. Often this is true, but they can be taught to do so. As a general rule, try to learn by observation how long the child can work at one sitting. Try to gear the amount of work and time required to that amount of time. His ability to work for longer periods of time can very gradually be lengthened or shaped.

Make sure the child knows what he is allowed to do when that work is completed. Frequently, if he receives immediate feedback on his completion of the work and its correctness, he will gladly turn to a *cushion activity* while waiting for the others to finish.

The cushion activities should be things the child enjoys doing that will not disturb the others. Listening to records with earphones, coloring, cutting, looking at books, puzzles, using favorite learning devices or clay, are all good possibilities.

When a child is given seat work and does one or two examples and quits, it may be that he looks at the whole page and panics. Try cutting the worksheet into strips. When one strip is completed, give out the next. He may be able to handle only one strip at first but gradually work toward completing two and then three. A good rule to follow is to give him the amount he completes with good attention and a reasonable rate of accuracy. Gradually work to increase the amount without sacrificing the rate of accuracy.

A kitchen timer can be very effective in encouraging children to persist or keep working. The timer can be set so that the child does not know when it will go off. If he is working when it rings, he can earn a reward or points or tokens to be exchanged at a designated time. Gradually the length of working time may be increased.

Be sure to start with work periods close to the amount he can handle at that time. It will be necessary to keep track of how long he can work alone for several sessions. It may be just a matter of a few minutes. Whatever the amount is, try adding another minute, or three minutes, or five minutes to that amount. As his ability to work for a longer period of time increases, make the intervals longer until he can eventually work for the desired period of time.

It is probably desirable to place the timer where the child cannot see its face. You can also try unpredictable periods of time. In this case, the child must keep working to get the reward because he doesn't know when it will go off.

The reward for working must be something that is pleasing to the child or it will not work. You can try candy, pennies, a special privilege, time for another favorite activity, or even just time off to do as he wishes.

Any time the child is working when the timer goes off, be sure to praise him for working hard or for being a persistent worker.

Children are usually anxious to please. When tasks are within their range of ability and they know what is expected, they will most often try to do what is expected. When they do not, there is usually a good reason why. Check the quantity and level of difficulty.

Sometimes all of these factors can be controlled and children will still have difficulty. Teachers frequently find that children will be slow getting started to work and/or will begin but not complete the work.

When children are slow getting started, try setting a kitchen timer for one minute when you assign a task. If everyone is working when the timer rings, the class earns five minutes of extra recess (Wallace and Kauffman, 1973). The child or group may also earn points or tokens for starting faster than the previous day.

It is also important to remember to give praise for starting to work. Ignore the children who have not started and heap praise on those who are working. As soon as a slowstarter begins to work, give praise for starting to work.

When children begin but do not complete work, remember *Grandma's Rule:* "You do what I want you to do and then you may do what you want to do."

If children have work to complete, it sometimes helps to list what must be done before a favorite activity can be undertaken. Tape the list to the child's desk. When the list is checked off, it may be exchanged as a ticket or pass to do what he would like to do.

Wallace and Kauffman (1973) have listed a variety of alternatives to try when children are having difficulty completing their work assignments. It is important to remember that this need not be a permanent problem. Some children do not develop good work habits without some assistance.

If It Does Not Work, Change

Nothing is more frustrating than to develop a beautiful plan only to find that it does not work. After a reasonable exposure, if you are not able to reach your objectives make a change. Flexibility is a necessity.

When you think you cannot come up with another approach, go back to your analysis of the task. Look at the kinds of errors that are occurring. Usually, here is where you will find the answer to what is going wrong. Is it a word that is not understood? Does the operation involve procedures that have not been mastered?

If you cannot figure out what is going wrong, move to another task. After the class, try to remember what you said and the children's reply. What were you really asking of them? How can you run a check to see what the trouble was? Put yourself in the child's place. If you knew nothing but what has been presented, could you perform the required task? What else do you have to be able to do? Was it stated in the simplest terms possible?

Perhaps the best way to deal with errors is to try to anticipate where they will occur and then make every effort to avoid them.

Do Not Allow Children to Practice Their Errors

Frequently, seat-work assignments will be made and a group of children will work the whole assignment with little or no monitoring. This is often true when children are expected to do a section or page of arithmetic problems.

Many children with learning problems tend to perseverate, or repeat the same error over and over, unless the pattern is broken. At times, it may be necessary to stop the activity and then return to it later. Otherwise, once they start making an error, chances are they will do it throughout the whole assignment. The result is an error that has been thoroughly *learned.*

This presents an additional teaching problem since the error must be unlearned before a correction can be made. It is easier to monitor the child's performance on the first few examples to be sure he gets started correctly. Observation while the child performs the work is ideal but not always practical. The next best approach is to be sure he gets started correctly and monitor as frequently as possible during the task.

When assigning seat work be sure it is work that has been taught. If the teacher will be involved with another activity and unable to give assistance, this is especially important.

Feedback Is Essential

Feedback between teacher and child is a necessity. When a child, group, or class gets into difficulty, the teacher must be tuned into what the children are trying to say. They will not be able to tell you exactly what is wrong, but their errors and behavior will give you valuable clues if you are looking for them.

Children having problems require as much feedback as it is possible to give. Give feedback as soon as a task is completed or whenever an error occurs.

Feedback, whether in the form of praise or a correction, should be specific. If the answer is wrong, *what* is wrong? For example: "No, you named the months of the year. I asked you to name the seasons of the year."

When you want to get a wiggler to sit still, catch him doing what you want him to do. Do not say, "Good!" Be specific and tell him what he did that was good. "That was good sitting still."

Feedback on written work is just as essential as it is with verbal tasks. Work should be checked immediately after completion, and the child should have his work evaluated. He should know what made his work incorrect and be able to make the corrections then. Many activities can be devised to be self-correcting to save the teacher time.

The golden rule is that feedback should be as immediate as possible, frequently given, and *specific*.

Be Positive

Handicapped children are very much like other children. They respond better to a positive approach than to a negative approach. Instead of saying, "You cannot play until you finish every last bit of arithmetic," you can say, "As soon as your arithmetic is finished, you may play." We have all experienced situations where someone got us going not by what was said, but rather the way in which it was said.

With a little practice, this becomes a habit and every time you slip and go the negative way, you end up giving yourself a mental black mark.

A positive approach usually brings about a positive response. After a while it becomes very easy to know when you get off the positive track. The behavior visibly deteriorates, and you know what has happened. The children take your attitude and follow your lead. A positive approach whenever possible results in a better learning environment.

Organization and Management

Many teachers with one or more handicapped children in their classes want to know how to organize and manage their classes. They worry about giving equal time and attention to all children. This is a legitimate concern. Unfortunately, there is no one cookbook prescription to solve this problem. How it is dealt with depends on the individual characteristics of each teaching situation. Here are some suggestions which may be helpful.

Team Up with Another Teacher

Many of the newer trends in education lend themselves to shared teaching responsibilities. Multilevel programs, team teaching, open schools, etc., provide for more flexibility.

You may be interested and talented in particular areas of the curriculum. Your teacher neighbor may be good at or prefer working with special problems. She may be willing to work with selected children from both groups on a particular skill while you work with the rest of the children in supervised seat work or some other activity suitable for large groups. Sometimes individual children or small groups can be exchanged for particular lessons.

Other teachers have been pleased with the results obtained by using older children as tutors. Most have found favorable results for the tutor as well as the child requiring the help. The book *Children Teach Children* by Gartner, Kohler, and Rusman (1971) contains an interesting discussion of possible uses for programs of this type.

Much has also been written about the use of volunteer parents to assist in difficult situations. Since greater numbers of exceptional children are being placed in the regular classroom, your school may want to investigate this as a possibility for a schoolwide program. When extra hands are needed, do not overlook any possible source of additional assistance.

More Than One Child May Need the Same Kind of Help

Teachers have said that very often when they begin to think through the problems of teaching a particular task or series of tasks to one child, they have found others who can use the same kind of help. If special attention is required, it can become a small group activity instead of an individual activity.

There can be no question that trying to meet the needs of a special child and twenty-five or thirty other children is a demanding situation. It need not be a chaotic situation.

If there is no way to form a pair or small group for instruction that includes the handicapped child, it will be necessary to alternate independent and instructional activities requiring teacher supervision. This requires extensive planning. Each child or group must be accounted for. The time spent in planning and selecting appropriate activities will help to minimize confusion.

It is always wise to remember that before you expect a child to work on his own or even learn to follow the routine devised, he must be trained to do what you want. Plan what all groups and individuals will be doing at a given time. Then, step-by-step train them to work as you expect them to.

Some people call this differentiated teaching when they talk about an average group of children. Why not differentiated teaching to assist the learning of children, both handicapped and nonhandicapped? Differentiated teaching does not mean one-to-one tutoring, but rather teaching to the different needs of all children in any group.

One way to move from the whole class approach to a differentiated approach is to gradually introduce pupil-team activities. There are two types of pupil teams. In matched pairs, the partners should be similar in skill abilities in the area to be practiced. This means that both partners will benefit from work on the same level and will be most likely to work at the same rate.

The second type of pupil-team is a heterogenous team of no more than four or five students. This type of team lends itself when a wide variety of responses such as planning and discussion are desired.

Activities designed for pupil-teams can be assigned for a single short activity, and other times they can remain together until a certain series of activities or materials are completed.

When pupil-teams are used for skill tasks, materials should be self-directing with instructions that are easily understood by children using the materials. Answer keys should be available to each team so that the activities are self-correcting. Periodic evaluation on an individual basis is critical.

Some suitable activities for partners include oral reading practice where each one takes turns reading to a partner for extra practice. This gives the teacher an opportunity to give extra help to those teams or individuals needing it. Flash cards, practice spelling tests, and classification activities are also easily adapted.

Heterogeneous pupil-teams can also be used for language development activities and practice or game-type activities. Team leaders can be appointed for periods or days. The only limit to the possibilities is the imagination of you and your class. The more creative and capable students do very well in this type of activity.

In actually beginning to shift from the whole class approach, keep in mind these four basic principles for initiating anything new into your program.

1. Start slowly.
2. State your objectives in terms of what the *children* will do.
3. Get yourself and the classroom organized.
4. Be flexible.

In putting these principles into practice during the first two or three weeks, it is best to plan a small variety of pupil-directed activities scattered throughout the week that are of the one-shot variety.

Your objective during this time should be to have the children try out and react to these kinds of activities. This will help to guide your future planning. The organization involves choosing the activities, planning how to space them, and the preparation of materials.

The second phase in getting started might be to train the students to work with one or two kinds of tasks or materials. The objective now is to have them follow the correct procedure for the assignment. The activities can be incorporated into the program as part of the regular routine. They need not be activities that are done every day, but should be done frequently enough so the need for instructions in getting organized is kept to a minimum.

In the early stages, many of the assigned tasks will be given to the group as a whole. Plan the level of difficulty low enough so that everyone succeeds. Your only purpose now is training.

The next step is to differentiate the tasks according to the needs of the children. Once you accumulate materials in one area on different levels of ability, you can work in matched pairs.

If the materials are self-correcting, you can permit the teams to progress at their own rates. While the teams work, you are free to teach new concepts to small numbers or give additional individual help.

Save large group periods for review purposes, repetition activities, training activities, etc.

In individualizing work, some kind of large envelopes or folders for each pair, team, or child can assist in simplifying the organization. Each folder should include the assignment, necessary materials, and some little device the child may use to indicate that help is needed. A cone-shaped piece of construction paper can be set up as a tepee or tent. This device alerts the teacher to who requires help. If more than one tent goes up, put the names on the board in the order that the tents go up. That way the child knows that his need has been recognized and you will get to him in turn. You can also drop names to the bottom of the list if the children get too restless waiting their turn. Remember to praise those children who wait patiently for their turn.

It also helps to have specific pick-up and return places for the folders. Two small boxes appropriately marked will do.

This one example illustrates some effective general rules for planning:

1. Recognize that all children do not finish a task in the same amount of time. Include a *cushion activity* between tasks that all children are required to complete. When you assign the general task, also assign a second task which they can begin as soon as the required task is completed. This also serves to reward hard work.

2. Plan for systematic reminders of what each child should be doing or is to do next. Use name tags with color codes, signs, lists on the board, verbal reminders, etc.

3. Be consistent in your day-to-day routine. The need for reminders is greatly reduced when the daily routine is consistent. The completion of one activity signals the beginning of the next. Good work habits are not enhanced by confusion.

4. Remember, motivation is maintained when the completion of one activity is automatically rewarded by the start of a new activity.
5. Plan for a periodic change of pace. Follow quiet activity with active, serious material with a game, setting by a few minutes of rigorous activity.
6. Go slowly at first. Lead into changes only after careful planning. Make changes whenever they appear necessary.

While these suggestions do not directly apply to the handicapped child, they do represent a sample approach to making maximum use of each student's ability to free the teacher to give more individualized attention to those children who require it.

In every way possible, treat the handicapped child just as you do your other children. They are more alike than unlike. Make exceptions and modifications as they are required by the particular disability. Try to focus your attention on what the child can do as opposed to what he cannot do.

What About Money and Materials?

There can be no doubt that money and a variety of materials can make your job easier. However, what is ideal and what is most often the case usually are poles apart.

Most state boards of education have consultant services available to local school systems. Some states have regional consultants who are able to work directly with classroom teachers. It is also common now to find state and regional instructional materials centers. These centers usually have a variety of materials and information to loan. Principals and superintendents should have information concerning the availability of these services.

Many different devices and teaching machines are currently available for specialized instruction. Many of these machines can be effectively used to improve specific skills in a specialized setting. Unfortunately, adequate funds and the lack of specialized training make them impractical for use in the average classroom. This fact should not discourage teachers since the same results can usually be obtained by the innovative use of more readily available classroom materials.

When all else fails, do not underestimate your own ability to modify and make use of what you already have in your classroom. When you have no other alternative, the materials you are using with your class can be modified and used. In this case, the way you use them becomes all important.

Know just what each lesson teaches and how it is taught. It is not enough to follow all the directions in the teacher's manual. This is where analysis of the tasks you are teaching can really help. There are several questions you should ask yourself when planning for children having difficulty:

1. How is the task taught?
2. Is the sequence logical in terms of learning?
3. What or how much can the child already do?
4. Is it possible to break it down into smaller steps?
5. How can the presentation be structured to accomodate the special problem?
6. Is this a necessary skill?

Perhaps the most important influence on the outcome of whether or not a given child learns is not what you use; it is *how* you teach it.

Acceptance of the child as an individual capable of being taught, patience and determination, and the willingness to approach the problem positively all will have a more significant effect. This is not only true of teaching handicapped children, but normal children as well.

Money and a variety of materials make it easier. If they are not available, the next best thing is to use everything you do have with a greater awareness of how it can be used to teach the skills that are not developed. It can be done. The materials don't do the teaching — the teacher does!

Chapter 7

INDIVIDUALIZATION IS ESSENTIAL

THERE is no way that we can overstress tutorial *individualization or personalization* in the teaching of handicapped children. It is the key to success. Leave it out or slight its use and one may as well eliminate the whole process.

Before we attempt to describe its use and function, may we clarify just exactly what we mean by individualization, or personalization. The term has come to mean different things to many people. Individualization as we will use the term:

1. Does *not* mean an open classroom where the children are permitted to do as they choose or study on their own whatever strikes their fancy no matter how many attractive learning centers are provided. *Handicapped children need a carefully structured, even tightly structured, learning environment.* They cannot yet choose and work on their own initiative. To start with, they are children in trouble educationally. They need the personal tutorial help of a good teacher to correct their deficiencies, and that takes carefully structured instruction and guidance.

2. Does *not* mean carefully prepared (or not so carefully prepared) work packets, units, modules, or text books designed to appear individualized.

3. Does not mean workbooks or the like where the teacher can turn the child loose on his predigested lesson for a long or short period of time. The handicapped child would be lost, confused, and frustrated.

4. Does not mean any other kind of teaching device or teaching machine, however sophisticated or simple, that the child can use or play with on his own. Again, the handicapped child needs careful guidance to avoid waste of time or probably worse, frustration and failure. On the other

hand we *do* mean just exactly what the term originally meant, *a child working with a teacher on a one-to-one tutorial basis at least for short periods of time.* The more the better at first, but we recognize the fact that in most cases the matter of time and numbers precludes any lengthy personalized endeavor.

Why It Is Necessary

For generations professional educators have observed differences among individual students. They noticed differences in physical characteristics and abilities, intelligence, interest, motivation, background, differences in aptitude for various subject matter areas, and great differences in children with learning handicaps. Even among children with more or less equivalent IQ scores, variation in rates of learning, differences in special talents, and differences in creative ability were observed.

When this concept of individual differences caught the attention of educators shortly after the turn of the century, it captured the imagination of many who were involved in teaching children. Here burst forth an insight to learning that could make a revolutionary difference in how children were *taught* and how they *learned*, which is the logical outcome of the portentous concept of individual differences in individualized or personalized instruction.

From ancient times to the present, teachers and learners have recognized and desired the ideal of a one-to-one instructional relationship. Special education teachers working with learning handicapped children have discovered that individualization is the only method of effective instruction. Enough recent research has been done to establish the efficacy of individualized instruction contrasted to group instruction.

Appallingly, although the idea has been talked about and written about ever since, very little has been done about implementing so tremendous and important a concept. As we, and others strongly concerned about the problems of our schools, observe the average classroom milieu, we almost invariably see a teacher instructing and communicating as if all the thirty (more or fewer) children were interested in the same thing, learned the same thing at the same rate, and could regurgitate the same amount on a test. Sometimes, particularly in the primary grades, we find a teacher who divides his class into three or four groups. but they still are groups taught as groups.

At the same time many, if not most, teachers are troubled and discouraged with schooling as it now functions. They see so many disinterested and failing students and have so many disruptive troublemakers to deal with. These teachers face physical and emotional exhaustion. Many are quitting the classroom for less demanding employment. Our schools continue to waste educationally and destroy self-conceptually millions of potentially worthwhile children. Tragically, all of the carnage piles up even though all have a means of rescue. Why?

Change in education always comes slowly, but it is hard to believe that three generations have been insufficient time. There must be other reasons, and there are. For one thing, we have discovered in far too many schools where the teachers sincerely desire to improve the effectiveness of their teaching and more adequately individualize instruction, the administration will refuse to cooperate with the teachers. This refusal may be more implicit than explicit and may take one or more of several forms. If they do not discourage the plan or forbid the teachers to teach in the manner they wish, they may refuse to furnish the extra and requisite resource materials needed to individualize, or they do not provide the time needed to plan and prepare for change. Lack of real support may be camouflaged by appearing to give consent with the statement, "If you want to individualize your teaching, work it out yourselves."

Cooperation Is Necessary

Most consultants refuse to work with a school system to help implement an individualized program unless they are guaranteed the full cooperation of the school board, superintendent, principals, as well as the teachers. (One wonders why, with all the concern for teacher accountability, we do not also stress school board and administrators' accountability.)

Another reason for the unfortunate lag in implementing individualized instruction lies in the fact that individual differences are greater, more divergent, and more extensive than most educators realize. Not only are there numerous and vast differences between individuals, but many significant intrapersonal differences exist with individuals. Too, medicine, psychology, and education continue to discover differences that no one suspected even ten years ago. For example, one such new category is specific learning disabilities due to minimal, ordinary unobservable, brain dysfunction. Still others recently identified are cultural deprivation, causes of social and emotional problems, and knowledge of when a child learns most and best.

Perhaps the culprit-in-chief has been the relentless and insidious pressure of the textbook, the highly visible but unsuspected enemy of individualized learning. Fantastic sums of money are made by publishing and selling textbooks. State boards of education adopt recommended texts, schools buy them, and state funds are appropriated to the schools which abide by the rules of their adoption and use. *Individualization of learning cannot be practiced when learning is based upon a uniform textbook approach to instruction.* The textbook was and is devised for groups of children; one or even two or three texts (usually one) cannot meet the diversified learning needs of twenty-five to thirty-five children, all of whom are different in so many ways. The textbook approach assumes the impossible: that all children can learn approximately the same thing at the same rate and pass the same tests. Nothing is more absurd.

Furthermore, some thoughtfully planned procedure and structure is necessary for maximum, even adequate learning. If a child were to discover by accident all he needs to learn in our highly complex culture, it would indeed be fortuitous, and highly improbable. Perhaps the most highly gifted may learn to read and do arithmetic on their own, but even they will learn these skills more quickly and more accurately if they are *taught* by a reasonably competent teacher. It is highly unlikely that even the most gifted can discover on his own the complexities of geometry or chemistry, for example. The slow or retarded pupils must have intensive training if they are to learn anything other than a hodgepodge of the simplest skills and concepts.

Some educators have promoted the mechanization growing out of educational technology as a method to accommodate the incredible differences among learners. Such attempts may vary all the way from the simple programmed instruction of cyclic teachers to complex computerized consoles costing almost $100,000 each. However, at best, such applications of technology have yet to discover any method to function well without the personal attention of skilled teachers. They are only partial answers, tools that may help good teachers to individualize more effectively. For most schools the cost of mechanization prohibitively exceeds the best budget possible. But if it could be afforded, it still fails the criteria of one-to-one type of teaching.

Individualized Teaching Does Something to the Child That Is Highly Therapeutic

If individualized learning did nothing more than provide a more effective and efficient mode of instruction, it would be worthwhile. If it merely reduced failure and frustration, it would be worth the effort, but it does something more.

Individualized teaching says to the child in a way that cannot be duplicated, "I think enough of you as a person to give you some of my undivided time. I want to help you. I think you are a valuable person who merits my time and attention."

Call it what you will, "Hawthorne Effect" or anything else, there are psychological forces at work that are therapeutic and inspiring, causing a child to work better and more diligently. It works!

In a study of increasing child suicide Fredrick Reese (1968) discovered a significant fact: "In not one case of (child) suicide was there any significant personal interaction between the student and teacher — there was similar absence of understanding of personal likes, ambitions, habits, and problems."

Failure because of any sort of learning handicaps brings about social isolation. Dr. Reese describes one such boy in the eleventh grade who wrapped himself in a shower curtain and hung himself from a coat bar. The boy was doing work well below his grade level. He was a moody, withdrawn boy who rarely participated in class unless called upon; but he bothered no one and was ignored.

The only exception was in the creative arts where he excelled. His friends saw him as very little different from the others, yet he was a loner. The general impression was that of a boy in a school environment foreign to his personal needs which no one seemed to do anything about. The end result was social isolation for which the solution was escape in death. Some individualization could have prevented both the social isolation and its end result.

What Are Schools For?

Schools not only exist for the purpose of teaching certain skills and knowledge judged to be essential in our culture. They exist also to develop social competency. No school worth its name can abdicate or neglect either role. Individualization could enhance both objectives, especially for learning handicapped exceptional children, or even the gifted.

Discipline Problems Vanish

While some of the children in our project developed notorious reputations for being behavior problems in their regular classrooms, *we did not have a single incident in our program.* This seems remarkable and can be explained by at least two facts. First, each child received the *personalized individual attention* of a concerned skilled teacher who accepted and tried to understand him. He was kept busy at tasks he could, at least for the most part, do. There was little or no failure as he had been perceiving it in the regular classroom, and socially he was made to feel that he counted for something worthwhile.

Discipline problems grow out of neglect of success experiences either academically or socially or both.

The Teacher Is the Key to Motivation and Learning

Motivation is not a new concept in teaching. The idea has been around for centuries that there is an intimate relationship

between a learner's motivation and his learning behavior. They
have known, too, that there is a close relationship between the
teacher and the learner's motivation.

They are not so sure as to what there is about that relationship
that stimulates or stifles interest. Some teachers attempt to use
gimmicks like an exotic chart or a complex diagram on the board,
a film, or a game to capture interest and inspire motivation. Other
teachers may find some fascinating gimmick an aid, but even
without such an attention getter they can cause these children to
sit on the edge of their seats waving their hands frantically in the
air hoping to get a chance to speak as the teacher stimulates a
hotbed of motivation and involvement.

Waetzen (1970) found that as emotional interest in discussion
rises in the hotbed of motivated interest, wrong answers *increase*
even among those who customarily give correct responses. As the
emotional tempo decreases, the percentage of correct responses
rises. *Paradoxically learning is significantly higher in the first
situation.* Perhaps this explains why some teachers avoid an
exciting discussion without knowing that learning flourishes
most when emotion runs highest.

A Teacher's Philosophy of Education Is Crucial

What makes a good teacher? Perhaps more than anything else it
is her philosophy of education. Some teachers minimize the value
of a philosophy of teaching as the product of a worthless ivory
tower of academia. Every teacher has a philosophy of education
whether she is aware of it or not. Let us suggest a simple but
essential philosophy without most parts of which a teacher will
fail to do an acceptable job of motivating and teaching. Teachers
should:

1. Foremost and most fundamentally, earnestly and
   enthusiastically, believe that all children (including the
   learning handicapped and exceptional children) can learn
   and learn well, provided they receive suitable and adequate
   instruction.
2. Realize that what constitutes suitable and adequate
   instruction depends upon knowing one's pupil and

diagnosing his learning problems. Objective assessment instruments will help, but they are only one small tool, which is the most one can expect from objective testing instruments. And may we stress the use of individualized diagnostic tests; group tests are so invalid both in content and administration that they are almost worthless, particularly for exceptional children. Reject their use with every fiber of your being. (The chapter on "Every Teacher Her Own Diagnostician" deals with this in a different way.)

Reliable and valid identification depends ultimately upon working with these children on a one-to-one relationship over a period of time as one observes not only *what they do* in a variety of tasks, but also *how they think and function*. Such essential analysis can be accomplished best by individualized contact.

Once these children are identified and diagnosed initially, and later, these diagnoses are *never* considered final; they are, instead, continuously hypothetical and must be modified as one observes performance. Therapeutic teaching must, therefore, be flexible (albeit highly structured), personalized, and individualized. In other words: prescriptive, but always represcriptive as necessary.

Any relationship with an exceptional child in order to be ameliorative must:

1. Be sincerely warm, understanding, and truly accepting.
2. Be patient but highly expectative.
3. Be firm but reasonable.
4. Be creative, inventive, and explorative, but never so without hopefully cogent and valid reasons.
5. Be positively reinforcing constantly as one sees to it that the child does not fail without a following success.
6. Use as extensive a variety of materials, devices and books as possible which meet learning needs at least partially.
7. Involve the parents in as many ways as possible.
8. Treat each child as an individual with unique and peculiar educational, psychological, emotional, and social needs.
9. Involve the other school personnel in as many ways as possible.
10. Realize that what helps the special child helps all children.

11. Share whatever will be helpful and useful with all who need (and are willing to use) what has been developed. In other words, effective techniques should be replicated.

How to Individualize in a Large Class

The question no doubt has been growing in the reader's mind, "How in the name of heaven can I individualize and help the exceptional children when I have thirty (or more) other children who need my help, too?"

Ten or fifteen minutes a day will do it. We have seen it done, we have done it, and it works. It does not take a long period of time to individualize tutorially. It does take some careful planning and preparation so that the ten or fifteen minutes are used well and wisely. (Much more about this in Chap. 6.) A short period of time on a one-to-one, or even in some cases a one-to-two-or-three basis, works wonders.

Marion Blank and her colleagues (1972) discovered in a controlled situation involving short periods of individualized tutorial teaching of fifteen minutes that disadvantaged children profited most from this type of teaching, raising both IQ and performance significantly. Longer periods of time and the conventional classroom situation were less effective.

Chapter 8

THE PYGMALION EFFECT:
THE ROLE OF EXPECTATIONS

For many years before Robert Rosenthal and his colleagues (1968) conducted their now classic research on the role of expectations in learning, it had been observed that a psychologist interacted in subtle nonverbal ways with his subjects so that he could get the response he expected to get. More surprisingly it mattered not whether the researcher and subject were in the same room or whether they were adults, children or rats.

Rosenthal reasoned if rats become brighter when expected to by their experimenter, is it not possible that children become brighter when their teachers expect them to be brighter? He designed a study to see if this were so.

Rosenthal's Research

He and Lenore Jacobson chose a school in the lower economic section of the South San Francisco Unified School District. Every child was given an unfamiliar, disguised intelligence test which they described as a "late bloomer" test. It would predict, they claimed, late intellectual blooming.

There were three classrooms for each grade, one for children of average ability, one for children with below average ability, and one for bright children. About 20 percent of the children in each classroom were chosen at random to form the group of late bloomers.

The teachers were given the names of these children and told that according to their test results this 20 percent would bloom this year in intelligence and achievement. They would show remarkable gains academically during the next eight months. In reality the only difference between these children and their classmates was in the minds of the teachers, *in their expectations.*

At the end of the school year, all the children were again given the same IQ test. And lo and behold! *The children chosen as late bloomers did bloom!*

Both Poor and Excellent Students Bloomed

Usually when educational theorists consider raising scholastic improvement and achievement, they are referring to improvement at the lower levels of performance. It was interesting to Rosenthal to find that the expectations of the teachers affected children who were at the highest level of intelligence as well as it did children at the lowest level.

At the end of the school year, the teachers were asked to describe the classroom behavior of all the students. The children described as late bloomers were seen as more interesting, more curious, and happier. The teachers also found these children more appealing, better adjusted and more affectionate, and needing less social approval.

Teachers React Negatively to Unexpected Improvement

Many of the other children in the classes also gained in IQ during the year, but the teachers reacted negatively to the unexpected improvement. The more the children not designated as late bloomers gained in IQ points, the more they were regarded as *less* well adjusted, *less* interesting, *less* affectionate, and *less* happy.

It appears that there may be hostility generated when children do not do what they are expected to do, whether it is better or worse than expectations. This seems to be particularly true of children in the low ability group. The unfortunate implications of this set of attitudes are quite disturbing. Both labeling and the halo effect rear their ugly heads to the perpetuation of poor achievement.

Research Replicated

The experiment was replicated in a number of different schools in different parts of the country, always with the same results. *Teacher expectations establish a startling self-fulfilling prophecy.*

Rosenthal's Findings Questioned

As with any discovery that upsets long-held attitudes and inserts a new dimenison into tradition-bound education, Rosenthal's and his colleagues' findings were mercilessly questioned, and his research attacked. Many attempts were made to replicate his findings, some without success, as well as many with corroborative results.

It is not within the scope of this book to discuss these research projects at length except for one explanative charge.

The Hawthorne Effect

In addition to charges of poor research design, insignificant results, and biased interpretation of test results, many attempt to explain his findings on the basis of the Hawthorne Effect.

The Hawthorne Effect grew out of research in the Hawthorne, New Jersey, plant of the Western Electric Co. In an attempt to improve production on its assembly lines, the illumination was improved on several lines. Production did improve, but unexpectedly, production improved also on the control lines. Then it was tried on lines in separate buildings with the same unexpected results. Finally they *reduced* the illumination on several lines and the output *improved* on these lines as well as on those with better lighting.

The explanation: give workers some added personal attention and they will improve their output, at least for a while.

Rosenthal and his co-workers rejected this explanation since the controls did not receive added personal attention in their research projects.

However, as we see it, the Hawthorne Effect cannot be considered all bad. It may explain to some degree why individualized or personalized attention improves school achievement. It certainly does not explain the full force of individualization, but it does have some beneficial effect.

Rosenthal Refutes His Detractors

Almost five years after Rosenthal and his colleagues proposed that students live up or down to their teachers' expectations of them, he comes again (1973) with reams of evidence to show that teachers express their convictions consciously or unconsciously by voice or gesture to their students. Teachers who believe that their students are bright expect more and teach harder, while teachers who are convinced that their pupils are slow teach with lower expectations and less effort.

By now, the theory has been tested in hundreds of experiments in the laboratory, classroom, factory, and office with the same results.

For instance, Pygmalion was generated in the swimming pool at a summer camp. The subjects were boys and girls seven to fourteen. Half of the instructors were led to believe that they were teaching a high potential group. Their pupils became better swimmers at the end of the two-week period than the regular group. Two weeks were enough time to show the results of expectations in developing a physical skill.

W.R. Shrank convinced the United States Air Force Academy Preparatory School to lend themselves to this research. He randomly assigned one hundred enlisted airmen to one of five math classes, and he told the instructors that each class contained selected students with differing levels of ability. The boys in the *supposed* high-ability classes improved their math scores substantially.

Pygmalion Does Not Always Work Out

We experimented in a small school in a poverty level environment. We convinced the teachers that some of their students were gifted even though it did not show up on the group tests used, saying it did show up on individualized IQ tests we used. At least we thought we convinced them of the brightness of these students.

At the end of the year there was no change of significance. The teachers expressed the viewpoint, "We have known these children for years, and they just are not that bright."

When we explained the experiment and its psychological principles to the teachers, they replied that they always had expectations higher than the students' performances,

Expectation Has Many Meanings

Not all of Rosenthal's research supported his hypothesis nor did other attempts of replication. Expectations of the researchers affect the other people involved just as the teachers affect the pupils.

Expectations in order to be effective must be of the sort that was expressed by a colleague of ours who stated that it must be a gut feeling. It is a kind of faith or sincere belief in someone's abilities; otherwise the Pygmalion effect will not work. There must be more to expectations than desire, want, wish, or hope or high standards. To paraphrase an ancient Hebrew teacher: "Expectations are the substance of things hoped for, the evidence of things not seen." It is faith in a child's ability to perform, together with the conscious or unconscious effort to realize that conviction.

NonVerbal Communication: Body Language

Rosenthal's experiments started out with research in the effects of a smile or a frown when tests were given. In nearly all cases the students performed better when the attitude of the test administator was positive and reassuring even though the other variables were kept exactly constant.

We all know that it is not *what* we say but *how* we say it that counts for the effect we produce on other people.

What is nonverbal communication? It is any message we send or receive outside of words. It may be as evident as the shake of the head, a frown or a smile, the shrug of the shoulders, or the unbelief expressed by an open mouth. It can be the clothes you wear, the uncut hair on a teen-ager, the books carried home by the gifted student, the number of books or kind of books in your home, the way you keep house or wax your car. It may be small, unconscious movements — the look in the eye, a raised eyebrow, the tenseness of the hand, the stiffness of one's shoulders, or the relaxed movement of the head.

Koch (1971) says that most nonverbal communication is unconscious but with a small sprinkling of the conscious mixed in. He tells of the patient sitting in a dentist's chair. He grips the arms of the chair tightly unconsciously telling the dentist that he is fearful and anxious. He says one may deny being nervous either because one is unaware of the fact or because one doesn't want to appear to be a sissy, but one's gripping hands tell the true story of how he feels.

Teachers Use Many Nonverbal Signals

Experienced teachers are skilled users of verbal communication or they probably would not be teachers, but they are also usually good at making use of the nonverbal communication of their students.

When giving a test they watch the eyes of their students and can tell whether the student is gazing up to think or to steal the thinking of another student.

The teacher can tell usually when a child is telling the truth by his ease or lack of ease, his looking her straight in the eyes or looking down at the floor or fiddling with his fingers. She has also learned that the clues vary from child to child.

She uses nonverbal language mostly to verify verbal statements and to detect sincerity and emotion. She can tell which students are about to do or have already done something to cause breach of behavior. She has a feel or a hunch that she depends upon a good deal of the time.

She knows which children try to butter her up, or polish the apple, and knows, too, by nonverbal signs which students are frightened and fearful, to mention just a few of the ways by which she reacts to nonverbal communication.

She Is Not So Skilled in Observing Her Own Nonverbal Language

Her pupils are, however.

Ask any child which student is the teacher's favorite, which subject she likes to teach and which she dislikes, and he can tell you in an instant. Ask the children who the teacher's pets are and they know. They know when she's happy and when she's displeased even though she may always wear a smile on her lips.

She may not know the answers. However, if she carefully reflects on the subject, she will realize that they are right. How do they know? Children are experts in reading the nonverbal language of parents and teachers.

Handicapped or exceptional children are most skilled. Although they are less adept at verbal exercises than normal children, they are more skilled at reading nonverbal signs. It is as if Mother Nature helped to compensate for one lack by increasing the efficiency of another method. However, this is not always the case. Occasionally one will find a special education child who has no concept that movements and facial expressions are sending messages. They are rare. Most academically handicapped children are extremely skilled at reading nonverbal language. They know if you like them, accept them, and expect them to learn. They respond exceptionally well.

Some Basic Nonverbal Language

Koch (1971) mentions various methods and techniques we use to communicate without words. Most common probably are *gestures*. One may immediately think of hand gesture, but we also use our eyes and mouth, face, as well as our whole head, and feet. The whole body conveys message by *posture.*

The way one stands or sits or even lies down indicates inner feelings of weariness or enthusiasm, acceptance or rejection. Sudden shifts in posture are significant to indicate impatience, anger, eagerness, or disagreement.

Recent experiments have discovered that the *eyes* are the best nonverbal cue of all. It is not by custom or accident that we watch the eyes of people we are communicating with or getting acquainted with. The pupils grow large with interest and small when there is lack of interest. Hostility (large) or fear (small) can be detected as well as sexual interest. Many people probably have used this technique for communication. Lies can be detected. Look at the eyes of the person who claims to like something but he does not. The eyes tell the truth.

Skin changes are commonly known from the blush of embarrassment to the red of rage or the pallor of fear. Perspiration when temperature is moderate tells its tale of nervousness. The lie detector depends heavily on skin dampness.

How *close we get to people* can communicate a liking or disliking of a person, or it can indicate innate distrust of everyone or a poor self-concept. Thus the closer one gets to a pupil, keeping in mind his own feelings about closeness, the better. This is why teaching on a one-to-one basis is most effective.

The politician or salesman knows the value of *touching* as he uses the handshake or pat on the back. Teachers of small children are aware of the effect of touching. It probably is out of place with older children except for the unusual sitaution. Hyperactive, learning disabled children can often be calmed by touching with a pat on the head or an arm about the shoulder. Mentally retarded children are usually affected positively by touching.

One word of warning is needed here, however. A male teacher was recently charged with sexually molesting a young girl by putting his arm about her shoulders. One needs to be careful about society's unwritten rules. Adults, not children, make and interpret these rules. Some other form of nonverbal communication like a smile or proximity or soft warm voice use may be a necessary substitute. We may add that so far as we have been able to observe, female teachers have far greater latitude in touching.

This brings us to the use of the *voice*. Fortunate indeed is the teacher whom nature endowed with a pleasing, well modulated voice. Everyone can develop a more pleasing voice, if necessary by using a speech therapist. At first thought, voice may seem to be entirely verbal, but it is far more than that. Tone, volume, abruptness, timing, pitch, hesitations, eagerness, interruptions, all convey something more than words. No one needs to be told that "No" can mean "Yes" by nonverbal inflections. Emotions come through one's voice as does boredom or enthusiasm. Encouragement or squelching an idea can be implied in voice use.

Even how you dress conveys volumes about the wearer; as Koch says, "Whole books have been written about dress." The carefully dressed teacher will have better attention and better discipline than the sporty or carelessly dressed teacher. Be careful, too, about overdressing. One would not wear a formal dress to school; neither should one wear sloppy casuals.

Punctuality and time tell the observant reader of nonverbal language volumes. Getting classes underway when the bell rings works better than dawdling around for a while. Keeping the lesson going, or hesitating; planning one's day carefully; rushing, or calmly teaching are all important messages. Being punctual says you care. Being early may suggest insecurity, as well as being late may say, "I don't like you," or "I resent this appointment." The teacher who has or takes time to listen to her pupils' questions or problems says a great deal about how important she feels the child is. The teacher who gets to class *before* the bell rings says, "I care about you," or, "I won't let the class out of my absolute control." Time and its use give more information than the hour of the day.

What do you think of the teacher who wants her room pin-dropping-quiet all or most of the time, or who allows some freedom and busy sounds within reason?

Some teachers make grades all-important and thereby tell the child that grades are more important than what one learns or the effort one puts forth. This is especially significant for special education (if not all of education) and will be considered in another chapter.

What kind of materials, supplies, lesson supplements, textbook, workbook, and busy work does the effective teacher use? Are the materials relevant, well-planned, and interesting? Some teachers want all themes typed and in a special folder. Some care more about misspelled words or smudges than they do about the idea and its development. What are teachers saying nonverbally when they give thirty identical topics to thirty students to write ten pages each or won't let the child take books home because they might get dirty? Such use of materials give real insight to the kind of a teacher one is and one's philosophy of learning.

This list of nonverbal communication is not exhaustive but merely suggestive. One could go on at greater length on methods and actions that speak so much louder than words.

What you *expect in sincere belief* makes for a self-fulfilling prophecy about what your child will learn. You communicate more by what you do than by what you say.

Chapter 9

MOTIVATION FOR LEARNING

IT is interesting, and disturbing, that school is the only place where the customer (student) is usually wrong. If he is not interested or motivated or does not learn, he is at fault. Rarely does the teacher examine herself and ask whether she may be less than interesting and motivating in her teaching. One wonders how many students would attend school or study if all of the punitive clubs (compulsory attendance, grades, failure) were removed. Just imagine for a moment that churches, merchandising, TV programs, and advertising operated like schools. Instead of changing to more interesting programs or making goods more attractive or devising more motivated advertisements or making religious services more meaningful, the customers would be forced to buy, watch, or attend, and be penalized and fined if they did not.

Most Teachers Inadequate Motivators

In probably no pedagogical endeavor are most teachers so inadequate as in the concept of motivation. A casual visit to almost any classroom reveals too many students apathetically going through the motions of being a part of the class, but in reality merely putting in time at best or tearing the class up at worst. Most teachers after contending with repeated student complaints, "What good will that do me?" "I can't understand it," "That's sissy stuff," or even more commonly just doing nothing, give up and rationalize their ineffectiveness. They point out that one child is absent a lot, another lacks background, a third is lazy, and a fourth's parents do not cooperate, that child is mentally retarded, or....

Other teachers do not give up easily; and by threats, appeals,

107

sarcasm, punishment, frequent quizzes, periodic rewards, and failing grades make frantic attempts to motivate. Their frenzied activities only serve to aggravate the problems. Compounding the problems are children who cannot learn, the exceptional and handicapped, under the usually prevailing learning situation. Sarcasm or failing grades or threats exacerbate their problems. They need help and motivation not usually given.

Under such circumstances when activity does take place, Mouly (1968, p.333) describes it realistically: "the operation seems to be powered by low octane mixture, complicated further by an unreleased emergency brake in the form of academic deficiencies, emotional blockings or lack of experience." Any careful observer will discover that laziness or lack of interest disappears when the child gets out of school or earns a few extra dollars at a paper route or grocery store. It is schoolwork that leaves him cold.

What the problem really amounts to is that most teachers do not understand what makes children tick. They do not comprehend that perhaps the student's self-concept has been destroyed by failure and criticism or that schoolwork is totally irrelevant. Nor do these teachers know how to effect a remedial approach.

It is both a travesty and a tragedy of education that the motivation most commonly used by teachers to stimulate learning is the least effective.

Motivation consists essentially of two kinds, *intrinsic* and *extrinsic*. Intrinsic motivation in education derives primarily from the satisfactions inherent in learning itself. Extrinsic motivation in education derives primarily from satisfactions associated with, but outside, the process of learning, and include such factors as grades, teacher or peer praise or blame, parental expectations, or mere scholastic survival. Furthermore, motivation may be either positive or negative for both kinds. The most effective motivation is probably some combination of positive intrinsic and extrinsic. The least effective is negative extrinsic, such as fear of failure, criticism, blame, low grades, or punishment of other kinds.

Unfortunately, negative extrinsic motivation may convert positive intrinsic to negative intrinsic because of associative factors. For instance, a student who has interest in a subject and finds pleasure in learning may come to detest the subject because of anxiety brought on by unreasonable demands, low grades, fear of failure, or criticism and blame. On the other hand, positive extrinsic motivation may serve to develop positive intrinsic motivation. Rewards, praise, success, even tokens of various kinds, have served to induce intrinsic motivation.

Every teacher ought to be aware (and beware) of this fact: for most children both grading and testing are methods of extrinsic motivation which may function in either direction, depending upon whether the student perceives them as reassuring or as threatening. The purpose and emphasis placed upon them, consciously or unconsciously, by the teacher determines whether they result in positive or negative motivation for the student.

No teacher should set unreasonable expectations for himself. It is too much to hope to motivate and interest every student. However, when more than a few are not interested and motivated, he should be seriously concerned. The issue of *Media and Methods* (April, 1969) invited students from schools of all levels across the nation to write about schools, and their replies would be published. There would be an issue on "Kids Talk About Schools."

The children surprised the editors both in volume of replies and consistency of attitude. Enough letters were received to make six large volumes. More significantly, they all said in effect, "School is a bore." The editors got their share of petty griping about lunch programs, buses, bathrooms, unfair grades, and too much homework, but students *were mostly concerned about the lack of real learning and poor teaching.*

Students were not negative because they were less inquisitive or more apathetic toward life. In fact, they were the very opposite. One cannot read their letters without immediately seeing that these kids *cared:* they cared very much! It would shake up concerned teachers to read what the kids said, and we believe most teachers are concerned.

What Research Tells Us about Motivation

Just as motivation has varying shades of definition, so there are various approaches to the problem of motivation for learning. In one school alone, the authors recently observed three approaches to the problem of motivation. One teacher regularly resorted to the use of what she sarcastically called "the board of education." Another teacher proudly explained how she lowered each grade a letter on the first reports sent home to "make the students work a little harder." A third teacher completely ignored the bored sleepers in her class. These teachers were exponents of the hard sell, the soft sell, and the no sell.

In our discussion of motivation, we presume that as a teacher you will be interested in selling learning and, therefore, will want to know as much as possible about establishing the desire to learn in others. So let us examine the kinds of methods, good and poor, teachers use to see what we can learn about getting students to *want to learn.* This is what motivation in school is all about.

Let us begin with a hard psychological fact: children start out in life and in school with a phenomenal drive to learn enhanced with an almost unquenchable curiosity. Yet, by the time the child gets to second or third grade, this complex survival drive is turned off insofar as school is concerned, and learning from there on for most kids most of the time is blood, sweat, and tears. This loss is not developmental, i.e. children do not outgrow the desire to learn. Our educational system does an effective job of squelching this tremendously significant drive.

To see what practices teachers do use and to analyze their effectiveness as motivators, Morse and Wingo (1962) conducted a survey of several hundred teachers selected at random, asking them how they motivated their students and observing their teaching. Frequently, the teachers were at a loss to explain what they did. In general their explanations were an oversimplification and belied the subtlety of the actual teaching skill that was observed. It is a rare teacher who has the insight and objectivity to evaluate validly his teaching skill or lack of it. Morse and Wingo found that students were far more able to make valid evaluations of teachers, at least insofar as they were able to interest and motivate the students.

Several years ago a study was conducted in California (Rosenthal, 1968) which speaks eloquently to this point. A little-known test of intelligence was administered to the pupils in a large school. The test was relabeled "Late Bloomer Test." Without paying the slightest attention to the test results, students from each class were selected at random, and the teachers were told that these students would "bloom" intellectually and academically that year. And they did.

The only factor changed was the teachers' expectations. By expectations we do not mean a hope or a wish or increased demands. It is more like a sincere faith or belief in the child which resulted in many subtle and significant ways of encouragement.

Morse and Wingo also discovered that a good many teachers motivate students by *expecting* them to work. Schools of all types are for learning; they never intimate that it might be otherwise. Such teachers motivate by their attitude and methods used in making assignments, asking questions, or presenting interesting information. In their opinion, most students really like to learn and, in general, enjoy learning. All that the pupils need, they believe, is to be guided through proper tasks reasonably and clearly set by an understanding teacher who anticipates student compliance. These teachers believe, and it works for them, that when students clearly understand just exactly what is expected of them, and furthermore, know that they have a good chance of succeeding, they will "work their heads off."

"I find something that interests him," is a frequent comment. These teachers tend to feel that there is enough intrinsic interest in most school tasks to motivate the average student. *Almost invariably these teachers also impart a feeling that success is possible.*

Probably most teachers who are successful with this method underestimate the basic importance of their own security and interest in their work, their ability to gauge the nature of their students, their ability to establish a secure learning atmosphere, and their ability to import the feeling that pupils and teacher are engaged in a mutual effort toward a worthwhile achievement. The student senses that the teacher is "with" him, not against him nor indifferent to him.

Some teachers consciously or unconsciously assume the attitude of a hurdle or obstacle over which the student must leap if he is to progress. Competition should never be with the teacher, but with goals, one's self, or other students. Good and motivating teachers are warm and understanding facilitators of learning.

Relevancy Motivates Learning

One of the outstanding complaints of the students mentioned earlier in this chapter is lack of relevancy and meaning for them. Relevancy is strongly motivational. Three of the best methods to develop relevancy are:

1. *Frequent use of carefully stated and meaningful objectives* which answer the question before it is asked, "Why should we learn this?" and answers more than, "Because it is good for you," or "Because you need it." Explain why it is good or needed. Good teachers make constant use of goals and objectives clearly defined and specific.
2. *Wide use of current events.* Here is the way to bring the big world outside of school into the school, or better yet, a way to take the school into the real world.
3. *Use of contemporaneous material.* Stories, poems, pictures, songs, art, TV programs. Why is only that which is years old good? Because it has survived by means of the artificial respiration given to it only in the halls of academia?

Curiosity Motivates Learning

One of the great mysteries is what happens to the insatiable curiosity of the small child as he goes through the school years. By some miracle a few keep their sense of wonder and their joy of inquiry. Tragically, for many more learning becomes dull, boring, routine, and even hated.

The only reasonable answer discovered so far states that the loss occurs because their teachers take over too much of the responsibility for learning. Teachers tend to substitute their own goals and incentives for the goals and motive power of the children. It is natural to follow the course of least resistance, and they do. The children become dependent upon the teacher to steer the course, ask the questions, devise or assign the (learning?)

activities, and motivate or prod them into action.

Any sensitive observer notices that this dependence increases as the children grow older and pass from grade to grade. They put forth fewer ideas and depend increasingly upon the teacher for predigested mental food which is to be regurgitated from time (teacher stipulated) to time. It reaches its peak in college; the students there are skilled followers, dependent upon knowledge poured forth, and experts in shooting it back in the required forms on tests.

Most students at the high school and college level require frequent quizzes and tests to keep them at the work of learning. Any teacher who recognizes the evil of dependency and who has the fortitude to try motivation for learning without the threat of frequent tests finds baffled and insecure students who lack the self-discipline to study and learn what they want to learn more or less on their own. They no longer feel the responsibility for their own learning! It is almost impossible to reestablish.

What a tragedy! And how unnecessary! The motivation of a small child is innate — his learning is self-propelled. He even finds school exciting, at first. He manipulates, explores, tests, feels, looks, examines, and listens. He is discovering a whole big new world. When he makes a discovery, he finds an elation and satisfaction which cannot be duplicated. There is no reason why such activities and rewards should not continue throughout life.

Any number of researchers have discovered that children, given the freedom to learn on their own, will learn. They will select increasingly difficult materials as they reach out and accept, *on their own,* the challenge that is in self-motivated learning. (However, this does not work well with learning handicapped children who need a highly structured learning environment.)

We have problems. It is hard for teachers to wait for children to take the initiative. There are precisely produced textbooks to cover. Teachers know that their own teaching ability will be rated by how well their students do on an achievement test. They are aware of the shortness of time. More than anything else, they think they know better than any child what he should learn, how he should learn it; the quickest, surest way to education for all is to devise a curriculum and put the students one and all through it.

How paradoxical and defeating this all is!

There is not the slightest question that what one learns depends upon not the motions one goes through nor the knowledge to which one is exposed, *but upon the meaningful experiences one goes through* as he is exposed to the knowledge, or as he goes through the motions. Too much stimulation dulls sensitivity. Ideas that come too fast cannot be absorbed. There is no incentive to put forth any real effort. All the questions are answered and all the facts discovered before any questions are asked. Nothing is left for youngsters to do but memorize — no one finds fun in this. Pupils learn to "put in time" at school, do as they are told, and save their ingenuity for out-of-school activities. (There are those who even propose to regiment this.)

Olson's findings (Olson, 1959) show that children go as fast or faster when they set their own pace as when the teacher tries to set it. Even more important, they show remarkably more interest and enthusiasm as they learn to feel responsibility for their own learning. If teachers would only let them learn what is meaningful as they guide, facilitate, set up problems without ready-made answers, rather than demand and dictate and prod children to learn what they dish out.

An encouraging trend is developing which capitalizes on the strong psychological drive of curiosity for motivation to learn. The technique is called variously, "Inquiry," "Discovery," or "Exploration." Many of the newer textbooks use such words in their titles and devote more or less space to the method.

Inquiry demands a great deal more time, planning, and freedom than most teachers, unfortunately, are used to allowing. They are bound by the textbook and having to cover a prescribed amount of material. As a result, more lip service than actual teaching is given to inquiry and discovery. Nevertheless this method possesses surprising potential for motivation largely neglected as yet.

The Carrot and the Stick

Other teachers do not expect school tasks to be self-motivating. They feel that there is not enough intrinsic interest in most school tasks and that students must be motivated by pressures and threat of failure or induced to learn by promises of enjoyment and reward — sometimes both.

A good many teachers report that they motivate pupils through tests, grades, and eventually fear of failure. "If you don't want to take this over again next year, you'd better get to work now," or "You'd better get on the ball, or you'll flunk out," are the spoken or implied threats.

Tests can be valuable devices for self-evaluation, and mild pressure certainly activates many a reluctant scholar — though not every one by any means. Tests are not always used for self-evaluation or even an evaluation of learning. Not infrequently they are used only for grades or as a reward or punishment. As pressure mounts, the results are not infrequently far from the ones desired.

Some pupils will work harder and harder to do what is demanded of them; others become discouraged and give up, particularly if they often experience failure or feel that the demands are unreasonable; and still others become rebellious and look for ways to retaliate against a system that makes them feel so uncomfortable. At any rate, only a few are motivated to real achievement by pressure and threats in this space age. When competition develops between a student and a teacher, cooperation and mutual encouragement is not likely to develop. A vicious circle, though, does develop; pressure and threats induce failure which produces more pressure and threats which produce more failure which produces......

Few teachers knowingly induce pressure to the point of producing real anxiety. Yet many teachers must make their students overanxious without realizing it, as examination tension and fear of failure are all too common among students. What such fear-producing stress does to pupil-teacher relationships was demonstrated in a classic experiment by Murray (1933). He found that when pupils were made fearful and then were shown a series of pictures, they imputed more maliciousness to the adults shown in the pictures than when fear was not first induced. *Teachers who, knowingly or unknowingly, cultivate fear can be expected to be perceived as threatening.* This response tends to broaden to a fear of school in general and a dislike of all school subjects and activities.

We know, too, from other studies that when an individual feels threatened, his perceptions become more narrow, his responses become more rigid and less flexible, and he becomes defense oriented rather than task oriented. This reaction can hardly be expected to improve achievement in school or college.

Pressure has another unfortunate result. It relieves the student of responsibility for his own learning. In working to meet the teacher's demands, the learner may fail to develop any feeling of responsibility for directing his learning or for setting up standards for himself. Instead of being self-propelled, he becomes dependent upon outside authority to keep him task oriented. When such students first encounter a situation in which they learn because of their own seeking, their satisfaction is dramatically different from the feeling they have under pressured learning. When students are given the opportunity to make a change from pressured learning to self-direction, they feel lost and insecure, but not for long. The new and more pleasant satisfactions from nonpressured learning motivate the new adjustment remarkably.

Many of the teachers studied report that they try to motivate by making the student's efforts satisfying and pleasurable. If the pupil likes the experience he will learn more, say these teachers. This claim is supported by considerable research. Swain (1956), for example, found that more was retained when the attitude was favorable. Tyler (1958) found that students did better in problem-solving tasks when they expected to succeed than when they did not, regardless of the difficulty of the tasks. Sears (1940) found that students who were motivated by pressures and fear of failure *began to express goals below their own actual accomplishment.* On the other hand, those motivated by anticipation of success and rewards tended to set goals higher than their level of accomplishment.

Teachers who try to make learning satisfying use a wide range of devices including teacher recognition, group acknowledgment, and parental support for work well done. Praise is their keystone. *Marks are thought of as symbols of reward.*

Teachers and psychologists alike have long emphasized the importance of rewards. Many experimenters have found that incentives can stimulate learning in both animal and human subjects. Rewarding a correct response seems to increase the likelihood that it will occur again. It has even been seriously proposed that a school be established where pupils would be paid cash to learn. The more one learns the more he would earn. This might be an interesting experiment in design, but no one expects it to become a pattern for American public education. Classroom rewards must usually be less tangible.

As a matter of fact, even such an apparently simple motivational device as teacher praise or blame is enormously complicated and may have varying effects under different conditions. Originally, Hurlock (1925) found that praise was more effective than blame in motivating pupil effort. Since this pioneer study, it has been discovered that a number of qualifications must be added to her conclusions. For example, it makes a difference who administers the praise or blame (Schmidt, 1941). If the person is one held in high esteem, praise can be potent, but if the person is looked down on, blame from him may be regarded as more desirable than praise — as proof that the recipient is in the "enemy camp." Praise given out by an unpopular teacher may thus have a negative result. Praise perceived as insincere or unearned is also likely to be ineffective.

Expectations, rewards, and pressures — these, essentially, were the three answers given by our teachers to the question, "How do you motivate students?" Yet they obviously used far more intricate motivational techniques than they listed. Some were master psychologists who could take a passive or even negative class of thirty-five and lead it to learning.

Some Recent Research

Many times you have heard it said, "You will reap what you sow." Educationally and psychologically speaking it would be truer to say, "You will sow what you reap." One of the most significant research discoveries concerning motivation clearly finds in behavior reinforced by positive or negative rewards *the second event always controls the first.* That is, what happens after you do something determines what if anything you will do the next time.

This concept is not new. Pavlov and Skinner clearly demonstrated its function. Some of the applications and implications challenge some long-held views of reward and punishment, particularly as they apply to a feeling of helplessness. Maier, Seligman, and Salomon (1969) stand among the leaders in this significant aspect of motivation. They start with an accepted law of behavior. All activity produces reward, punishment, or sometimes nothing at all. In other words behavioral response is satisfying, adversive or neutral. Stimuli can also be so categorized.

One of the most unpleasant forms of pain that can be experienced is that which is produced by an electrical shock. Yet strangely most animals can learn to like, or to even seek, an unpleasant shock — *provided it is followed immediately or shortly by a desirable reward* such as food, sex, praise, freedom, or anything perceived as desirable.

However, if the order is reversed (that is, if the shock *follows* the desirable behavior), no matter how intensely satisfying or pleasurable the behavior may be, the animal will quickly learn to fear and detest that which was once desirable.

To put it specifically, shock a rat then give him food and he will seek more food and will even come to seek the shock that produces food; but give him food followed by a shock and he will seek to avoid food, or if he gets hungry enough he may eat but he does so with great anxiety and fear.

Now apply this same principle to children. Have a child perform a task, even one which is onerous, which is followed by a desirable reward such as play, candy, even sincere praise, and he will learn to like the work. However, if you put the reward first followed by the task, a negative attitude or hostility develops toward the task. In some cases it will even badly color the play or other reward. Follow the work with criticism or more work or ignore the child, and he will soon learn to hate the work.

To apply this to school, study that is followed by an acceptable reward enhances study. However, when the study is followed by adversive reinforcement such as criticism, a test with the threat of low grades, the child soon learns to detest studying. The only exception, of course, is the child who gets the grades or praise that he wants. Tests motivate only the good student, but even some good students develop severe test anxiety because of the implied threat of low grades. Yet we wonder why so many students dislike school.

Primary or intrinsic rewards work best to reinforce desirable behavior, but secondary (extrinsic) rewards should not be ignored. What are secondary rewards? This is a difficult question to answer, but generally speaking, a reward is anything that has been shown to function as a reward: anything that is satisfying, desirable, or pleasing. Some combination of intrinsic and extrinsic rewards probably provides the most effective reinforcement. But remember, *the second event always controls how one feels about the first.*

Find out what a person wants, or wants to do, and then let him have it — *after* he has done what he may not like to do. Destroy or inhibit a desirable response (or an undesirable one) by following the response with some adversive kind of reinforcement.

Activity that reduces an adversive or painful state can become rewarding *if,* and only if, the adversive state is reduced consistently by the activity. A child may study to reduce criticism or improve poor grades, *if* more study actually accomplishes those aims.

You can get an organism (a rat or a child) to learn some response to escape punishment. Rats can be taught to press a bar in a cage to escape punishment or to obtain a reward. The latter will display eagerness and joy at the sight of the researcher, while the former will snarl at the researcher and bite him if he gets a chance.

You can cause a child to play a piano with praise and reward or by threat and punishment. In either case he will learn to play. In the first case he will do so eagerly and joyfully. In the second case the child will have to be pushed and pressured into playing. One will like his teacher, and the other will hate his teacher.

You can cause a child to study and learn by rewards such as

praise and good grades and other desirable results. You can also cause a child to learn to study by pressure, threats, scoldings, and threat of low grades. The first child will enjoy study and like his teacher and will usually become a well inner-motivated student. The other child will dislike study, will do so only if pressured, will usually dislike his teacher, and will cheat at the first opportunity. The child may be turned off completely by the second method. Nothing the teacher can do will motivate him to study and learn. He has dropped out of school intellectually and emotionally long before he drops out socially and physically.

Why this happens is explained by Maier and his colleagues' research. The results are startling and disturbing. Dogs were placed in cages with no excape from a series of mild but unpleasant shocks. The dogs jumped and barked and squirmed, but nothing they could do led to an escape or turned the shocking current off. All they could do was take it and take it.

These same dogs were next placed in cages from which they could escape easily by jumping over a moderately high threshold. Again they were shocked. They made no attempt to escape. Even when the researchers helped them out, showed them the way, and gave them food many times, the dogs never learned to escape. They had learned *not* to learn.

Children are in the same straits who find a classroom painful for any reason: scoldings, embarrassment, failure, low grades, ridicule, painful tests, learning handicaps, from which they cannot escape. They have to stay there and take it. Day after day, week after week, year after year. They may try a variety of ways to get a reward or escape, but they fail and fail.

Then perhaps a few years later they are placed in a class where they can succeed if they try. There is an understanding, accepting, and stimulating teacher, or the demands are now reasonable and rewards possible, but they do not try. Like the dogs, they have learned not to learn. They cannot learn. They are helpless.

Think of the student who is placed with harsh, unreasonable teachers, or who is retarded or perceptually handicapped or culturally deprived or with a speech, sight, or hearing problem. He cannot learn. He cannot escape. He does, however, learn not to learn.

Fortunately the case is not as hopeless as it seems at first glance. Children are not dogs; they can with great patience, understanding, and consistent rewards for the slightest progress learn again to learn. But it is not easy and the situation must change before the child reaches adolescence. There does come a time of no return.

When one uses adversive motivation and reinforcement, one must be *very* careful how, when, and on whom it is used. In all cases there must be provided the alternative of an escape or reward *perceived by the child* as possible to attain. It is not enough for the teacher to see it (or think he sees it); the child must be able to see it, too.

How unfortunate, indeed, it is that most parents and teachers use most frequently the kind of reinforcement that is poorest. The carrot always works better than the stick to motivate acceptable behavior, including learning, in school.

Punishment and pain are useful to inhibit, reduce or destroy a response, *if and only if:*

1. *It is truly painful.* Some children who feel a need for attention find painful attention better than no attention. Therefore, some teachers (and parents) actually reinforce undersirable behavior by means of punishment.

2. *It is consistent and inescapable.* Haphazard punishment actually teaches a child that he might get away with misbehavior at any time because he is allowed to do so sometimes.

3. *Most importantly, the behavior threatened by punishment presents an alternative response that is truly rewarding.* Escape, or better yet, reward must be possible.

In the eyes of children, parents and teachers are powerful and important beings who control their very being. For good or ill these awesome creatures enhance and strengthen with positively rewarding reinforcement the self-concept of a child, or they weaken and debilitate with negative and adversive reinforcement what a child believes about himself. *Negative reinforcement over a period of time destroys the most important possession the child will ever have, a good self-image.*

The child with a good healthy self-concept learns and grows as he should. On the other hand the child with a poor self-concept grows poorly and learns little.

The most important teaching a teacher (or parent) will ever do is that which makes the child feel that he is worthwhile, a person who is worth something; motivation by pain and pressure and punishment will never accomplish this overriding goal. Success and rewards will.

Teacher Warmth and Understanding

Even though the teachers interviewed did not list interpersonal relationships as motivators, experience shows that such relationships are prime factors. Perhaps without realizing exactly how they operate, many effective teachers depend on a personal relationship of mutual interest and confidence in which they provide emotional support and bolster the pupil's confidence in himself. Liking and admiring a teacher provides an incentive to do well and live up to his expectations. Undoubtedly, too, many effective teachers make learning satisfying by supporting the work impulses already present in their pupils, by kindling new interests, and by holding to requirements suited to the capability of their students.

Several definitive studies of teacher effectiveness show clearly that teacher warmth tends to motivate students to learn (Reed, 1962; Ryans, 1960; Christensen, 1960). Children study harder and learn more when they know they are accepted, liked, and respected by their teacher. Research has never supported the view expressed in this statement: "I know they do not like me, but they will thank me later."

Motivating for Creativity

Most susceptible to fatality in the "pressurized fact factories" are the creative students. Most likely to survive are the skilled conformists who have learned that it does not pay to be a thinking and creative individual with divergent viewpoints. They have learned how to digest facts and how to store them so they can be easily regurgitated upon request. Those who possess a good measure of "the most valuable ability given to man," creative thinking in all areas of learning and living, cannot succeed in an environment they perceive as hostile. They depend more upon the ability to think and synthesize than upon the ability to memorize long lists of facts (Witty, 1960).

Critical, discriminating, and creative thinking abilities are developed more by the conducive *processes* or *methods* of learning than by the content. This is not to minimize the importance of knowledge or facts, but to stress *how* these facts produce understanding and creative thinking. Witty (1951), Torrance (1962), among others, have emphasized the importance of a warm, informal receptive, and exploratory atmosphere in which the teacher becomes the accepted sponsor of creativity.

Motivating Underachievers

Every teacher is familiar with the underachiever or low producer, the student who is achieving far below his potential, Gallager (1964) has discovered much to give the concerned teacher some help with these troublesome and troubled students. Without detailing the impressive research conducted, he found that the methods of motivation *least* successful were:

1. The inspiration talk, or "get-in-there-and-fight-fellows" approach.
2. Personal counseling of various types.
3. Pressures of every kind.

However, when these underachievers were given a warm, accepting, flexible, and skilled teacher, they responded by higher achievement. When in addition these underachievers were grouped with other students of similar abilities who were also good students, achievement was even better. This study indicates that it *is* possible to improve learning by modifying attitudes (motivation). This can be accomplished not by attacking poor learning and poor attitudes directly, but rather *through modification of the educational environment of the student!* In these experimental classes the underachievers were introduced to a warmer and more accepting environment and more stimulating ideas and individualized help than they had experienced before.

These studies indicate beyond question that the single most important factor in motivation for learning is the teacher.

There is hardly an educational problem or troublesome child who will not respond positively to individualized constructive attention consistently given in an interested, warm, and accepting manner.

Summary

No matter how thoroughly motivated a student may be (self-actualized or teacher motivated), behavior may not be realized nor the motivation result in fruition. *Motivation results in goal-directed behavior only when certain requirements are met;* the most important of which are these:

1. *Knowledge of how to satisfy the motive.* While the motivation for learning is both innate and induced, one must also learn how to learn, how to attain the goal. Many students could profit much from instruction in how to study — how to learn. It is also imperative that teachers give explicit directions (assignments). A student must know *exactly* what is expected of him and how to do it. Just because the teacher *thinks* he knows is not enough. It must be clear in the student's own mind.

2. *Absence of strong conflicting motives.* It is impossible to remove all conflicting motives, but in order for the motivation to learn or study to result in study, either the study motivation must be stronger than the conflicting motive, or the conflicting motive must be reduced or removed. Habit and self-discipline play important parts in this. Any valued reward or reinforcement will help to overcome the conflicting motive; punishment in itself often serves to have a reverse effect, that of reducing the study motive and strengthening the conflicting motive. Associative pain or distress motivates escape from the causative motive which in many cases may be perceived as the study motive. Rewards work far better.

3. *Incentives.* Even when motives are strong, one knows how to satisfy them, and conflicting motives are overcome, one

must also have incentives. Incentives are additional motives often extrinsically related to, attached to, and reinforcing the initial motive. In education these may include desire for prestige, a better job, pleased parents, making an impression on a peer, winning a prize, more money... Incentives vary with different students depending upon other operating motives.

4. *A reasonable chance for success.* Even if the first three requirements are met, motivation is not likely to result in any goal-directed behavior unless the person believes he has a reasonable chance for success. In education, failure experiences or the prospect of them constitute the most debilitating obstacle to achievement. This is why low grades tend to reduce motivation to learn. It also explains why students who never appeared even to want to learn do so when placed in a situation where they succeed. The nongraded or continuous progress class (highly structured for handicapped children) effectively motivates chronic failures because now they can only succeed; the risk of failure is eliminated.

5. *Freedom from anxiety.* The manner in which vague fears and the premonitions of anxiety prevent many strong motives from producing desirable behavior can be observed in even very young children. Anxiety produces strong avoidance of even that which may be highly desirable. For instance a child separated from his mother for some time developes anxiety to such an extent that he probably will actually avoid her for a time after she returns.

In education anxiety from whatever cause will produce avoidance drives; even if the child is physically present, he may escape into fantasy or withdraw into himself. Fear of ridicule, failure, criticism, nonacceptance, for instance, are strong producers of anxiety and reduce interest. Some anxiety will improve test performance, but a point is reached (which varies for individuals) beyond which anxiety reduces test performance seriously. Any teacher who wishes to motivate for achievement must watch carefully for any behavior of her students so that she can be sure of her own responses which induce anxiety. It does not matter how the teacher feels about it; it depends upon how the student perceives it.

Exceptional Children Need Special Help
in Addition to Best Motivational Practices

There are some students who fail to respond to even the best teacher who practices all the best motivational procedures. We are referring to

1. The slow or retarded child whose learning needs are for simpler tasks, and less of symbols and abstractions. His greatest need is for more spaced drill with concrete materials which stimulate his mind through his senses.
2. The gifted child who is bored with what is good for most of the class. He may need more freedom, depth, independent studies to motivate him and capture his interest.
3. The child with subtle perceptual learning disabilities for whom most of what is done in the average classroom merely serves to confuse and frustrate him.
4. The emotionally disturbed (and disturbing) child who needs the best specialized help available.
5. The culturally disadvantaged child who has not developed the learning readiness skills teachers take for granted. In addition he may lack the vocabulary and word knowledge of the other students. His stimulation index may be very obstinate; his home environment may be hostile to learning.

Most children are motivated to learn when they can learn what has meaning and relevancy, if it meets their educational needs, and satisfies their own purposes. Differentiated methods and materials are the only answers to motivation to learning for these children.

Motivation to learn consists of meeting the psychological needs, finding the interests, and using the innate drives of children as learning opportunities are presented in a warm and accepting and individualized situation. Also, it must be done in a challenging way that provides relevancy and successful experiences.

BE CAREFUL WITH GRADES

No ruler of a nation exerts more momentous power than the average teacher in a classroom as she gives out grades. She can determine whether a child passes or fails and whether his self-concept grows or diminishes.

She probably is unaware of the momentous influence she has upon the lives of the children in her care. Yet by the stroke of a pen she can make or break a child scholastically, vocationally, or even personally. Grades have become the all important mark of scholastic success or failure.

Yet Only in School Do Grades Have Meaning

Only in academia (school) do grades have any meaning, but even there they do more harm than good. No aspect of education, as it is commonly practiced, produces more failure, distorts and prevents learning more, and damages more children than grades. Most unwittingly but critically injured are our special-need children, helpless in a devastating system designed for average children.

Yet, probably no aspect of education is more sacred and revered and time-honored by conventional educators than the prevailing grading system of percentages and A-B-C-D-F. Most people have become so brainwashed and accustomed to grades that anyone who suggests some better evaluation system immediately finds himself assaulted on all sides by parents and teachers and traditionalist educators who cry out, "What shall we do without grades?"

It's sobering to note that very few students like grades. As a matter of fact, a number of studies made (Stallings and Leslie, 1970; Hazen Foundation, 1968; Morton, 1967; Peterson, 1966,

127

among others) find that students would eliminate or strongly modify the present grading system. Significantly, the better students, those who seem to profit most by the traditional grading system, cry against grades the loudest.

There is a rapidly growing body of outstanding educators who are saying, "Grades must go!" Slowly the idea is taking hold in some of our major universities as well as in a growing list of public schools.

Those who would perpetuate the grading system as most children know it, complain, "If we do away with grades, how can we know what they know?" "How can we motivate (force) students to learn?" "We will lower educational standards." "How can we prevent students from goofing off?" "How can I tell if Johnny is smarter than Jimmy?" "What will I do without this primitive and punitive club that makes me feel so in control of learning?"

How Did the Grading System Begin?

How did it all begin? Grading by percentages and letters began in the early part of this century as an outgrowth of the industrial revolution. It was education's attempt to appear as efficient as the mass production of industry.

Thorndyke got the assembly line of education moving with his seductively reasonable generalization: "If anything exists, it exists in some quantity, and if it exists in some quantity, it can be measured." He proposed a number or seemingly objective processes. Soon everyone jumped aboard his deceptively facile grade assembly line and has been riding it ever since.

A great deal has been written down through the years with sincere attempts to modify the evils of the practice, nearly always with the idea of revision. A system that is inherently malignant will not yield to palliatives; it must be excised. Therefore, within the last five years concerned educators and psychologists in considerable numbers are crying, "Grades must go! We can no longer support this destructive and worthless practice."

If you will hear me out, I will show that the prevailing grading systems only *appear* to do what their proponents want them to do.

More significantly, grades do atrocious harm to personality development, intolerable violence to real learning and sinister mischief to motivation.

Literally, not a shred of research evidence supports the conventional system. In fact research supports the opposite view: *learning improves when grades are eliminated.*

The only seemingly genuine function of grades serves certain administrative functions by making it easier and apparently more objective to decide who is on probation, who can take an honors course or a "bonehead" course, who is promoted or failed, or who can go to college or graduate school, and the like. Some elementary and high schools, colleges, and universities have discovered that they can function more effectively without grades. In any case, grades are too destructive and defeating to be allowed to continue to prostitute and profane what education could be. Especially it is true for handicapped children that one must be careful with grades.

Twenty-five Reasons Why (With the exception of the first six, they do not follow any order of importance.)

1. Some realistic assessment of the worth of grades is revealed by the fact that research study upon study strongly supports the sobering conclusion *that there is little or no correlation between grade point averages and successful achievement after graduation from high school or college!* (Holland and Richards, 1965, 1967; Hoyt, 1966; Wallach and Lutz, 1967; Holland and Austin, 1962; Getzels and Jackson, 1962; Price, Taylor, *et al.*, 1964; Taylor, 1966; Torrance, 1962, to mention a few.) The literature is replete. One cannot help but wonder why so much emphasis is placed upon GPS's in the light of the wealth of devastating research. For those who support grades, Werts (1967) is frequently quoted, but his research is strongly questioned. His reported results have never been supported by subsequent replications.

   Our own experience with hundreds of student teachers supports the findings of the above researchers. There is no correlation between grades made in college and ability to teach. We have had good and poor student teachers with high GPA's and good and poor with borderline GPA's. The correlation is not significant.

The most recent research was done by the American College Testing Program who publish the widely used and prestigious ACT college entrance examinations. One would expect such a concern with so much at stake in scores used for college entrance purposes to support testing and grading, but they do not. Thirty-seven recent research projects sponsored by ACTP support previous findings: *grades have no relevant correlation with job success, professional achievement, or any other out-of-school performance. Grades do not count for anything except in school!*

2. *No practice of contemporary education has a greater effect upon a child's self-concept than the grades he receives.* To the student, the grades he receives are usually equated with what the teacher thinks of him as a person. Thus, the student who gets good grades thinks the teacher rates him highly, while the student who gets poor grades thinks the teacher rates him poorly. Now add to this self-concept forming effect the pressure of peers and parents, and you have a most powerful personality forming force.

Probably the worst effect upon the gifted student may be feelings of superiority or lazy learning habits that develop if he does not need to work at getting high marks.

On the other hand, low marks tell the poor students (or the ones rated and labeled poor), consisting mostly of special-need children, that they are dumb and not worth much, with devastating results. Contrary to the attitude of some teachers (and parents), low marks do not motivate students to study harder and learn more. Quite the contrary, as many researchers have discovered, failure or the perception of failure causes the failer to reduce his goals or set them so high that no one will blame him if he fails or causes him to quit trying, period. Other studies show that the person who cannot escape from an adversive and painful situation soon learns not to learn and will continue not to learn even if he is placed in a different situation conducive to success in learning. This explains at least partially why underachievers so rarely become learners. For all practical purposes they have been destroyed as worthwhile persons. (See chapter on motivation for treatment of this aspect.) Achievement correlates strongly positively with self-concepts held.

The student who is not doing as well as he likes, or feels others wish him to do, and who feels that he cannot do any better, will not be moved to try harder. Instead, he will probably try to rationalize his grade. He may blame the teacher, but more likely, if the pattern persists, he believes he is poor in that particular subject. In other words he is helped to develop a negative reference to self.

Most children who develop real emotional and personality problems (and those who do not stand out as so serious but who nevertheless have poor self-concepts) have a history of failure in meeting demands whether in school or at home. One of the most successful forms of emotional therapy so far developed rewards even the most miniscule achievement. No failure is possible because expectations are only whatever the child *can* accomplish. It works upon the theory that achievement is therapeutic.

Where did we ever get the idea that only those persons who achieve above a certain level, 70 percent in popular grading scales, are recognized as achievers and anyone making less than that is a failure? Has not the child who rates a 40 or 50 percent or even less learned *something?* Many psychologists (Hewett, 1968) think so and suggest that children can be rewarded for "thimblefuls of achievement as well as for bucketfuls." Most children who fail assume an apathetic attitude of resignation, others become hostile, and still others regress into some psychotic state; they believe they have very little chance to succeed or be happy in the world as they see it.

Much more could be said about the horribly destructive force of failure in school which shatters children's self-concepts. For those who may wish to pursue this further, may be recommended William Glaser's *Schools Without Failure* (1969), especially the first few chapters, or La Benne and Green's *Educational Implication of Self-Concept Theory* (1969), as well as others also listed in the Bibliography and Additional Reading List of this book.

3. *Grades separate students and teachers into two warring camps, both armed with dangerous weapons.* If any one thing precludes a "community of scholars," this is it. "The grades keep students from teacher and teacher from student as effectively as if each wore the sweaty jerseys of two arch-rivals each fighting for a bid to a bowl game" (Simon, 1970).

The student soon learns of this situation and learns how to do battle. If he feels he has a chance to win even a little, he sits in his seat trying to outguess and outthink his opponent. As the teacher teaches, he keeps asking himself, "Will that be on a test?" Or, "Will I be graded on that?" He says and does what he feels will get him a good grade. He does not dare to brown-nose too much or other students will not like him, and the teacher may even get suspicious.

All the while the teacher fortifies her position with as many defenses as possible so that the student, "will not get away with anything." No student will get a good grade who does not meet her standards. Tests rate high in her arsenal of war.

If it is not war, it is strong competition. If Carl Rogers (1969) and others are right, the teacher is a helper, facilitator of learning, fellow scholar, even friend. Not in classes where grades are prized by the student and guarded by the teachers who act more like roadblocks to see that no one gets by who makes less on a test than they arbitrarily determine.

This competition (or war) exists at all levels of schooling, but reaches its zenith in college. Impersonalization on college campuses has many causes. Size is not the least of the causes, but impersonalization flourishes on the campuses of small colleges, too.

The problem grows out of the dual role of the teacher at any level of learning who must be both *instructor* and *judge* (grade giver). In her role as judge she is charged with the responsibility of rewarding and punishing students as she is pushed in the opposite direction. One is able to teach a friend — as a matter of fact, it may not be really possible to teach one who is not a friend — "but one does not comfortably give an 'F' to a friend" (Axelrod, 1968).

Many teachers, at all levels of school have grown wary of showing or encouraging any sign of friendship , or even friendliness, between themselves and their pupils. This plain fact is undesirable, and perhaps the teacher is fairer to everyone when grades are given if she has been impersonal with all her pupils. Riesman (1964) says that the grading relationship "tends to contaminate the teaching relationship."

The students who suffer most from this contamination are the gifted creative student and the special-need student. The former needs the personalized teacher-student relationship most as he offers divergent viewpoints, hopefully without fear of reprisal, and the latter has even greater need for individualization in a one-to-one learning situation.

Eliminate grades and you eliminate the policeman-judge. How much more effective learning might be with the help of a friendly helper who evaluates and furnishes feedback without the contamination pressure of grades.

4. In a (September 6, 1970) cartoon by Shultz, Linus, in the "Peanuts" Sunday feature, is shown back in school writing a theme "On Returning to School after Summer." He writes, "No one can deny the joys of a summer vacation. . . . It must be admitted, however, that the true joy lies in returning to our halls of learning. Is not life itself a learning process? Do we not mature . . . "

The teacher likes it, so Linus concludes, "As the years go by, you learn what sells." *Most conventional education encourages conformity which grades aggravate.* Students soon learn to feed back to the teacher what they think the teacher wants to hear. It is true that this could happen even in a nongraded system, but as long as good grades are as highly prized and emphasized as they are, conformity will be stressed, too. Most tragically, the brightest students are most affected. Those who have the ability to do the best thinking and creating bow to the system most rigourously. Many studies support this observation (Price, 1954, p. 46; Getzals and Jackson, 1962; Torrance, 1962).

Education motivated primarily by grades and objective testing emphasizes memorization of facts because facts are what objective tests are designed to evaluate. A teacher determines by the kind of tests she gives more than she may know the kind of learning that takes place in her class. She may *say* she wants critical and creative thinking, but if grades are based upon objective tests, memorization of facts will be actually what takes place. If, that is, the student has the ability to memorize easily; if not, as is the case with most types of special-need children, he suffers frustration and failure.

This is not to imply that facts are not important; they are. Facts are the foundation upon which real learning is built. Too much of education today is merely knowledge gathering and test regurgitation. Problem finding and problem solving, critical and creative thinking, never strong parts of our education system, are consistently downgraded (at least by implication) by our testing and grading procedures. The few rare courses that require thinking are evaded by the very students who should take them, the college-bound (or in-college) students, because they fear the possible low grades, or the insecurity engendered when they are no longer operating with the *certainly principle*.

According to the certainty principle, everything has a right or wrong answer and education is to find out what that is and reproduce it on a test in order to get a good grade. Even when the teacher allows free discussion, they are guided by that teacher "until we arrive at the right answer." Most students stay with the safe, predictable memory courses, reducing the risk of a low grade, and reducing the human potential to think.

Thus, conventional education consistently emphasizes a lesser function of the human brain, memory, while relatively neglecting its major function, thinking. Even when thinking is taught, it usually is that required to solve problems in math or science for which there are definite answers. Much less a part of the school programs is thinking about problems for which there is no definite or right answers. We desperately need thinking and inquiry about political, social economic, educational, and even scientific problems for which there are at best a series of possible alternatives, none perfect, but some, we hope, better than others.

Most teachers will never allow this as long as they have to grade precisely, for such kinds of thinking cannot be objectively tested nor graded mathematically.

5. *Grades have become a substitute for education.* Ask any student what he wants most of all to know after he has taken a test or finished a course. What does he work for? What does he think about during class and while studying? Yes, there may be rare students who care about what they have *learned.*

6. *Grades simply do not do what they are supposed to do.* What are they supposed to do? In 1947 William Wrinkle discussed this question in a book that became the "grade user's bible." Whether most educators are aware of it or not, Wrinkle's philosophy on grading controls what they do and why they grade. Here is Wrinkle's list:

A. *Administrative functions:* Grades indicate whether a student has passed or failed or is on probation, whether he should be promoted or retained, and when he should be graduated. They are used in transferring a student from one school to another and in college admissions. They may be used by employers to evaluate prospective employees.

B. *Guidance functions:* Grades are used in guidance counseling, in defining areas of special ability and inability, in deciding which courses to enroll the student in and which to keep him out of and in determining how many courses he may take.

C. *Information functions:* Grades are the chief means employed by the school to give information to students and their parents regarding their learning progress, success or failure in school.

D. *Motivation and discipline functions:* Grades are used to stimulate students to make greater effort in learning. They are also used to determine honors, school activities, eligibility for extracurricular activities and athletics, and in winning prizes and scholarships.

That simple numbers or letters can carry so much information useable for so many purposes is unbelievable! Indeed, it is unbelievable and the reason for not believing is that grades do not do what Wrinkle and all his disciples say they do.

In 1966 the Association for Supervision and Curriculum Development of the National Education Association appointed a prestigious committee to study and report on the matter of grades and their function. Their *1967 Yearbook* is devoted to this topic, and what follows (continuing under 6) is condensed from this report:

Administrative function. Marks are used for the purpose suggested by Wrinkle, but they do not succeed in this function. Few colleges, if any, still depend upon grades alone for admission or dismissal, but rather use a wide variety of information. Increasingly, public schools also require many sources, such as intelligence tests, reading ability, personality inventories and teacher recommendations. Few employers including school administrators, are still interested in grades when considering a candidate for a position.

Possibly it is only at graduation time that the grade point average reaches full flower. The moment of graduation is often where schools stand most squarely on credit hours and GPA's. (Most special-need children are not even considered for this.) Awards and honors, indeed, even graduation itself, are often based upon a hundredth of a point. In order to cut the points even more finely, some schools record numerical grades. But it is an unequivocal fact that such use of grades do unconsidered violence to any valid concept of evaluation. For one thing few teachers, if any, take into consideration the very real unavoidable standard error of measurement (see item 20).

For another thing, GPA's take no cognizance of teacher vagaries and variability. It is a known fact that different teachers grading the same test or paper seldom agree on the grade. And for still another thing, GPA's do not take into consideration the varying difficulty of different courses of study. While the GPA looks valid and can be arrived at mathematically, it is nothing more nor less than the chance result of a long set of arbitrary teacher-made decisions.

Guidance functions. Similar conclusions can be drawn about this claimed function. No careful guidance counselor or psychologist relies upon grades as sufficient evidence for making decisions about a student's abilities, vocational or course choice. Of all the information available, grades are the least reliable.

Information function. This is a bad joke. Many studies have shown that no two people seem able to interpret a set of grades or even a simple grade in the same fashion. When different persons are called on to give marks to students, even under standardized conditions, they tend to vary greatly in their judgments.

Most confusing is the common practice of combining into a simple grade many different considerations such as group expectations, individual expectations, progress, effort, conduct, neatness, skill, form, content, spelling, grammar, originality, attitude, participation, absence, and tardiness.

No single grade, however carefully calculated, can possibly convey all or even part of that hodgepodge lumped-together information. It is strongly debated whether a number or letter can give adequate information about any *one* bit of information. Yet many special-need children are capable of perhaps only one or two types of achievement. To be held responsible for all of them is unrealistic, especially if improper (for these children) teaching methods are used.

A grade cannot give needed information about strengths or weaknesses (Which? In what? Why?); progress (How? How much?); spelling (In what? Which kind of words?

Carefulness? Ignorance?); content (Like what?); and so on.

Grades are at best confusing and ambiguous. Communicate? Absolutely not! For the sake of argument, let's assume that a grade represents a single bit of information such as relative class standing. Even here it is impossible to know what it means. For instance, does a "B" represent an "A" student not working up to capacity, a "B" student doing his best, or a "C" student overachieving, or an "A" student who dared to disagree with his teacher, or a "C" student who looks and acts as his teacher wants him to?

Furthermore, different teachers have different standards. Consider the teacher who says, "My 'C' is worth an 'A' in any other teacher's course," and the teacher whose "A" can be earned without real learning? How do you compare an "A" in shop with an "A" in physics?

Grades represent an effort to reconcile the irreconcilable which results in the ciphering of the indecipherable.

Motivation and discipline. Even Wrinkle questioned the reliability of grades to serve the first three purposes he proposed! He says, "Of all the functions marking and reporting practices are supposed to serve, they actually serve only one degree of effectiveness — motivation."

As a matter of carefully considered fact, grades do serve to motivate students — the good ones. *Grades do not motivate the poor or failing student,* many of whom are special-need children. He either rationalizes his grade, or lowers his goals, or gives up.

We know a principal who for years every fall has told his teachers to lower every student's grade at the first grading period one letter from what he actually earns, "He will work harder next time." The man really is quite intelligent and should have discovered by this time what actually happens. If he were to examine the students' grades, he would notice that except for a few of the braver, hardier, and more self-motivated students the grades *tend to remain constant.* If the scheme worked, grades would be *more* than the one lowered letter higher next grading period. This grade constancy infers permanent damage to student goals.

Needless to say, the endless belaboring of students by teachers through the marking-grading system leads to considerable student grade sensitization, even neuroticism. Still teachers will appear to be surprised at students' overconcern with grades. The ceaseless emphasis, explicit or implied, on grades results only in children's being adversely affected permanently, and in far too many cases destroys the very taproot of their motivation.

Even when motivation is achieved, and it is often only in the better student, a serious question lies in the manner in which motivation occurs. The process is based more often than not upon fear of failure, fear of humiliation, fear of loss of privilege. In only a few cases do some good students find reward and desire for achievement in lowered grades; the failing student, never.

For many years this writer has made it a practice to discover how college students feel about tests that are graded. It is sobering to note that among these students, the cream of high school crops, ones who above all others should have found tests and grades motivating, this writer has found more than 95 percent who fear and hate tests.

Even when the effect is positive, in these few cases, the view of learning is not one of a joint search for learning and truth by student and teacher or by students together. Rather, it is mostly like an ant-pile of scramblers fighting one another for the few positions at the top, with self-interest the most prominent motive, and little time or room for the luxury of cooperation and concern for others. (Item 10 discusses this further.)

Psychologists and psychiatrists have long noted the undesirable effect upon the self-concept and mental health of many children caused by an overemphasis on grades. Educators have long noted the stress created during the grading process — distress evident in teachers as well as in students. Is this not too high a price to pay for a mostly *negative* kind of motivation? Research has repeatedly demonstrated better and more positive means to stimulate learning quickly and permanently. (Of this more will be said in the latter part of this chapter. See also the chapter on "Motivation.")

7. *Since grades do not accurately report educational growth and give the information needed to make sound decisions, the relationship between grades and ability is even more distant.*

    Brown, 1962; Getzels and Jackson, 1962; Heist, 1962; Price, et al., 1964; Torrance, 1962; as well as others have shown that grades do not reflect the ability to create or think reflectively.

    Further support for this contention can be found in the extraordinary records of these poor grade getters: Edison, Einstein, Churchill, Salinger (*Catcher in the Rye*). Many more could be named.

    Creativity and thinking are penalized since these students are apt to give highly original meanings to questions, even the so-called objective type, which are then graded on the basis of predetermined answers stipulated by the teacher. Moreover, the thinking and creative student does not respect the testing and grading practices of most teachers. If he voices this attitude to his teacher — which he often will not hesitate to do — he alienates and exasperates the teacher still further, and endangers his grade even more.

    Most tests are not designed or used for the purpose of ascertaining learning but for the purpose of getting a grade and/or erecting a high fence. As a result, the tests have very little relationship to the verbalized objectives of education, and the grade does not (cannot) validly reflect the learning; it merely is the arbitrary mark made on a test, nothing more or less.

8. *Most teacher-made tests have low validity and reliability coefficients.* In our profession, we have come to know many teachers both in the public schools and in college. We are sorry to say that we do not know a single teacher who does an item analysis of his tests and determines validity and reliability coefficients. At the college level very few teachers ever had even one course or read one book on the principles of test construction. Yet the academic lives and self-concepts of students depend on the grades obtained from invalid and

unrealiable tests.

If the teacher does not make her own tests, she probably uses textbook publishers' tests. This is even worse. The most important kind of validity is curricular validity which simply stated means that the test items are taken directly from what is taught, and only from what is taught. *If* the teacher sticks precisely to her text and teaches no more or no less, and *if* the publisher has the services of a trained professional, the test may be valid. But these are tremendous and elusive "if's."

Furthermore, no teacher-made test and few textbook tests have been normed, that is, the probable score of an average group of students determined. The test probably is graded on a teacher-set standard which may well be too difficult or too easy. A grade *is* arbitrarily determined, which may or may not have a real correlaiton to student learning; if it does, it is most likely a lucky chance.

Consider this, too: the *very best* standardized tests, carefully constructed by experienced professionals, tested and revised several times with careful item analysis, and having validity and reliability coefficients that are in the order of .7 or .8 or higher — *these* tests have a standard error of measurement of *no less* than plus and minus three. That is, a test score, say, of 78 may just as reasonably be 81 or 79, a spread of six points, or on some scales, a "C" or a "D."

A teacher-made test or textbook publisher's test undoubtedly has a much higher standard error of measurement. How, then, can any reasonable teacher claim her test grade is what it is, and most ridiculous, how can anyone give valid, meaningful pluses and minuses? As a matter of hard fact, no teacher can reliably grade accurately enough to say a test score is worth the grade she assigns to it rather than a letter above or below it. The *most* anyone can say realistically and truthfully is that a grade is somewhere near the range of a letter or percentage point, give or take three points.

Yet students' very lives often hang on a grade differential of one point based on a test with a standard error of measurement of *more* than plus and minus three points! This kind of grading is the bread and butter of most education today. Furthermore, even *if* grading were valid and reliable, such precision could not be justified.

9. *Except in rare cases, current methods of grading practices do not allow for individual differences.* Popular practices in grading do not allow for the fact that learning is a highly individualistic process with varying interests, peaks, and valleys peculiar to each person alone. Right here, then, lies the cause of much of the unthinking damage done to special-need students.

No concept of popular education is more fallacious than that which presumes (or functions as if it presumes) that all students learn even approximately the same things at the same rate in the same manner. It is assumed, therefore, they should perform on the same test in a manner that will permit a uniform (fair) system of grading.

Most teachers give easy lip service to the concept of individual differences without really comprehending just how different individual differences are and how those differences affect learning not only quantitatively but qualitatively as well. How dare all children be graded according to the same or even similar standards!

Grading, as it is usually done, facilitates evaluation of large numbers of students with as little trouble as possible; only the convenience is considered. The individual as a peculiar person with peculiar learning patterns is usually overlooked. This assertion applies even to the children we consider normal.

To further complicate matters, about 50 percent of all children are in one or another of the categories we call exceptional: retarded, gifted, culturally disadvantaged, perceptually handicapped, learning disabled, emotionally disturbed, socially maladjusted, children with medical problems as well as those with chronic speech, hearing, and sight problems. In most schools these children are mixed in with all the others and tested and graded alike.

What a travesty and tragedy of most schools' favorite function!

10. *Grades, as commonly used, promote dangerous and unrealistic competition.* One of the most popular arguments in favor of grades supports the concept of competition. Life is a competitive process; therefore, children should learn how to compete and get used to it.

This argument needs careful examination. (For a more thorough treatment of this aspect of education, see the chapter on competition.) First of all, grades are not a realistic model for the competition found in real life; they are not analogous to salaries or promotions which are based upon training, experience, proficiency, and fixed schedules rather than upon the ability to memorize and pass tests.

Nowhere else in life does the retarded person compete with the bright and gifted, and the bright and gifted compete with the slow and retarded, except in school. Once out of school, the laborer competes with other laborers, the skilled craftsman with other skilled craftsmen, the businessman with other businessmen, and the professional with other professionals. Not only for jobs, but for homes, positions, status, possessions, clubs, recreation.

We take for granted the concept of fairness in competition in sports. Tennessee Wesleyan does not play basketball with the University of Tennessee, nor does a Bronx sandlot team play the New York Mets, and so an *ad infinitum.* Players and teams are carefully matched, and we all take it for granted and call it sportsmanship. Why, then, do we pit IQ 75 with IQ 140 in the classroom?

It is said that if we single out the slow from the average, from the gifted intellectually and academically, and put them in to special groups, it will damage the ego and self-concept of the slower child and give the gifted a sense of superiority. Yet no one feels this way in athletics. Do you feel bad that you cannot run the 100 yard dash in less than ten seconds, or bat .300 with the major leagues, or play golf with a 70 score on a tough course? Then why do we do it academically?

Dr. Orville Johnson of Syracuse University puts the point straight home with this statement: "No child is more cruelly segregated than the child in the regular classroom who perceives himself a failure." Do not think for a moment that the child who fails, whoever he may be, wherever he may be, does not know he fails and does not suffer ego damage. If we want competition in school (and we are not at all sure we do), but if we want it, why not make it fair and realistic? Let the slow compete with the slow, and the gifted with the gifted, and the learning disabled with the learning disabled. Some realistic measure of success and reward will then be possible.

Secondly, even for the few perpetual winners in academic competition, one or more of several highly undesirable attitudes usually develop. The student may become insufferable in his supposed superiority. He may feel that he has to win at any price, and that price far too often is the squelching of reflective and creative thinking and individualistic viewpoints as he conforms to win.

If the going is rough, he will cheat to get a good grade. He learns to exploit people, fellow students, and teachers, in order to obtain that all-important grade. There is no question that traditional grading practices are the primary source of unwholesome competition in school.

11. *Grades pervert students' attitudes and habits of learning.* A comprehensive study made by Stallings and Leslie (1970), disclosed the disturbing consequences of the current emphasis upon grades contained in items 12 through 17.

12. Emphasis upon grades restricts study to what is likely to be tested. Relevancy to student and the quality of learning are rarely considered. Students quickly learn to study for the kinds of tests used on them. Thus, it is possible for the students who get the best grades to have studied not what was most relevant or exciting to them, but what the teacher tested for. It is also possible for the student who profited most in meaningful learning to end up with the poorest assortment of grades. In spite of the teacher's claim that she does not teach mere facts, most grades are based upon fact

orientated tests.

13. Where students have a choice of courses, the emphasis upon grades encourages students to enroll in easy, or safe, courses and tends to keep them out of more interesting and significant but more difficult (in terms of grades) courses.

Grades based upon tests force students to conform to teachers' ideas and emphases. Few teachers accept divergent viewpoints on tests, and few students will risk them.

14. Grades do not provide useful feedback for better learning. This might be accomplished if the teacher went over the test items soon after giving the test, but many teachers do not do this. Even when they do, most students, so grade orientated, pay little attention to what was right or wrong about their responses. Research strongly supports the practice of giving tests without grades to provide meaningful and accepted feedbacks. Contrary to the popular opinions of many teachers, such testing methods do not cause study and effort to deteriorate.

15. Cheating is largely the product of emphasis upon grades. Cheating varies directly proportionally to the pressure of grades. This also is the finding of other studies, such as Bowers of Columbia University (1964).

16. The pressure of grades does not prepare a student for the pressure of the real world. Getting good grades depends as much or more upon skills of how to please a teacher and in how to study for tests and how to take them — skills that likely will never be used outside of school — than upon ability and relevant competencies.

The grading system rewards the conforming noncreative student and penalizes the most creative student. This study, we as well as others mentioned earlier in this chapter, found that the best grade getters were inferior in the ability or skill of creative productive thinking. They were good memorizers and problem-solvers, but we need creative thinkers and problem-finders. These latter were rarely recipients of high grades.

17. Students often see no relevant correlation between grades and what they believe they have learned (earned). As a result,

attitudes toward study, course, teacher, and motivation to
learn deteriorate lamentably (Jackson, 1970).

18. *The usual teaching, testing processes reinforced strongly by
grading practices reduce the need for students to make
independent choices and shape their own values.* In self-
defense they adopt their teacher's values. It does not take
long for students' sense of shaping and controlling their
world to dry up. They become robots in a numbers game
called grading.

19. *Extreme test anxiety is produced by prevelant grading*
practices. Debilitating, frustrating, and stifling describe this
very real syndrome. Its ill effects affect the conscientious and
hard-working student most severely. The American
Association for Higher Education of the NEA and the
American Pscyhological Association are concerned about
the increasing incidence of student suicides which has more
than doubled percentage wise in the years between 1952 and
1968. Although it affects students at all learning levels, the
overall GPA of suicides is 3.2 and is highest in the better
schools.

    Of course, only a relatively few students go that far in the
throes of test anxiety. More find themselves unable to
perform at a level reflecting their actual competency. Most
students just learn to hate tests and to hate school.

20. *The need to continually justify and support grades develops
a self-perpetuating vicious circle.* Since objective tests
appear to justify grades, teachers safeguard themselves by
using few open-ended tests that stimulate reflective and
creative thinking. Result: proliferation of objective fact-
centered tests which are easily graded and which produce
clearly delineated scores easily converted into grades. Thus
we have a seemingly defensible but wholly vicious circle of
grades and objective tests, each supporting the other as they
both pervert the true intent of learning.

21. *In order to make testing easier and more grade-productive,
teachers tend to shy away from learning activities producing
responses that are not objective.* For instance, discussion, a
most valuable and interesting form of inquiry learning,

cannot be mathematically calculated. Free-form art work, student-chosen topics and forms for papers, in fact creative approaches to anything cannot be precisely graded. Therefore, teachers tend to stipulate carefully and exactly how the student is to do it, "because, otherwise, there are not standards by which the work can be graded." If the work is done without careful conformity, the easy precision and deceptive validity of grading disappears.

22. *Grades fool the teacher into believing that he is teaching and evaluating learning* when all he is doing is setting up carefully controlled response situations that can be objectively graded. In other words, the *grading system,* rather than valid and desirable objectives *controls the form of what is taught.* If meaningful objectives are considered at all, they are distorted and twisted to allow objective grading. The influence of this factor is far greater than most teachers suspect. They dish out information or make assignments which the students can regurgitate in varying amounts which furnish grades that are the evidence that learning is taking place — the grades made by the better students are the evidence used to support this unfortunate hypothesis.

It matters not that the less able or more creative and independent students are destroyed in the process as the teacher defensively says, "If some students can get it, so could the others, if they tried." Get what? Have meaning, relevance, independent thinking, and creative activity no place in learning? Should these desirable objectives continue to be replaced with memorizable facts and stereotyped learning activities which can be easily tested and assigned grades which prove that children are learning?

Perhaps this is a major reason why nongraded and pass-fail approaches to learning are so vigorously opposed by traditional educators. It is far more difficult to teach reflective thinking, creative activities, and independent inquiry. Plus the fact that these open-ended goals of learning are impossible to grade objectively; one has no way to prove exactly what and how much is learned.

Changes in attitude and behavior are what education is all about, but these are difficult, if not impossible, to measure. Therefore, the content, the facts the teacher and/or textbook writer thinks are important, become the basis for teaching and testing. Mere knowledge has little or no effect upon attitudes or behavior. Far too often forgotten: *how* a child is taught is more important than what he is taught.

23. *Grades actually lower academic standards!* One of the popular arguments against nongrading or pass-fail educational programs states that such practices will lower the standards of education. As a matter of sober fact the reverse of this is true. There are at least two reasons why this is so. First, since grades determine promotion and graduation, and since all children except the very slowest must sooner or later get a high school diploma, and since many poor students are included, grades must be manipulated and adjusted or standards lowered so that most children will get through high school. Every teacher knows of students who graduate who cannot even read above the primary level.

This aspect of lowered standards may not be common at the college level, but colleges as well as public schools are guilty in another way of lowering standards because of prevelant grading practices. As long as grades remain as important as they are, few students will study course material that will not be covered in a test and thus lead directly to a grade. Students learn quickly to ask, or discover in other ways, what will be on a test. We know many teachers who tell the students whether material will or will not be on a test. If it is not on a test, students may pay little attention because they do not want to clutter up their notes or their minds with anything not directly related to a test grade.

The counter argument, that if it were not for grades students would not study or listen at all, is part and parcel of our flagrant use of grades in an attempt to force irrelevant learning on students. As was presented earlier in this chapter, grades motivate only the good students, and motivate them the wrong way.

Tests or no, students listen and learn when the material is relevant and interestingly presented, and *they tend to learn more when they are not graded.* Dr. William Glaser (1966, pp.65-67), an outspoken opponent of grades, relates an interesting experience.

He had been invited to speak to a group of parents, teachers, and students about grades. Discussion followed in which nearly all participated vigorously defending grades as valuable indicators of "how we are doing." They even went so far as to say they would change schools if the school were to experiment with a nongraded system. The climax came when Dr. Glaser asked, "Since you all believe that grades are so valuable and important, would you like to have the teachers grade your discussion tonight?

That tore it. There were moans and groans all over the place. A number of the children (and parents) said that if they had known they were to be graded, they would not have spoken so freely, in fact many would not have spoken at all.

There was complete agreement that this had been a profitable experience long to be remembered. There was also complete agreement that discussions of that type would never occur if they were graded. Significantly, from that moment on the discussion turned to how to change the school to a nongraded program. No one defended grades further; they all wanted to make learning at that school more meaningful thereafter.

While there are more and more people who will agree that nongrading may work for elementary and high school, very few seem to think it would work in college and graduate school. However, an increasing number of colleges are turning to a pass-fail, no-grade system.

An excellent example of what can happen if grades and tests are abolished is found at one of the nation's outstanding medical schools, Western Reserve in Cleveland, Ohio. For more than twenty years grading has been abolished. It was felt that students spent too much time and became too anxious about grades to really learn well, thus reducing genuine thought and inquiry about medicine and surgery. With this worry gone, Western Reserve medical students were able to broaden their educational outlook and professors were able to *raise* standards considerably. In national and state testing after graduation, Western Reserve physicians rate far above average. In addition they remember their medical school experience as a pleasant time, in sharp contrast to the majority of doctors.

The faculty of Western Reserve believe that objective tests discourage research, discourage thoughtfut reading, discourage listening to anything but facts, induce debilitating anxiety, and discourage individualized study. Dr. Glaser (a graduate of Western Reserve Medical School) says about objective testing: "Students learn to read their books by memorizing the words in italics, as if the author wrote all the other words just to use ink." Yale University Medical School also has a program similar to Western Reserve's.

We would hate to read all the magazines, journals, and books we do with the threat of objective tests hanging over us. We would hate to be endlessly asking ourselves, "Will this or that be on a test?" We are sure we would read far less and enjoy what we did read much less. This is, we are sure, a universal attitude which can in no way be interpreted to support the hypothesis that grading motivates or improves learning.

24. *Grades have become moral equivalents.* A good grade is equated with good behavior. Not only is this a widespread practice perceived by all concerned but affecting most unfortunately the special-need child. Indeed, the abstraction goes further as grades become equivalents for good and bad without relation to behavior.

25. *Last but by no means least, grades have no correlation with real life.* In no place but academia, in no other area of endeavor, are people graded. Evaluated, yes, but not graded; and there is a very real difference.

Think for a moment on just what life would be like if we continued to grade people as we do in school. Husbands grade wives and wives grade husbands, parents grade children and children grade parents, employers grade employees and employees grade employers, and so on without letup. At the end of each grading period, everyone would get his report card with its letter or percentage grades. It would be interesting to see what you would get (as a husband) in shaving, hair grooming, picking up after yourself, promptness, money earned, love-making, and remembering special dates. A man would not dare say nice things to his wife, pat her on the fanny, or buy her candy or flowers — this would be "apple polishing," working for "A's." How about throwing in a few objective tests to make the grading less subjective? Furthermore, if the wife assumed the role of a proper grader, she would see to it that he did not goof-off. Maybe she could lower the grades a letter or so to make him shape up.

Apply our prevelant grading system to any endeavor in real life you can think of, and the whole process falls apart with *reducto ad absurdum* in complete control. It is unfortunate, indeed, that more educators cannot perceive that giving grades in school is also a farce!

Why Do We Continue Giving Grades?

In spite of the fact that many teachers are disturbed by current practices of giving grades, plus the many recommendations which have been made for change and the extent to which the system has been so discredited, little change has taken place. Why?

1. *It is the way it has always been done.* Inertia and resistance to any change are widespread. Most people prefer the evil they know to the possible evils they do not know. It is as if most educators have been hooked on a drug they both hate and enjoy. It is difficult to amend or abolish a structure so widely used and so familiar to so many people and upon which so many practices (however defective) have been built. The system has acquired the status of a complete monster that almost destroys local control of its record-keeping processes and leaves an individual teacher or school almost helpless. It is as if everyone had his hold on the long tail of a

monsterous lion — everyone will have to let go at once; a large-scale effort is needed. However, a number of public schools and colleges have led the way without falling prey to the system no one really likes but most are afraid to turn loose.

The Committee of the National Association for Supervision and Curriculum Development to which we referred earlier in this chapter (*ASCD 1967 Yearbook*) states categorically that they find the popular grading system "undersirable and inherently useless."

2. *Those who win in the system have a vested interest in its continuance.* Those most rigidly resisting change are those who have won good grades or who see opportunity to do so in the future. Among these must surely be included most of our schoolteachers, administrators, and all college professors whose own performances in their school days place them among the academic elite of our society.

3. *Grades satisfy the need for simple, precise answers.* So much of life is unpredictable and uncontrollable and complex. How nice to find simple, apparently controllable answers! How often, too, do we accept simple answers that are not answers at all!

4. *Grades obtained by objective tests appear so reasonable and correct.* They take teachers and administrators off the hook. "See," they say. "Figure it out yourself; this is what they earned. All I do is record their marks."

5. *Teachers feel a need and a wish to justify their evaluations.* Especially is this true, if, as it often happens, the teacher has some deep-seated doubts and fears with perhaps some guilt when it comes to grading. Conscientious teachers feel humble in the face of this responsibility. They know only too well that they do not possess either the objectivity or the omniscience which the grading process demands. Comfort can be found in the delusive mechanical and arithmetical approaches, in order to be at least objective and fair.

6. *Grading systems help to facilitate mass-produced learning with mass teaching.* Mass grading is a way of dealing with many students at one time with as little sweat as possible; it

matters little that the practice is invalid and worthless. It is acceptable and seems fair.

7. *College entrance and graduate school admission policies have tended to perpetuate the common grading systems.* Colleges' and universities' demands for transcripts, GPA's, and class ranks have led public school educators who may want to change to conclude that the system is a necessary evil and must be continued. This in spite of the fact that some schools and colleges, even graduate schools, have found a better way.

8. *Grading is highly charged with emotion.* People are usually reluctant to face up to areas of great emotionality. Grading certainly qualifies on this point. Such behavior is most frequently ignored, postponed, and/or rationalized.

9. *Educators are not alone in resisting change; parents often make the loudest noise when grades are eliminated.* They cry, "How can we tell how Johnny is doing?" The most desperate shouts are usually from parents of good students. Do they *really* want to know how Johnny is doing? Grades do not have that much to say, as we have shown earlier in this chapter. Could it be that what they actually want to know is, "Are Johnny's grades better than Tom's?"

Many parents, especially of the middle class, attempt vicarious fulfillment through their children as they premiumize promotions, honors, awards, and scholarships, all of which are contingent upon the fool's goal of good grades. Thereby, they emphasize grades rather than growth, value high marks instead of learning, and stress report cards as a substitute for true intellectual development.

For far too many parents, grades are status symbols. So great a premium is placed upon marks that these parents bribe, nag, cajole, and even threaten their chilren to obtain those all-important good grades.

Underlying the pressure imposed upon children is the assumption that most, if not all, can obtain high marks if only they would work hard enough. Not only does this assumption violate the very concept of individual differences, but also the resultant overemphasis and pressure for grades produces lower marks than ability and industry would normally permit. So great become the grade and test anxiety that it actually impedes learning as it interferes with concentration in study. The concentration centers on tests and grades. Constantly before the student's mind, conflicting with learning, is the overriding question, "Will this be on a test?" or "Will the teacher ask for this?"

Many pupils whose schoolwork has become grade oriented are unduly disappointed as they perceive failure to get a good grade as complete failure. Hence, they lose even that which is within their grasp. Although one cannot accurately assess the degree to which preoccupation with grades retards learning, most psychologists agree that it is significant.

All grade-conscious students are to some degree hindered by their perverted concentration and excessive anxiety, but the weaker student suffers the most damage. The very ones, such as our handicapped learners, who can least afford the loss and who need help most, are forced to endure failure over and over again. This not only negates motivation, lowers goals, but the blighting effects upon personality development of constant frustration and failure cannot be overstated.

10. *There seems to be inability to agree on a feasible substitution* for grades. And perhaps that's the problem — find a *substitute!* Let's abolish them in any form or substitute! We do not need them.

If a student learns at his own rate in his own way, he doesn't need a grade to tell him how he is doing any more than a baby needs grades to tell him how well he learns to walk or to talk. *He knows when he does it!* When he has learned to walk, he tries to run — without grades.

A growing number of schools and a few colleges are using performance and accomplishment as the only needed criteria for advancement or graduation. It works successfully!

Reports to parents and notes to counselors are really descriptive explanations. Administrators find in permanent records "completed the course" adequate. Best of all, the student cannot fail. If he is unable to accomplish what he is guided to do or that which he himself has chosen to do, he is not given any mark or grade that represents failure. Either he is given an easier task or is encouraged to try again and again, if necessary. Failure is so final. To try again is encouraging and far more lifelike and realistic; it allows for individual differences in rate and style of learning, and never shuts the door to development. He learns at his own rate, and even a thimbleful of learning, as well as a tubful, is acceptable and rewardable. Most importantly, he learns to like himself, school, and society.

If you *must* give grades, be careful; they are dangerous as commonly used. And doubly so for handicapped learners.

COMPETITION CAN BE DANGEROUS

A NOTED educator was speaking to a group of high school teachers. His topic was "Grades and Competition." He based his lecture on the widely accepted assumption that competition over grades in school provides a healthy method of training children for the real competition forced on them when schooling has been completed. True, he said, the student who makes less than the highest grade may feel badly, but he can feel superior to all those who get lesser grades than his, and so on down the scale. Everyone is superior to someone else. Everyone, that is, except the poor fellow at the bottom, "And he is too dumb to know the difference."

Is Competition in School
Training for Real Life?

This assumption unquestionably reflects an extreme attitude, but it does no violence to the popularly held position with which he started his discourse; namely, competition in schools is realistic, an excellent motivation which provides helpful training for the dog-eat-dog world in which we live as adults. The purpose of this chapter is to examine carefully this widely held viewpoint.

First of all, it is only in school that mentally retarded persons compete with gifted people, or even with those of average ability. Only in the regular classroom does a perceptually handicapped child vie for rewards with a perfectly normal learner. School, with its emphasis upon grades and competition, pits the gifted child from an affluent suburb with the culturally disadvantaged child from the slums. (Even if we have to bus the children from school to school to augment this brutal process of learning.)

It is time we take a closer and harder look at this beneficial, real life competition. With whom does the mentally retarded adult compete for jobs or social position? With other similarly retarded adults, of course! With whom does the gifted adult compete for jobs and social position? With other similarly gifted persons. The laborer competes with other laborers, white-collar workers vie with other white-collar workers, and professionals contend with professionals. Where did we ever get the idea that the artificial competition in school even approaches training for the real world? Let us take a further look.

Competition in Sports More Realistic

In sports we are far more realistic. Podunk Center, Ohio, competes with Podunk Center, Indiana; and Metropolis, New York, struggles with Metropolis, Illinois. Tennessee Wesleyan College tangles with Carson-Newman, and the University of Tennessee plays the University of Georgia. It is big league against big league, and little league against little league. But not in the classroom; here the competition must be "realistic!"

There are those who decry and scorn any attempt at any ability grouping in school. They say it is unfair, unrealistic, and stigmatizing. Dr. Orville Johnson of Syracuse University countered that argument well: "No child is more cruelly segregated than the child in the average classroom who perceives himself failing in that class." He does not realize his limited abilities and failure to keep up when he is in a regular class? His peers do not call him a "dumbell" there? Placement in a special class will hurt his self-concept? If he can learn and succeed in that class, who is kidding whom?

Few gifted children really learn what competition is all about until they are put in a class with other gifted children or discover that there are many other bright kids as they battle for their academic lives as freshmen in college. If competition in school is training for the competition of real life, why not even up the odds? We have rules against competitive disparity of skill and ability — except in the classroom.

How Realistic and Beneficial Is Competition Between Comparative Equals?

Consider further the assumptive claim that since the out-of-school world is competitive, therefore competition in school prepares a child for that world. It is true we live in a constant, all-pervasive atmosphere of competition for the individual and groups from the cradle to the grave. It is also true that competition seems to improve effort and achievement in most of life's activities. Therefore, we work at making children feel that they should be better than anyone else in school, in the club, in sports, in dress, in love affairs, in social positions, and in jobs. When they grow up, they should have the best positions, live in the biggest house in the best neighborhood, drive the best car, and belong to the best social organizations.

It should be obvious that it is impossible for everyone to reach all, or in some cases even one, of their goals. For every winner there are many losers. Too, every social class has its own set of bests and status symbols. Furthermore, as Lewin and Hoppe (1930) discovered in extensive research which has been supported by many studies since, the *occurance of success and failure is independent of actual achievement. It is determined, rather, by the goals, expectations, and aspirations of the person at the time of the action.* They found that after a success experience, aspirations were usually raised, and after a failure experience the goals were either lowered significantly or raised to such an impossible level that no blame could be imputed for failure to reach them.

Differences Between Aspirations and Achievement Psychologically Significant

Although differences between aspirations and achievement may not be great in a quantitative sense, they are psychologically extremely important. When success and failure are evaluated, "a miss is as good as a mile." This difference in relation of aspiration to achievement is aggravated by the social pressures of the school situation which often operate to throw off balance the protection mechanism of the level of aspiration. Thus, children are subjected to exaggerated failure and success experiences.

Competition Builds Harmful Classroom Pressures

Let us examine how these pressures arise in most classrooms. Social acceptability in so intimate a group as a school class requires a high degree of conformity to group standards in all sorts of behavior. The first step to social acceptability is to set goals in accordance to the group standards (often teacher-made standards). Since in most schools evaluation is largely (even totally in some cases) based on grades or achievement, the poor students are forced by the social pressure of the classroom to set goals they cannot achieve or else to admit that they do not belong. Both are unacceptable alternatives from a mental hygiene viewpoint.

Pressure is exerted upon bright students also to set their goals and reduce their levels of achievement in conformity with the achievement of their roommates rather than with their own higher possibilities. Competition, on the other hand, exerts its pressure to excel. Thus the bright student is placed in the middle of two strong pressures. He conforms or becomes a maverick. His position from a mental health standpoint is no more desirable than that of his less able fellow classmate.

Compare Classroom Pressures with the Real World

Let us take a look at that real world for which school is a preparation. Adults are not frequently subjected to such pressures for long periods of time. Adults are able to hide from others certain crucial symbols of their divergence from what is considered good or desirable (such as age, income, family background, status symbols bought on credit). Too, they are able to withdraw when the pressures are too great. The association or social structure is not nearly so close and tight as that in a six-hour-a-day, five-day-a-week classroom where everyone is constantly evaluated and graded.

Furthermore, achievement in most adult activities is not

estimated (graded) with nearly the arbitrary precision (one point can make the difference between failure and success) that most teachers attempt. For instance, let us momentarily take a look at the college professor, considered by most people as near the top of the educational ladder. If he writes a letter or a paper or a book, if he cannot spell a word, he either marks it with a question mark and/or hopes his secretary will catch it. The same for punctuation. For much of the knowledge he was supposed to have absorbed in his seventeen or more years in school, he turns constantly to reference sources. If he is really on his toes academically, he has discarded much of what he learned to accommodate the change and increase of knowledge in his discipline. *And most importantly, there is no one standing over him constantly pointing out and evaluating what he does or does not know.* Neither is he under continuous pressure of time externally applied. School is similar to real life? Constant meticulous search for error is realistic? Competition in school resembles competition out of school? Not by a long shot!

Doctors, lawyers, teachers, bakers, plumbers, housewives, can vary within a considerable range of effectiveness and no one is the wiser; they are still adequate. This gives a fundamental security which is denied to students who are frequently and publicly evaluated and thereby acclaimed or humiliated by an authority from whose decisions there is no recourse and by a group from which there is no escape!

Moreover, the doctor, lawyer, teacher, baker, plumber, or housewife does not live or die on the single criteria of professional competency. The rewards in the classroom are all centered about a very limited set of achievements — all academic. Competition is narrowly circumscribed. Therefore, the child who is relatively dull or uninterested in academic activities must experience continual failure. He will fail even though he is kind or good looking or has a sense of humor or has physical prowess or leadership ability or mechanical aptitude. He will fail in school even though he is energetic, graceful, courageous, or friendly.

Although these other characteristics are highly valued by other institutions and by the clients of the doctor, lawyer, or teacher, the student will fail in school if he cannot make the grade academically. He will continue to fail until be becomes mature enough to establish other more rewarding relationships. However, that may never happen, for continual failure such as suffered by the handicapped usually crushes self-concept and self-confidence irretrievably.

Not only does the adult in the real world find that nonacademic achievement is rewarded, he also can balance failure in one area of his life with success in another area. Unlike the student who is the captive of one closed society, the adult has a variety of institutions (family, job, club, avocation, church, union) with varied values which have somewhat equal potency in his life. He is not at the mercy of a single source of reward or failure as is the child in school.

Middle-class children are unusually sensitive to these pressures. Not only do they have to contend with the demands of the competitive classroom, they have to contend with the goals of the family as well, for in most cases they are one. The family supports the school. This means that the pressures, the demands, the rewards and punishments, the successes and failures of the school are reinforced by the family. There are no substitutes and no escapes; the values reach a level of overwhelming importance to the child. No one with influence will question the righteousness of the school's verdicts or the correctness of its values. How long will we allow education to perpetrate its scurrilous claim that the classroom is a microcosm for the real world?

Competition as Motivation to Learn

Another vigorous claim made by proponents of competition in the classroom states that children are motivated to learn more and learn it better when stimulated by the scramble for grades (or other rewards for achievement). It is assumed that if the pressures of competition for extrinsic rewards were removed, students would reduce their motivational levels. To make this assumption oversimplifies the process of motivation to learn. As a matter of fact, competition motivates only those who win or who feel they have a good chance of winning.

The student who puts out his best effort and continues to lose and the one whose self-concepts have been shattered by repeated failure are motivated to fail even more. Nothing succeeds as well as success, and nothing fails as miserably as failure. The idea that if we push a man down, he will try harder to get up is true only if he has the ability to get up and is not pushed down too often. Farnsworth (1965, p.46), Torrance (1962 and 1969), Rogers (1969), to mention only a few, have found that the most effective pressures toward excellence have no competition for grades or other fixed rewards, nor is there competition between teacher and student.

The best competition is that of the student with himself. The learning experiences are so structured that there are exceedingly numerous channels of communications between all members of the class which provides immediate feedback by and to all students and teacher. Consequently, students and teachers regard each other as colleagues rather than as opponents or competitors.

The point of this view is in sharp contrast to that found in most classroom situations where students hold that it is smart to get away with as little work and as much deception as possible, while the teacher assumes the positions of various attempts to see that his students "do not get away with anything." An all-pervading competitive battle of wits arises which undermines and discourages a climate of excellence.

An Experiment in Reducing Competition

We have been experimenting with some of our college classes, those which are small enough (fifteen to twenty) to allow discussive channels of communication and feedback to develop without the pressures of competition for grades or competition between teacher and students, as each tries to outwit and outguess the other. Many different methods of evaluation have been used but have not include the usual series of paper and pencil graded tests. The methods used include evaluation of discussion; papers and projects; rough notes on reading; a final comprehensive essay examination using broad, open-ended discussion questions which allow for pursuit of individual interest; and student evaluation of the course. Letter grades are used which stand for highly satisfactory, satisfactory, or unsatisfactory work, and a statement of why the work is so considered.

Very little lecture is used, and where we believe some area of learning needs our exposition, we have prepared a number of papers which can be read by the student far more quickly and accurately than any lecture and note-taking. Time that might have been taken up with lecture can then be used for discussion, reports, projects, microteaching experiences, and the like.

In all such classes a semicontractual agreement has been made in which a good grade is guaranteed if the students participate within a broad and extensive outline of studies (readings, papers, reports, discussion, projects, etc.). Minimum standards are set and top grades are promised to those who exceed the minimum. Careful and frequent checks are made to evaluate the work done. Competition no longer is a factor — every student "has it made" if he does what is expected of him. We strongly feel that what we have done has exceeded our wildest expectations. Part of the success is due, we are sure, to the fact that every student knows what is expected of him; he is allowed freedom to pursue his own interest within a broad spectrum of learning possibilities carefully structured. He has not one, but many ways to fulfill his responsibilities. He has great freedom, but also enough structure to provide security.

The atmosphere of these classes includes a sense of freedom and informality, even comaraderie. Discussions reveal interest, involvement, and wide reading. One of the most difficult problems we face is that of convincing the students that they can express any viewpoint, hypothesize and guess without threat, reprisal, or criticism. This took longer than we had anticipated, at first, so conditioned were the students after more than a dozen years in teacher dominated and competitive classes. They did loosen up and open up when they discovered that we actually meant what we said about welcoming an idea, right or wrong, just because it was an idea.

Some idea of the feelings of the class can be seen from comments made by students in their evaluation. Here are several reactions:

> I appreciate this course because I feel that it is the *first actual college course I have had, and I am a senior!* For

once the students have been treated and trusted as responsible adults instead of irresponsible children pressured to
learn almost solely by means of tests and grades. At first I was
frankly skeptical as to how much value the course would be
to me. I know my previous attitudes well enough to fear that
I would not do the work without the gloomy pressure of
frequent tests and grades hanging over my head. However, I
found myself studying and working harder than I had ever
done before. The class inspired me to work on my own or feel
left out completely. In this I believe I have discovered the
ultimate goal of good teaching, that is, to inspire the
students to self-motivated, self-disciplined study.

It makes me sick to think that until now, as a senior, I have
had only the old traditional courses in which I was supposed
to do nothing but absorb what the teacher poured out and
give it back when I was squeezed by objective tests, most of
which never really indicated how little I really learned. It
works the other way around for some other kids I know, but I
was a good temporary memorizer; a day or two later I
couldn't have passed the test. But at the end of this course I
can even remember most of what we discussed in the first few
classes. I sincerely hope that similar methods of learning
will spread into our entire education system — then, only
then, will we really have an *education* system.

A young lady had this to say,
When I heard about this course and how you had been
teaching it, I thought to myself, wow! this is a way for me to
get a good grade withoqt working. But I soon found myself
working harder than I've ever done before, and because I
wanted to. I am enchanted with the freedom and challenged
by the opportunity to pursue some of my own interests. I
usually am rather quiet, but as you know, I have been saying
a great deal. I still find myself, occasionally, fearing to say
what I think. Then I am reassured by the freedom that
pervades the whole class. I have learned, really learned, more
than I have in any class I have ever had.

The benefits are not only those to the student. We find ourselves enjoying teaching more (and that is saying something because we have always enjoyed teaching). The give and take of idea exchange stimulates other ideas. Misunderstanding and misconceptions can be reasoned through rather than marked wrong on a test. Above all we like the freedom from competition between oqrselves and the students. They no longer sit trying to outguess us as to what might be on a test, and we no longer need to act as judges, critics and guardians of grades, but rather as helpers, guides, facilitators of learning.

A student put it this way:

> I felt as if I were a part of a committee with the teacher acting as chairman as we shared information, ideas, formed answers, solved problems, reached conclusions and hypothesized implications. What we came up with was the product of the whole class, teacher included, instead of only what one or two persons believed. As a result, what we learned became ours, not just yours or a textbook's that we were supposed to remember long enough to pass a test. It was greatly satisfying!

However, we found ourselves spending far more time in preparation, structuring the information, writing well documented papers in lieu of lectures, and framing questions. To satisfy our objectives (which are mostly behaviorial) requires questions which not only stimulate discussion, but go far beyond *who? what? when? where?* to *why? so what?* plus questions that stimulate creative synthesis. This keeps us on our toes continually, since feedback and student response are immediate. We find it much easier to evaluate our own teaching as well as the preparation and involvement of the class. If a lesson or part of one falls flat on its face, we know it immediately. In lecturing one has only the periodic checkups that tests provide, and then it is far too easy to blame the students for our failure.

The Effects of Reward and Punishment on Competition

Hurlock's classic study (1924) on the effects of reward and punishment (praise and blame, high and low grades) has been replicated many times. (Cofer and Apply, 1965; Kennedy and

Wellcut, 1964, to mention some of the most recent.) Put briefly, they find that rewards increase achievement, punishment causes a decrease, and reproved children stop trying even over as short a period as five days. An occasional failure and reproof does little harm, apparently; therefore, the successful student seems to work harder. In other words, competitive grades serve only to motivate the better students. Even they do not require such competition to learn well. Considering everything, it is too high a price to pay in the damaged ego and reduced effort of the many who fail.

Especially since we do not need such motivation. Lewis Goldberg (1965), using a large sample of college students, compared the effects of five grading policies: strict, lenient (pass-fail), normal, bimodal, and rectangular. He discovered no significant differences in achievement, as disclosed on a final standardized test, as a result of the five different grading policies. He believed that his discoveries "should force proponents of a particular grading policy to make a thorough reappraisal of their beliefs." Especially should they "be wary of including *motivational* rationales as part of their arguments."

When grading practices *seem* to be motivational, a careful examination will disclose, said Goldberg, "That type of detailed feedback had been used which enhances learning and motivation." In other words, meaningful and detailed feedback motivates grades, but competition does not. Gross (1946) discovered this some time ago. It is really tragic that teachers pay so little attention to research findings and so much attention to traditional hearsay, whether in a college classroom or in early elementary learning situations.

Competition and Cooperation

Deutch (1060) and Marquart (1955) compared the effectiveness of competition and cooperation in problem-solving. The competitive group arrived at individual solutions, while the cooperative group was rated as a group. Deutch found that the cooperative group surpassed the competitive in nearly every respect; in addition the communication and feelings were far friendlier, more open, effective, orderly, and productive. Marquart discovered that neither the competitive nor cooperative group was more effective in solving problems than the single problem-solver in it. The cooperative group, however, did just as well as the competitive group and had in addition all the other not insignificant benefits. Conclusion: we do not need competition to motivate. *Children who succeed invariably raise their level of aspirations,* unless the goal of the aspirations is painful or meaningless. *Children who fail or who are made to feel as if they fail lower their level of aspiration.*

The implication these psychological facts of motivation have is tremendous. It explains why, contrary to the fears of competitive traditionalists, the ungraded and continuous progress type of learning experiences, where every student learns at his own rate *without failure* as we usually define it, succeeds better than any other method yet devised. And it is a must for exceptional children.

Competition Makes It Difficult If Not Impossible to Realize Other Valuable Educational Goals

Adequate learning demands something more than acquisition of knowledge and the desire to come out on top. In spite of many puritanistic educators who feel that the only worthwhile learning is that which is mostly blood, sweat, and tears, learning should be pleasant, joyful, even ecstatic. Anyone who has watched the face of a child as he joyously cried, "I get it! I can do it! I understand now!" can never deny the ecstatic satisfaction that comes with the insight and discovery of learning.

You can force a child to learn some things, or you can guide and lead him to discover truth. In the first case he will also learn to hate both what he learns and the one who pressures him. In the second case, he will like both what he learns and the one who stimulates his learning. Unfortunately, too often what the student has learned is a lesson in expediency. He learns that science or history or English is drudgery, boredom, and skilled cheating.

This gratuitous lesson is not what his teacher intended to teach. Yet the proof of the perverted lesson is sadly demonstrated only when the disillusioned student turns his back on the dreary subject forever. However, by that time his teachers are busy teaching the wrong lessons to new students, usually unaware of the nature of their own spurious achievement. Or, if they should be aware of the negative attitude incited against what they themselves love, the teachers will salve their consciences by the attractive rationalization, "It was just too tough for him."

The pressure of grades and competition has destroyed love of learning for most students, and the many chronic failures learn rather permanently not to learn. Such are the sobering findings of recent research by Mair and his associates (1969). We cannot afford the waste of allowing potentially fine quality children to develop under the influence of inferior and often degrading stimuli. In some fashion we must develop an all-pervasive climate of opinion that excellence is desirable, necessary, and enjoyable. This cannot be done as long as learning is pressurized, not unlike that of a fine steak in a pressure cooker, by competition for grades or other extrinsic rewards.

Creative Thinking and Competition Antagonistic

All children were born with remarkable ability to think creatively, and the more intelligent, generally, the more ability to create, innovate, and do imaginative things. However, by the time children reach third (or fourth grade at most), this God-given talent has literally disappeared in most of them. No knowledgeable educational psychologist considers this developmental; the child does not outgrow his ability to do creative things.

It has been discovered that divergent innovative thinking does not usually get the best grades; it does not lend itself to objective evaluation. Whether they enjoy it or not, children soon learn what is profitable. This explains the discoveries of Getzels and Jackson (1962 and 1965) and others, that the best grade getters in the competition for status are not very creative. A few hardy children with excellent self-concepts survive both educationally and creatively. The poor and handicapped students die out in all respects early.

Competitive Adversity Destructive

A popular philosophy of pseudopsychology claims that suffering, hardships, frustrations, and the painful experience of failure prepare a child to handle adult adversity more adequately. No single bit of research evidence supports this misconception. On the contrary, those adults most able to handle failure, frustrations, and adversity are those in whose childhood these adversive states were minimal. These are the adults whose emotional resiliency and ego strength withstand the "slings and arrows of outrageous fortune." Psychiatrists' couches, mental hospitals, prisons, and slums are filled with those whose childhoods were full of failure and frustration.

While the home environment plays a significant role in ego development, school plays a larger part than most parents and teachers realize. In addition to the frequent adverse grades, children who are asked to read aloud but who have reading problems, the unsolved problem put on the board, the wrong recitative answer, or unacceptable creative response, criticism, sarcasm, jeers of peers, all take their deadly toll.

Beatty and Clark (1968) present a dynamic self-concept theory of learning which explains much of what happens, or does not happen, in emotional development and in motivation to learn. As the child grows, he receives constant appraisals from parent, teacher, and peers of what he is like. He also receives appraisals in terms of what he could or should be like. Even more important than this, he has the models of mother, father, and teacher who appear to be so much more effective than he is. This leads to the development of the part of the self-concept which is called the "concept of adequacy," which is the way the child perceives what he should be if he really is going to be adequate and effective.

These two parts, the perceived self and the concept of adequacy, make up the self-concept. In some ways these two parts are alike, in other ways different. The individual continually strives to become more like his picture of an adequate self. He formulates goals, things to accomplish in the world to decrease the discrepancies, and takes action which he hopes will succeed. These actions are responded to by himself and by others.

Consistent responses indicating that he is becoming more adequate reinforce the new behavior and lead to a change in his perceived self. He becomes more like his concept of adequacy. *This change we call learning.* On the other hand, if his feedback is not reinforcing, or is negative, he does not make that change. If this happens a number of times as in the child who often fails, is criticized, is unaccepted, makes no friends, wins no games, and the like, the discrepancy becomes greater instead of smaller. He will reduce his goals or raise them impossibly high or quit trying. Classroom competition reduces this discrepancy for the consistently successful, but increases it for the many failures; it may help a few but harms many, mostly handicapped children.

Children Do Not Fail Often in the Real World

In the real, outside-of-school world few children fail completely and always; but in terms of competition, acceptable grades, and progress, as they are usually determined in most classrooms, they consistently fail. If expectations are realistic and any progress, however small, is rewarded, as it is done in nongraded, noncompetitive classrooms and especially individualized teaching, the discrepancy concept will be reduced, the child learns and is motivated to learn more by the simple agency of success.

What Happens to Curiosity

One of the most perplexing of educational mysteries poses the question: What happens to the insatiable curiosity which all normal children have in abundance to start with but which usually disappears as the child goes through the school years? True, a few children keep their sense of wonder and joy in finding out, but for most, learning — supposedly their main occupation during these years — becomes dull, routine, humdrum, if not actually painful.

There are no simple anwers to explain why the most powerful of motivations to learn, curiosity, seems to fade away in school. However, part of the answer undoubtedly, can be found in the substitution or extrinsic rewards (grades, winning competitively, or failing) for the intrinsic reward of curiosity satisfaction. Furthermore, too often teachers substitute their own inducements, goals, and methods for the innate motive power of children. As a result, students adapt to what is. They follow the line of least resistance and minimal pain as the teacher steers the course, poses the questions, prods them into action with artificial motivation, and competitively grades their responses.

Atkin (1958) compared the learning behavior of second graders with fifth graders. He discovered that the older children as a group were far less motivated by curiosity, put forth fewer ideas of their own, and were far more dependent. By the time students reach high school and college, they need the constant pressure of tests and quizzes and grades to keep them going; the good students do, that is, the poor student has given up entirely or does only enough to get by. Many gifted students become chronic underachievers.

Atkinson (1966) and his associates in a study of motivation in older students found that fear of failure became the dominant drive. The unsuccessful (by school standards) were poorly motivated, period.

What a tragedy! How unfortunate and unnecessary. The learning of the curious little child, which he finds so ecstatic and exciting, is self-propelled. He manipulates, explores, tastes, feels, looks, invents. He wonders, imagines, and asks questions. When he makes a discovery or develops a skill, he is elated! He has a sense of new power. His ego is given a boost, and his self-confidence grows. He is motivated to learn more and more. *There is no reason why such activities, rewards, and motivation could not (should not) be continued throughout school, and for a lifetime!* It usually does not happen in the traditional learning situation at any level of schooling. Some measure of what learning can be is found in increased achievement and personal satisfaction developed in the newer approaches with freedom to learn, at the student's own rate, what interests him without grades, fear of failure, and competition.

Competition and Aggression

Any society that encourages competition encourages

acquisition which encourages aggression. On the national scale it becomes the drive to acquire territory and power by means of war or colonization. Preparing young men in the behaviors needed for these activities demands strong emphasis upon competition together with a reduction of imagination and self-awareness to a minimum. One could best lie in an alien land as part of a military occupancy or fight to the death against an impersonal foe by conceiving one's self as an instrument of one's country. This trick of detachment has been taught in various ways. Stereotyped behavior grows out of the mass-producing classroom or the close-order drill of basic military training. This male bias of education explains a good deal.

From the individual's viewpoint, competition stimulates and reinforces right answers, standardization, eager acquisition, status, aggression, and "win at any cost" attitudes. Until recently it appeared that such goals and attitudes were what was needed and wanted. It is safe to say that such human characteristics will no longer work for the world in which we live. Already they are both inappropriate and destructive. In other words, if education continues along the same old track, humanity, sooner or later, will destroy itself. Not only by the possibility of atomic fission but with all the refuse, water, and air pollution produced by making and using all the things a competitive and affluent society wants without real concern for others. Competitive success declares that one has every right to what he has won.

Furthermore, competition emphasizes *getting* rather than *being*. To put it another way, competition distorts goals, such as grades instead of growth, the trappings of status instead of real character, "asking what your country can do for you rather than what you can do for your country." The difference should be so obvious that further discussion of this point is unnecessary.

Competition Emphasizes the Completion Complex

Like the overemphasis upon grades as goals, competition emphasizes the *completion complex*. The completion complex makes the assumption that getting through a course; completing a textbook; getting so many hours, credits, or degrees, or putting in so many years constitute the goals of education. In other words one is more interested in having a lesson done, a course completed, or a degree earned rather than in learning itself, which is never completed.

A culture such as ours is beginning to be must live with constant change, exploding knowledge and multiplying problems; it demands a learn*ing* rather than learn*ed* society, even if the latter were possible, which it is not. An individual must learn that the usual words of commencement speakers are not clichés; the education he has received *is* only the beginning. Failure to keep on learning in terms of new developments can only mean unemployment and social disorientation. Somehow we must stimulate students to view learning as a continuous process rather than so many courses and grades and degrees completed.

The completion complex is reinforced by parents who continually cry, "Get your work done!" and teachers who prize work that is finished and courses that are covered.

Many colleges give credit for so many contact hours or classes attended, clock hours of student teaching, and the like. As a matter of fact, no equivalency can be assumed even if one considers only the rate of speed of lecturing which varies greatly from professor to professor. If one also considers organization of material, interest, involvement, supplementary reading, and independent projects, equivalency-based hours are impossible.

The completion complex is an anachronistic carry-over of the days when learning was equated with mental discipline and the accumulation of knowledge (when the body of knowledge was relatively stable and fixed). That completion is not necessarily learning has been demonstrated many times as has the fact that enforced learning often develops antipathy.

The most important misconception fostered by the completion hypothesis is that *knowing* rather than *learning* is overemphasized; the *end product* rather than the *process* becomes the goal. It is the product that is evaluated rather than the resultant behavior. If learning is modifying behavior, and most educators give at least lip service to this definition, then the product has no meaning other than what one did to satisfy requirements for a certain course. For instance, when a student writes a paper, it is the paper that is evaluated, not the attitudes, thinking skills, or creativity or development of the student. It is not what the student *becomes,* but what he *produces* in an expedient manner.

As a result the student, in his eagerness to finish a nice-looking product and hand it in, will employ any shortcuts he can devise rather than develop the subject in meaningful depth. The process is reinforced by teachers who ask for certain lengths of numbers of words, as if this were the optimum treatment but which in fact may be minimal.

Again, let us emphasize the fact that in teaching, the method used is more important than that which is taught *if* one is concerned with behavior modifications as one's learning objectives. To put it another way, the manner in which one is taught is more important than the product contrived. In still other words, the answers are not as important as the processes used in deriving solutions if one learns how to learn, think, and create.

The emphasis upon completion encourages haste (even carelessness), and the attitude of finishing one thing and getting on with another until completion becomes a veritable complusion by which one comes to view achievement as that which one has completed or finished. Instead, learning should be (must be in these times) viewed as a never-ending process. If anything is finished, it is only bits and pieces.

We can be certain that the only certainty for the future of tomorrow is adult change, and the result of the change is especially uncertain. Precisely because that is true, our schools (all of them) must abandon the concept of completion and retention as the epitome of education purpose.

To attempt to predict the unpredictable is far too prophetic for the teacher. We cannot predict answers to questions our children need to know for the future. We do not know what knowledge will be of most worth for the certainly uncertain future; in fact we probably do not even have that knowledge — it is yet to be discovered. Hence, we must desist in emphasizing the accumulation of facts soon out of date, incomplete, and forgotten. No longer dare we assume that the future will be a repetition of the past. We can only prepare youngsters for the future by teaching them how to learn, how to solve problems, create and innovate, and most importantly, to like to do this.

If classes were to become places where one experiences the hypothetical mode instead of the didactic expository mode, students would become learners rather than retainers for antique stores. This requires that instruction move from the teaching of facts, which will soon be forgotten or become irrelevant, to the *manipulation* of ideas and concepts. To do this, teaching objectives must move from the low intellectual levels of fact retention to the higher levels of comprehension, application, synthesis, or evaluation; the classroom environment must be such that students are consistently encouraged to manipulate information at these levels, without pressures of competition.

Teaching for Thinking Not Competitive

The results in achievement produced by different forms of teaching are known and supported by valid empirical research. If facts are taught and tested for the student, he will develop only recall skills; if teaching is for manipulative (thinking) skills and testing is done at the same level, the student will develop the abilities to confront problems and make rational decisions. However, if the teaching is for thinking and creating at a high level, but the testing is for retention and recall of knowledge, the latter will be the skills and abilities developed. Teachers determine by their competitive tests more than they realize the kind of learning that takes place in their classes.

If educational achievement will benefit future (continuous) personal development, certain of present-day school practices must be revised. Perhaps the most important of these is that we consider growth and adaptive processes as educational ends in themselves rather than the usual elements (products) considered as educational achievement.

Since growth and adaptive processes are personal, we can no longer consider progress determined apart from the individual.

Competitive (with others) processes of evaluation have no validity or meaning. In this context, self-appraisal becomes a more legitimate and tenable base for the evaluation of educational achievement than any judgment from competitive and external sources.

What Is Taught Compared to What Students Become

Up to now, most educators are more interested in *what* is taught to students than in what students *become*. With this approach the rationale follows that only the teacher is able to properly assess how much of what was taught is retained, or what progress is made. The verb *to educate* is not only transitive, it is also reflective; it is not something we do to a child, rather it is something the student does to himself. It is based upon a purely reflective thinking process. An essential part of education is learning how to evaluate one's own advancement — knowing what one has learned and what one needs to learn in order to satisfy one's self for mental well-being; therefore, it can best be evaluated by its possessor.

No method of testing and evaluating learning has yet been devised that can be used by a second party to ascertain what another person actually has learned. The best that can be said of a test score is that it is a score made on that test, no more and no less. It may or may not reflect test-taking skill more than anything else. It may indicate what has been memorized. It is difficult, if not impossible, to assess the *true aims* of education — modifications of behaviors.Only the individual can be certain to any degree, and even he may not always be completely right. He knows better than any second party.

What Can Be Done to Remove Harmful Effects of Competition?

It probably is impossible to eliminate all competition in the classroom. It may not even be desirable, but the destructive effects can be reduced significantly.

First of all, competition in the classroom should be made

reasonably fair. If students must be pitted against each other for grades or other rewards, then the odds must be reduced and equalized. Let the gifted compete with other gifted students, average with average, and slow with slow. Be sure there are no other handicaps such as perceptual problems, mental retardation, emotional problems, cultural deprivation, or sight or hearing handicaps. It should be obvious that such children cannot compete on anything like a fair basis with normal children.

The most effective and fairest competition is that of an individual with himself. It actually is the form most people use — *if* they are free to choose. Think for a monent of all the things you have learned, the skills you have developed in this manner. This is the way you learned to talk, walk, ride a bike, drive a car, and read. How competitive with others is your hobby? Not very likely. Do you fish to beat a buddy or hunt to outdo a friend? Most of the learning you have done before you went to school, outside the school, and after graduation was motivated by interest and a desire to improve your past performances. True, there is competition of sorts with others outside school, but rarely is it the do or die, pass or fail variety encouraged in most classrooms.

A few teachers have discovered that competition with one's self can be used effectively in school and used without the threat to one's ego so often imposed in competition with others. This is even more true *if progress in any amount is accepted and rewarded.* Why does it have to be more than 70 percent or above a "D" to be acceptable? This is why ungraded, individualized, or continuous progress programs are so effective and motivating. Any amount of progress is acceptable; the student competes only with himself, *and he always wins.*

A further step in the right direction would develop what is sometimes called a positive approach to failure. In most classrooms failure is the worst possible happening. Low test scores, wrong answers, and incomplete results are bad, explicitly or implied.

The normal human tendency reacts to failure with a feeling of discouragement, particularly if one has worked hard over a long period of time. If the failure to get the right answer or solve the problem or see progress occurs more than two or three times, discouragement may be accompanied by loss of self-confidence and ego. This latter effect is not a little matter; it is cause for serious concern.

Develop a Positive Approach to Failure

A more helpful approach is possible. Scientists can teach us a few things here. All scientists who deserve the name overcome this problem by adopting a healthy and realistic approach to failure. They view their work as a never-ending-continuum. At any given point they see their task (learning, research, discovery) as incomplete because later on they will know more about what they are attempting to do. Failure in that light is not failure as we usually think of it; it is a step along the path of discovery and problem-solving.

Failure says to the inquiring scientist, "At least you now know what does not work; this is not the answer. Try another route to resolve the problem." He may not have gotten what he wanted, but he did get information, and all information is valuable. From this perspective failure becomes a type of success because it tells the scientist his hunch or hypothesis was not the right one. He at least discovered what would not work. As a matter of fact, the failure could be considered an addition to the storehouse of knowledge of cumulative scientific information.

Many instances of this principle at work can be cited. Here are several noteworthy examples: The Salvarsan treatment for syphilis is also known as "606" because Dr. Ehrlich failed 605 times before discovering a formula that cured the disease. The Polaroid Land Camera® has changed the entire concept of candid camera photography, but Dr. Howard Rogers spent fifteen years and developed more than 5000 compounds *before* he actually invented a new molecule that revolutionized picture taking. His 5000 failures add to the storehouse of chemical knowledge. Dr. Fleming discovered penicillin and opened up a whole new world of sickness therapy because a bacterial culture he wanted would not develop properly. He failed in his original intent. Babe Ruth's name will live long in baseball's Hall of Fame as the "King of Swat" in spite of Henry Aaron because he set a record of home runs. What are not so well-known, but which also set a record, are his strike-outs.

All career scientists follow the path of uncertainty guided often only by the light of failure, fully aware that failure is just one place in the continuum of discovery. The scientist then accepts his work as both uncertain and unfinished. He may arrive at a point where he can make certain conclusions from his collected data. As he answers one question, others arise unanswered. There is always one job to do because of the continually revealing nature of the scientific enterprise. Problems are solved eventually, but in the process others are uncovered.

From the child's and student's point of view, failure has several important dimensions. Failure is a part of learning what one can and cannot do. Adjustment is essential for good mental health. However, adequate adjustment is impossible if all failure is labeled bad and if failure is not followed by successes. Success derives its joy from overcoming previous defeats. We are all aware of progress made in other areas of human endeavor, in addition to that made in science, in which failure after failure was met with "try, try again" and eventual success.

Several cautions need to be observed carefully. *First, in such cases there was always the hope of success.* Such men felt confident that they had a chance to succeed. *Second, these persons were highly self-motivated;* they were not prodded and pushed by someone else. And, *third, no one was continually labeling them failures* or calling attention to lack of immediate success by such important criteria (in our school culture) as grades. Any accomplishment, however small, was acceptable and motivating. No one was constantly saying or implying, "Come on now, you can do better than that if you only try to work a little harder."

Contrast that with the usual classroom situation. The failing student may not now be putting forth his best effort, but he once did, and it did no good. There was no hope of success. He was pushed and prodded and reminded by grades over and over again that he did not measure up on the competitive scheme of progress. Success was measured by whatever the teacher decreed. He was called lazy, disinterested, and a poor student. More students are in this defeated dilemma than most teachers know or are willing to admit. Without question the slow, retarded, perceptually handicapped, emotionally disturbed, and environmentally handicapped fail hopelessly over and over again. The ego of no child can survive this continuous frustration. How many such children are there? No fewer than 50 percent in most classes think of themselves as failures, and it may run as high as 75 percent. Nothing contributes to this dismal sense of failure more than the popular competitive evaluation of achievement.

A positive approach to failure would say, "We do not have it *yet*, but we will get it. You have done something worthwhile." It accepts wrong answers as a good try. It encourages hypothesizing and innovative approaches, and rewards them because they are ideas, right or wrong. Evaluation encourages and stimulates rather than defeats or deflates. At the very least, the student will have learned what errors he has made without feeling a dunce for his mistake; he will try again. At best he may come up with a really good idea. But he must operate and be encouraged to think in the secure atmosphere dominated by a positive approach to failure.

Students' Methods of Learning Vary Greatly

Teachers ought not to feel threatened by what appears to be student failure. There is no reason to be antagonistic toward pupils who are unsuccessful in one's classroom. Accepting them as they are, one can extend sympathy and understanding. Let me say again: children are all different and although they are more alike than different, *the differences are all important.* For instance, boys as a rule do not develop as rapidly nor do they learn as fast as girls. Only in the upper levels of college do boys really begin to catch up. Some children learn best by visual stimuli, others by auditory stimuli, and some others learn best by manual manipulation. There are variations of combinations to add to these differences, together with giftedness and mental retardation, and other specific learning disabilities. *It is utterly absurd and damnably devastating to compare in any respect children with each other, and to encourage classwide (or schoolwide) competition.*

Each child ought to be allowed to learn *as he learns best, and at whatever rate that best is. The most effective and harmless competition is that of a student with himself.*

Any number of instances come to mind, but perhaps this one illustrates our point best. Once, while I was observing one of my student teachers, the regular classroom teacher took me over to meet one of the students. "John," she said, "has been having a lot of trouble with writing, but I want to show you how much he has improved. Here is his paper for today." She pulled a paper out of her desk. For a fifth grader it was very poor. If she had compared him with the others, he would have gotten an "F". But she pulled out another paper. "Here is one he turned in a month ago. I wanted you to see the difference, the improvement he has made." John beamed.

There was competition here, and it was effectively motivating and ego-enhancing. John was afflicted with a specific learning disability, a handicapped child. He never learned to write well in comparison to other children his age. In this teacher's class he learned more than in all the other previous four grades put together and learned to write well enough to be read by most teachers. Later on in high school he learned to type. He is now a junior in college doing very well. Think for a moment about what would have happened to John if this teacher had used the usual sort of classroom competition. "That is different," you may say. Yes, it is, but are not all children different?

Chapter 12

DISCIPLINE AND
BEHAVIOR MODIFICATION

PROBABLY no aspect of teaching causes teachers more concern, causes them to expend more effort, and induces more teachers to quit the teaching profession than the problem of classroom discipline. Some teachers seem to have more and some fewer problems and trouble than others. It all comes down to three primary issues: teacher personality, classroom management, and personal teacher-pupil relationships.

At the unfortunate risk of making it *the* major issue, may we interject a fourth issue, the child himself. Everyone *knows* that children come from different kinds of homes and that some seem to have no training at home in discipline and are incorrigible right from the start. This is true in a few cases, but it gives the teacher who is looking for an excuse the very thing she is seeking — an excuse for the poor discipline she has in her classroom.

It has become a popular heresy widely accepted that exceptional children are for the most part trouble-makers. We stated earlier in this book that even chronicly troublesome children caused us no problems.

If exceptional children are serious discipline problems, it is not because they are exceptional, but simply because one or more of the primary issues or causes are being violated.

Teachers with Personality Problems

This was discussed somewhat in an earlier chapter, but let us briefly restate several of our major premises. The insecure, nonaccepting, cold and loveless, rigid, impatient perfectionistic, and impersonal teacher inevitably will have trouble and actually has no business teaching even normal children. Above all she should not have anything to do with exceptional children.

General Classroom Management Principles

1. Set up, with the aid of the students, clear rules where such rules are needed. This includes such parts of the daily routine as putting away clothing and personal belongings, use of the toilets and drinking fountains, access to school supplies, special books, special audio-visual equipment, independent work, free time, recess, meal time. Be careful of regimentation.

   Whenever a rule is needed, it should be simple and clearly understood by all, both as to what is stated and as to why it is needed. The rules should be delineated as soon after school gets started as possible.

   It always is easier to prevent problems or induce good behavior than it is to change undersirable behavior once it has started.

   Rules are means to ends, and therefore they should be presented as such to the class. They should be understood as to why they are needed.

2. Minimize and reduce disruptions and delays. When the bell rings, be prepared to start with the schoolwork. Work out some system whereby attendance checking, money collecting, announcements can be held to a minimum, done by a capable student, or carried out after the work has begun.

   Problems start easily when the children have time on their hands and there is no clear task to occupy their busy minds and bodies. There is no better cure for minor (or some major) discipline problems than productive activity.

3. Plan independent activities as well as group work. Allow some time for independent seat work or at an interest center. Be sure they have something else to do when they have finished. Many disruptions originate when students have completed their seat work or independent studies.

   Never assign what is called *busy-work*. Students should understand that whatever work they have to do is a part of the curriculum and not merely a time-filler. It should be an opportunity to practice skills, obtain information, or practice solving problems. Our observation has been that when students resent work to be done, it is either busy-work or the teacher has not clarified the objectives for the work being asked for. Tell your students often why they are to do their work or study a certain subject or read an assigned book. It should be far more than, "It's the lesson," or "It's good for you," etc.

4. Encourage questions whether they are questions for information or questions of procedure; students should feel free to ask those questions. This is one sign of good rapport within a classroom and another sign of high interest and of confidence in the credibility of the teacher.

    This does not mean that the teacher should do the work for the student. There is a fine line between help and doing a student's work.

5. Stress positive rather than negative statements and classroom behavior. Everyone finds it more pleasant and rewarding to be told what *to do* rather than to be told what *not to do*. Good and Brohphy (1973) give (p. 179) a number of illustrations of positive language such as: "Close the door quietly," rather than, "Don't slam the door." "When you finish your work put the scissors back in the box and the bits of paper into the waste basket," rather than, "Don't leave a mess."

    This does not mean that negative statements have no place in teaching. They do, but they should be used where appropriate and at a minimum. It takes more thought to use the right approach, but practice makes it easier, and a better classroom atmosphere makes it worthwhile.

6. Praise behavior that is good — catch the child doing what he should do. It is a travesty of classroom management that teachers use the stick more than the carrot, when it has been shown in research study after study that the carrot works far better than the stick.

    For praise to be effective, there are certain criteria that must be followed:

    a. The giver of praise must be respected. Praise given by

someone not respected has a reverse effect; it proves that the giver is insincere and is trying a "rip-off."

b. Praise should be sincere; flattery is worse than nothing. Children do know the difference.
c. Try to find *something* that is worthy of praise. Even a poor lesson can be praised for the effort. You no doubt have heard the story of the boy who brought home one day an ugly mangy mongrel. Every member of the family found something wrong with the dog the boy obviously liked. Finally, he said when they had finished their disparagements, "But don't yoq see how nicely he wags his tail!"
d. When praising an accomplishment, be as specific as possible. What in particular did you like? Such praise is far more effective than some general statement such as, "That's good work." *What* is good about it would be far better praise.
e. Use both verbal and nonverbal praise. Sometimes a pat on the head or some reward other than a verbal statement would mean more. Variety is indeed the spice of praise. Sometimes use both verbal and nonverbal praise.
f. Praise given where others can see it or hear it means more than that given privately. Far more.

Punishment May Be Needed Occasionally

As a general rule, punishment is used as a last resort and only with chronic misbehavior. It is not a step a teacher should take lightly since it indicates that the problem has gotten out of hand and cannot be coped with by either student or the teacher. It is an expression that states that the student is not trying to improve and that the discipline break is deliberate. It can be damaging both to the teacher and to the student. It can harm further what probably is an already damaged self-concept. Never should it be used when the student is trying to improve.

When punishment is used, it should be swift and sure and appropriate. It can take many forms, but the form most often used is physical punishment, because it is most common and is easiest to administer. It is not recommended by most educators and psychologists because:

1. It is quick and final — there, that's it. Therefore, attention tends to be focused on the punishment itself rather than the misdemeanor that caused it. It becomes an end in itself, rather than a means to an end.
2. It is difficult to administer objectively. Usually there is a good deal of emotion and feeling before, during, and after the incident.
3. It removes the feeling of guilt quickly (and may substitute resentment). The culprit feels no remorse or responsibility for what he did to bring punishment upon himself. It therefore has few lasting qualities. It is temporary at best.
4. It is interesting and sobering to note that the students who are most often the victims of physical punishment come from homes where beatings are frequent and severe. Criminals convicted of violent crimes and assault almost always show a history of physical punishment. Seemingly, it teaches that violence is the solution to unwanted behavior. It does not teach desirable and appropriate behavior nor self-discipline which is what is wanted in the long run.

Prescription for Disruptive Students

As a part of this chapter we wish to reprint this article.* It is one of the best treatments of discipline and behavior modification we have seen.

It could be almost any class at any level in just about any school. A disruptive student is causing a commotion and though the teacher is knowledgeable and experienced, she is poorly prepared to handle the situation. Few have the training they need to equip them to deal with chronic disrupters, according to two Seattle educators, and thus complaints about poor discipline continue to mount.

In Mrs. Edwards' fourth-grade class at Ridgecrest School the ruckus is taking place at the rear of the room near Tommy Benson's desk. Mrs. Edwards grows more and more angry as she

---

*Reprinted for Vivian Hedrich, "Prescription for Disruptive Students," *American Education*, 8:11 (July, 1972) with permission from the author.

attempts to ignore the noise which has been erupting off and on since recess, when Tommy had a brief scuffle with another boy. Now the hitting has covertly resumed while most of the class watches, their arithmetic assignments forgotten.

Finally, reaching the end of her patience, Mrs. Edwards announces in a loud voice that there will be no further recess privileges for Tommy that week. Her "victory" is temporary silence.

As the children file out for lunch, however, fighting breaks out again in the hallway just outside Mrs. Edwards' room. True to her expectations she finds Tommy the prime culprit. His next stop is the main office, where he sits dejectedly on a bench waiting to be received by the principal. Probably there are several others ahead of him, so he has time to think.

Tommy's emotions are a smoldering combination of anxiety and anger. What will the principal say this time? Will his parents be called? Will he be suspended? Whatever happens, the five-minute interview with a harried administrator that follows does little to restore Tommy's enthusiasm for returning to class. He has long ago identified Mrs. Edwards as unfair, the arch-enemy.

Mrs. Edwards also has been analyzing the situation, over lunch. Tommy is a born troublemaker. She has seen "his kind" many times before. If he were not in her class, she would be able to accomplish twice as much with the children who really want to learn. Tommy sets a destructive example for the rest.

As the weeks pass and further incidents occur, the relationship between the teacher and pupil goes rapidly downhill. Where originally Mrs. Edwards had seen Tommy as an irritation, she now begins to feel open hostility toward this child who complicates her life and hampers her teaching efforts. The cold war is on. Just before spring vacation the teacher requests that Tommy be reassigned.

While that move at least temporarily restores peace to Mrs. Edwards' classroom, Tommy's problems are just beginning. At Ridgecrest he will likely repeat his performance in another room and may eventually be moved to a different school or to a "special education" class. By age ten he may already be on the treadmill that leads to dropping out.

Psychologist Wayne Foley and counselor John Willson, who work as a pupil guidance team in the Seattle Public

Schools, find situations such as the conflict between Tommy and Mrs. Edwards something less than constructive, but understandable nonetheless. Tommy, anxious and frightened, believes that everyone hates him. Beyond her protective feeling for the class as a whole, the teacher feels that her authority and competence face a threat that must be removed. And so Tommy is shifted elsewhere, a transaction that may serve a short-term administrative purpose but is not well calculated to contribute to the youngster's education.

Foley and Willson are convinced that most of the situations teachers find so frustrating and defeating are in fact well within their power to alter and improve. And yet, they say, most teachers — even experienced teachers faced with almost continuous student disruption — never learn how to cope with the problem. Foley and Willson are strong advocates of "preventive medicine" for potential disrupters, and a major part of their daily work is helping teachers learn how to apply it.

"Many erroneously assume," says Foley, spokesman for the team, "that disruptive students are inherently unable to function within the classroom, perhaps because they come from an 'inconsistent' home environment, and that nothing can be done about it." Thus students like Tommy are punished or banished on the shaky assumption that the experience will somehow promote an improved performance. A much better approach, Foley and Willson say, is for the teacher to control and modify behavioral problems before,

OUNCE OF PREVENTION VS POUND OF PENALTY

they become unmanageable.

"Teachers can accomplish this by systematically varying the magnitude and timing of their attention and by using approaches that encourage and reinforce productive conduct," Foley says. "And for their efforts the teachers can receive visible rewards in the forms of improved academic work and a generally better learning environment."

Tommy's chances for making a success of the fourth grade, Foley and Willson feel, would have been immeasurably enhanced had several conditions been different.

At the beginning of the year when the children were new to the room, an open discussion of the types of behavior that are considered disruptive and the kinds that are appropriate for the classroom would have given the students a clearer understanding of the rules under which they would operate.

Also a daily effort on the part of Mrs. Edwards to watch for and reward children who showed they were willing to comply with the negotiated rules would have had a cumulative and beneficial effect on the class as a whole. By intentionally focusing on the positive and by identifying the particular rewards to which individual children were likely to respond, she would have been well on her way to teaching potential disruptors that good behavior has benefits far beyond avoiding a teacher's displeasure.

"While Tommy's trip to the office accomplished very little in modifying behavior in itself, it did set the scene for a positive more," Foley says. "If the teacher, instead of ignoring his existence when he returned to class, had made a point of noting and rewarding his new and more appropriate behavior, Tommy would have gained a more balanced view. He would have seen his teacher as someone who wants him to improve, and himself as a person who could succeed as well as fail."

As full-time staff members at Seattle's Bailey Gatzert School, located in a low-income, high-minority population area, Foley and Willson are frequently consulted by teachers who find themselves frustrated by persistent behavior problems.

"Our first move in offering help is to relieve some of the tension and pressure that has built up between teacher and child," Foley says. "Both of them need a 'breather,' and we offer to take part of the responsibility from the teacher's shoulders in order to start building a more objective relationship. Particularly if the youngster has had a history of misbehavior, the teacher may have lost sight of the child's true potential and the kind of academic performance she should be able to expect from the classroom."

Foley and Willson point to three essential elements in successful behavior modifications. First, the teacher must be sincerely concerned with improving her ability to work with the child. Second, the teacher herself must be the prime agent for promoting student change.

CATCH THE CULPRIT IN THE ACT OF BEING GOOD

Third, the engineering of change must take place in the

classroom setting where the undesirable behavior was exhibited, not in a principal's office or other "neutral" location.

The psychologist and counselor provide a temporary support service for the teacher, working with her in the classroom to advise strategies for spotting and fending off potential problems. They find that most teachers, when they have reached the point of requesting help, are anxious to cooperate.

Although most school officials are clearly aware of the need for more effective preventive programs in dealing with disruptive students, Foley and Willson say, there must be equal understanding that effective teaching training in this area requires a new emphasis and a much broader approach to discipline.

"Punishment following a disruptive act does nothing to anticipate or even to prevent future outbursts," Foley says. "In itself punishment only tends to suppress deviant behavior temporarily, and does not teach or strengthen appropriate new behavior."

As educators recognize, the use of force or power generally requires a continued and increased use to suppress bad behavior. It can mainly be imposed to intimidate younger children. As children become older they increasingly resent such controls and may in time actively rebel against them.

"Clearly, if a teacher for some reason needs from us punitive control to eliminate specific behavior problems," Foley says, "there should be an even greater effort to promote and strengthen the kind of conduct that is appropriate. After a student has been punished and is at least trying to cooperate, the teacher should make an effort to 'catch him being good.'"

The Foley-Willson approach to behavior modification offers students an opportunity to contribute to the establishment of classroom rules. Their subsequent willingness to comply with these rules is rewarded by the teacher on a regular basis and in a number of ways. Many teachers award one point at the end of each class period to all students who have not broken any of the agreed-upon rules, the points being accumulated throughout the week until Friday, when they may be converted into time spent on an activity the student himself selects.

Most of the students decide to visit the "Gatzert Store," a

popular facility opened two years ago in a portable building on the school grounds. Here children may play with an attractive array of toys and educational games. The "store" has proven so successful that this year four other area elementary schools elected to open similar facilities following a period of inservice training in the Foley-Willson behavior,

FIRST STEP IS TO ESTABLISH GROUND RULES

modification approach.

"While under certain conditions children's behavior can be motivated by almost anything, by far the most powerful and effective reward is praise," Foley says. "This can come from the teacher, the principal, or any other adult, and can be the 'payoff' for any accomplishment, no matter how small. A teacher who knows how to capitalize on that fact and use it in developing models of appropriate behavior in the classroom, has the power to turn peer pressure (which so often works against her) to her own advantage."

Given the proper follow-through, the child will come to see the teacher not as an enemy but as someone who treats him fairly at all times. Such follow-through bears on another essential aspect of successful behavior modification — consistency. Inconsistency breeds confusion. Under a consistent teacher the child can make the discovery that appropriate behavior "pays."

In a large-city ghetto environment children's school problems are often compounded by the struggle of their families to survive, by a higher incidence of broken homes, and by the greater mobility that often characterizes low-income families. Foley has no question that despite these kinds of handicaps, such children can learn to function effectively in school, and many are doing so. In a sense, they put on a "school hat."

"Even the most 'ghettoized' child can be motivated to make the most of his school opportunities everyday," Foley says. "It is simply not realistic to be satisfied with a token effort and blame school failures on the "problems that exist in the home." Our responsibility is to help today's children in today's classrooms."

Foley and Willson say that although prospective teachers emerging from colleges and universities today are much better informed about tested behavioral concepts than their predecessors were, application of these concepts is still a rarity. That being so, they recommend a major expansion of inservice classes and demonstration pilot projects.

"Any teacher who attends such a program with the sincere desire to help children improve their behavior," Foley says, "can learn the skills and strategies necessary to achieve success in her own classroom. Only in rare cases of severe emotional disturbance is removal of a child from the classroom the appropriate way to try to help him solve his problem. Our experience strongly suggests that what used to be called the 'incorrigible child' is virtually nonexistent."

An example of how behavior modification can help even a serious behavior problem is seen in Darrel, a nine-year-old who arrived at Bailey Gatzert last winter as a disciplinary transfer from another Seattle school.

"It wouldn't be too strong to say that the teachers and staff of his former school intensely disliked, even hated, him," Foley recalls. "Darrel's reports indicated he had done absolutely no work during the year before. He intimidated nearly everyone with whom he came in contact and had spent nearly half of the previous year at home on disciplinary suspension."

A range of tests given to Darrel when he first arrived at Bailey Gatzert indicated that, his irritating conduct aside, he was a bright youngster who could be expected to do well in school. In the classroom Foley helped him to prepare a written contract for a specified amount of work to be accomplished in return for time to spend in the Gatzert Store, and his teacher was in turn advised on precisely what to expect from her new pupil.

"Within two weeks we were seeing some gratifying results," Foley recalls. "Darrel completed at least 90 percent of the work agreed upon and was regular in attendance. After a time he decided to test us and briefly reverted to his old habits. When our response was 'no payoff' and no special attention, he soon went back to doing his schoolwork."

NO REWARD FOR SEEMLY CLASSROOM CONDUCT IS AS POTENT AS PRAISE

On Friday, when Darrel collected play time and was headed for the store, his teacher made a point to walk with him by the main office and to stop there and tell the staff how well he was doing. On several occasions Foley or Willson telephoned Darrel's home to tell his mother, in the boy's presence, how much he was accomplishing.

Although Darrel's about-face was perhaps unusually dramatic, the effectiveness of the program has been such that it is being expanded. With a $65,000 grant under Title III of the Elementary and Secondary Education Act, supplemented by district in-kind funds, a three-year demonstration project will begin at Bailey Gatzert next fall.

Part of the money will help establish an "intervention classroom" in which teachers may observe behavioral specialists demonstrating techniques of proven success with problem children. Four rooms have been selected as model classrooms in the initial year's program, with all of the school's 35 teachers and approximately 650 children eligible to participate.

The new intervention classroom will be much like a typical room, with two exceptions. A one-way glass will enable observers to be present without distracting children from their work, and a videotape machine will be available to film segments of the instruction for later discussion and training.

In September, children from the four pilot classrooms will be tested and placed in appropriate levels for individualized basic skills study. Teachers may refer children to the intervention center (staffed by a trained teacher and an instructional aide) at any time for reasons of poor academic performance, lack of motivation, or antisocial behavior. In preliminary consultations with the staff, teachers will be asked to pinpoint the problem and back it up with classroom data. Agreement will be reached on the magnitude of the behavioral change expected.

"We in no way demean a teacher by offering help," Foley says. "In essence we are saying 'You've got a problem; let's work together to solve it.' When the change we are looking for occurs, we will have met our part of the bargain."

The teacher, for her part, agrees to regular weekly meetings with the student and the guidance team to discuss the youngster's progress during his assignment to the center. The teacher also agrees to attend a minimum of three one-hour observation and training sessions on individualized instruction and behavior management, with the project teacher acting as her substitute during those periods. Return of the child to his regular classroom is geared to his progress at the center together with the teacher's completion of the training sessions.

Parents also will be involved in the new program and by now have received a written description of the project and an invitation to attend a meeting in September at which they will be introduced to the intervention facility and the staff. Later, each parent will have an opportunity to attend five one-hour training and observation sessions aimed at helping them contribute to their child's progress.

Summing up the work of the Bailey Gatzert program, Foley says: "Disruptive students present problems that are difficult to understand and that continue to occur with high frequency throughout the year. It is not surprising that after a series of unsuccessful attempts to relate to and change such students, many teachers simply give up. In this situation, the psychologist-school counselor team can make a strategic contribution. Because of our training and experience and because we are a part of the school staff, we are in a position not only to recommend effective tactics and techniques but to demonstrate them firsthand."

Foley and Willson dismiss the notion that there is anything magic about their approach, noting that it is based on well-established psychological and pedagogical principles. They see their job as being to help teachers learn how to apply those principles in the classroom — routinely. If the teacher does so sincerely and consistently and learns to "individualize" her expectations for success — to reward and punish based upon what the child is capable of — she will build a positive and honest relationship with her pupils. She will succeed — and so will her students.

WITH SKILLFUL HANDLING FEW
YOUNGSTERS REMAIN "INCORRIGIBLE"

"As more and more teachers become actively involved in preventive efforts," Foley concludes, "we will without question see higher morale, measurable growth in academic achievement, improved student self-perception, and a new view of school as being relevant, rewarding, and fun."

Summary

No teacher, however competent or skilled in handling discipline problems or managing the classroom, escapes minor instances of misbehavior or an occasional major breach of misdemeanor. Children are sometimes unthinking or testing the teacher or untrained. There are a few chronic cases of hard-core delinquency around.

The teacher who has few personality problems, who understands and loves children (and lets them know it), accepts the unacceptable child, who knows how to manage her classroom for maximum learning, gives individual attention to her pupils sometime during the day, and maintains a healthy and understanding relationship with her pupils will generally have good control of her class and a good learning situation.

Chapter 13

DO NOT FORGET THE GIFTED

IN a study of exceptional children, the gifted are as important as those at the other end of the scale. Possibly it might be said that they are more so because of the fact that they are more likely to be the individuals who will supply the innovations and leadership necessary to the survival of human society in a civilized state. Therefore, while the school is seeking the best possible program for the other exceptional children, it is imperative that the needs of the gifted be met also.

The Thorniest Problem in American Education

The thorniest problem in American education today is the underachievement (low production) of children who appear by every available identification procedure to have adequate or more than adequate intelligence for learning. In the U.S. Government Report *Education of the Gifted and Talented* (1972) we find that more than half (54.6%) of gifted children are underachievers.

This is tragic when one considers their potential for outstanding achievement in all areas of worthwhile human endeavor. It is even more tragic when one considers that the gifted child is the most neglected child in our schools. We are concerned, as well we should be, about handicapped children, but ought we not to be concerned about the gifted underachiever whose extraordinary talent is wasted because it is fallaciously assumed that because he is bright, he will learn no matter what one does or does not do for him? *He is a child who needs help to learn, as does any child.*

The underachiever is as handicapped as any child who needs special attention to learn as he could. When we said he constituted the thorniest problem in American education today, we did so

196

because most efforts to help him to become the achiever that he could become have failed.

Why Have We Failed to Motivate the Underachiever?

We have failed to motivate the underachiever because we have not understood his problems. Any study of the literature of underachievement will reveal that most educators consider these students a more or less homogeneous group whose self-concepts for one or more of a variety of reasons have been severely damaged and who actually believe that they cannot produce. They can come from any type of home, but most of them are from what we call the "better homes," and they are ten boys to one girl. Such is the brief classical picture of the gifted underachiever.

We are convinced that there are at least six rather distinct types of underachievers:

1. One is the classic type described above. His damaged ego interferes with his learning although he has the ability to learn easily and well. No one knows really why he is as he is. Hypotheses abound but much more research is needed here.
2. The gifted child from the culturally disadvantaged home will obviously have problems because of his restricted environmental background. We might say he is environmentally handicapped.
3. Creatively gifted children are far more independently minded than most children, and when they have an excellent teacher or are studying a subject in which they are interested, they often do well. When they are bored or disinterested, they are poor students indeed. They can most easily be identified by their on-again-off-again record of scholastic endeavors.
4. Some gifted children have been pushed and prodded and nagged until they have lost all interest or have rebelled against the prodding. One cannot push a student to the top of his class. Nor can one set unreasonable expectations without doing real damage to the motivational powers of his personality.
5. It is an interesting and disheartening fact that underachievement among the gifted usually does not show

up until about the third grade. It may occur sooner or later, but this is an average. There is little doubt that poor teaching, being bored with the "same old stuff," has turned a lot of students off who could do excellent work. It just may be that gifted children with other problems are pushed over into the morass of underachievement by a boring educational experience.

6. Children with specific learning disabilities are also found among our group of gifted underachievers. They are sometimes identified by the fact that of all the gifted low producers they are usually most highly motivated. They want to learn but cannot.

All of the problems faced by gifted underachievers are aggravated by the unfortunate attitude that they are just lazy and uninterested, which is summed up by the attitude toward the child, "You could learn if you really tried." The fact of the matter is that the child probably could, but he unconsciously is handicapped by one or more of the problems outlined above.

How to Help Underachievers Easily

This writer has had unusual success in helping gifted underachievers by a warm, concerned, and individualized approach. Using some of the methods suggested in Chapter 6 will help. More than anything else they need someone who cares about them enough to help them with a personalized approach. It does not take hours and hours; a few minutes a day will usually accomplish the objective. It does not make any difference as to why the child is a gifted underachiever if you approach *his* problem in learning warmly, appropriately, and individually.

Who Are the Gifted?

The purpose of this chapter is to present some important facts about the gifted and their education with emphasis upon what the teacher needs to know in order to meet their needs. How can the school best help the gifted? If it serves them as it should, there are some specific steps that must be taken.

First, these children must be identified. Who are they? How do they differ from other children? How can they be recognized so that a program can be prepared for them? What type of program is best for them? How can they be taught in order to realize their greatest potential? Of course, there are no absolute answers to these questions, but there are indications and known facts which can be of great help to those who teach the gifted.

Because of the wide variety of giftedness, there has been considerable disagreement in defining this quality. One commonly used definition is "A talented or gifted child is one who shows consistently remarkable performance in any worthwhile line of endeavor" (*Education for the Gifted,* Witty, 1958, p. 19). However, this would exclude the underachiever and very probably the underprivileged as well. Perhaps Sumption and Lueecking (1960) are more encompassing and suitable: "The gifted are those who possess a superior central nervous system characterized by the potential to perform tasks requiring a comparatively high degree of intellectual abstraction or creative imagination or both."

When IQ's are used as a measure, there is wide variation of opinion in where the cutoff point should be. It has varied from 115 to 180. Hollingworth (1942) studied those with very high IQ's, 180 and above. Terman, in his famous long-term pursuit described in *Genetic Studies of Genius* (1925 to 1959), used subjects with IQ's of 140 and above. Frequently the lower cutoff point is 130. Some states use 120 as the lower cutoff point. Since it has been learned that the IQ is not the static absolute, at least in function, that it was first thought to be, it has ceased to be used as the only important determiner of giftedness.

The percentage of identified gifted in the general population varies with IQ cutoff points and with means of identification. The government report *Education of the Gifted and Talented* (1972) states that the gifted are classified as 3 to 5 percent of the population. For educational purposes De Haan and Havighurst (1957) divided the gifted into two groups: "first-order" are those rare ones in the highest one-tenth of one percent. "Second-order" compose the remaining upper 10 percent. With these facts two important points should be remembered by the teacher: there are many more gifted needing attention than may be known. They are frequently neglected. "Contrary to some popular notions, intellectually superior children are often the most neglected children in the classroom" *(Education of the Gifted and Talented,* 1972, p. 52).

Although it is dangerous to equate certain characteristics with certain levels of intelligence, since there are no absolutes here, a number of prominent authorities such as Lewis Terman, Willard Abraham, Paul Witty, E.P. Torrance, J.J. Gallagher, and Walter Barbe have agreed upon some traits which might be called a signpost of giftedness. What follows is a summary of these findings.

Some Popular Misconceptions

Some are in direct opposition to popularly held conceptions about the gifted. For example, it is frequently assumed that the gifted child is an undersized weakling wearing think glasses who studies constantly, spouts polysyllabic words, and will eventually burn out or become insane from too much study. It has also been thought that he is inclined to be a troublemaker by nature and that he lacks practical knowledge or common sense.

Conversely, it has been believed that the gifted person will learn regardless of the kind of teaching he receives and that he will respond to unlimited expectations. Generally it has been accepted that the gifted are easily recognized by looks and conduct.

Some Signposts of Giftedness

However, according to these authorities, such popular ideas are usually false. The gifted child is not easily recognized; he is more like the average child than he is different. However, physically he is inclined to be above average for his chronological age in height, weight, physique, and endurance, and to mature early. He will probably be less prone to mental disorders than others, nor does giftedness decline rapidly with maturity or age. He is not usually a discipline problem, although he may become mischievous if bored; and his giftedness serves him in good stead here, as he can think of many ways to amuse himself at another's expense.

His intelligence is inclined to be general in quality and applies to all areas of cognition and understanding. He will not achieve well regardless of bad teaching or neglect. In fact the tragedies of underachievement and failure often result from such false assumptions.

A number of other characteristics which seem to belong especially to the gifted have been noted by the specialists and are important in identification and instruction. The gifted child usually learns to walk and talk early. His use of language in involved sentences may be striking. With a broad, intense intellectual curiosity, he has diverse and frequently self-directed interests. Often he learns to read before entering school and almost always he has an early desire to read. Furthermore, his reading skill is higher than average, both in quality and quantity. His vocabulary in reading, writing, and speaking is beyond that of his peers, and he uses picturesque ways of getting an idea across. His reasoning power and his ability to handle abstract concepts with creative and critical thinking are premature for his age. Frequently he shows special interest in a subject such as mathematics, science, or music.

Learning easily with fewer explanations and less repetition, he may be less accepting of drill or busy work than others. If he has had good experiences, he likes school and does exceptionally well. He will learn without prodding and often takes difficult subjects in school because he likes them. His hobbies may seem numerous and precocious with a number of them going on at once, while his games and amusements may be in advancement of others of his age.

Often he enjoys playing with older children. Generally he is well-liked by other children, but he may be impatient with those who are slower. In character studies he has been shown to be more trustworthy when under temptation to cheat, higher in honesty, and higher in emotional stability, as well as more adaptable in social situations. He also shows an earlier and deeper interest in religion, God, reasons for being, and questions of right or wrong. When he analyzes his own abilities and limitations, he is prone to be more objective than the average. If he has such undesirable characteristics as negativism, antisocialism, or an undesirable personality, these are not part of his giftedness. Nor does he necessarily have all of the traits mentioned. Very likely he will look much as other children do and frequently act as they do, for he is after all a child. Herein lies a problem: he is easily overlooked by everyone, including his teacher.

Teachers Not Expert Identifiers of Giftedness

How, then, can his teacher discover him? The teacher is handicapped by a tendency to think of the meek, studious conformer as the gifted. Moreover, it is much easier to think of a clean, attractive child from a good home as intelligent than it is to so consider the dirty, unattractive child from a poor home. Gallagher (1964) states, "It is rather sobering to note that presence on the honor roll was a better indicator (of giftedness) than teacher ratings" (p. 9). Pegnato and Birch (1959) in a study discovered that from a total of ninety-one children with an IQ score above 136, teachers identified only forty-one; they also classified as gifted 113 children who proved not to qualify according to accepted standards. Many other authorities have confirmed these statistics.

Nevertheless, the teacher can identify gifted children. Without doubt he will need help from the testing services of his school system. *Education of the Gifted and Talented* (1972) recommends the use of multiple means for identification, such as intelligence, talent, and creativity tests. In addition to testing, and sometimes to initiate it, the teacher needs to be aware of what to look for. Specialized reading and special training are important. There should also be sensitivity toward these children.

Who Can Teach the Gifted?

Contrary to popular opinion, it is not true that anyone can teach the gifted any more than anyone can teach any child. Furthermore, as we pointed out in an earlier chapter the teacher is especially important in the school experience of children. Some educators have insisted that a teacher of the gifted must be a highly gifted person. Although this might be helpful, others feel that any great degree of giftedness is unnecessary.

However, the teacher must be imaginative, flexible, open to new ideas. He must be comfortable enough with himself not to feel threatened by intellectual challenges from students. He must be able to say "I don't know; let's find out." However, he needs to be an expert in the subject matter he teaches. Gallagher (1964) states, "Every teacher has only so many 'I don't know's' to expend before he loses the intellectual respect of his class" (p. 82). He also may need special training in how to teach the highly gifted. Another very important characteristic of this teacher is a sincere respect for these students and a desire to help them use their capacities as fully as possible.

Many Teachers Fear Teaching the Gifted

Many teachers fear that children with outstanding ability are almost certain to be conceited and difficult, using their superior traits selfishly. This need not be true. Educators suggest, as in the Cleveland Major Work Program (Mike Wirick in an unpublished lecture at Kent State University, 1963), that these children need to be taught early that their ability is a trust, and that those who have much owe much to the society in which they function. History is filled with records of gifted people who learned to use their gifts for great good.

How Are the Gifted Taught?

How does the school need to modify its program to meet the needs of the gifted? What approach and what techniques does the teacher need? Goertzel and Goertzel (1962) devote an entire chapter to "Dislike of School and School Teachers" (pp. 241-270) in which they show that resistance to formal schooling of most kinds has been common among outstanding individuals. Their subjects found the average classroom regimented and dull and preferred tutors, including parents. The government bulletin *Education of the Gifted and Talented* (1972) states the thinking of modern educators:

The major thrust in American education today is to free all students to learn at their own pace — and to place on them more responsibility for their education.

....

From all available evidence, some kind of grouping is needed for the nurture of the abilities and talents of the gifted, accompanied by quality control with well prepared teachers and staff members, consultant assistance, and careful evaluation. Special grouping and special planning carefully conceived and executed provide opportunities for the gifted to function at proper levels of understanding and performance (p. 39).

Klausmeier, in the book of readings by French (1960), makes some recommendations which are still considered classical: have a systematic and continuous program for identification of the gifted. Watch for high achievers in kindergarten and see that they have suitable attention. Place the children in the elementary grades in classes with a wide range of talents and group within the class or individualize instruction within the class to meet their needs. In the elementary grades there might also be some segregation, as in reading, arithmetic, or library work. (Klausmeier feels that complete grouping in the elementary grades might produce social maladjustment.) During the intermediate grades and junior high, accelerate by double promotions those high achievers whose physical, social, and emotional development are in harmony with their intellectual level. Encourage potential high achievers to complete high school early or provide enriched training in areas pursued. Adapt the school program throughout with various curriculum patterns and approaches to meet the needs of the gifted. In addition he urges full utilization of community programs. Individualization is still the best method of teaching the gifted.

The teacher of the gifted in the classroom needs various techniques. According to most experts, the term *enrichment* has been much overworked while its practice is neglected. Giving the quick learner an additional load of the problems being solved by the average child is a very harmful procedure because it will almost certainly antagonize him and is worse than useless. He needs drill, but less, not more of it. These children need a creative flexible approach, with guidance to learn on their own. They need to learn to consider and evaluate ideas, to pursue their own special interests, to use various approaches to learning. In teaching them, the discovery approach is particularly adaptable. In this method the student is encouraged to find facts and solutions for himself. For instance, a problem may be set up, a question asked, a result demonstrated; the student finds the answer to the problem or the cause of the result.

In-depth work may be encouraged in an area of interest so that the child engages in research, possibly with experimentation or help of the library or the community. Open-end questions with no set answer are useful. Several authorities suggest the practice of brainstorming as one good incidental method. Here an idea is presented for general consideration and comment, with all contributions, no matter how far out, accepted for evaluation.

There are many ways to teach these children in an effective manner. The plan should have definite objectives that are worthwhile for these students' development. The program needs to be structured but with much room for adaptation. At all times the teacher must seek to develop creativity and to meet the unique needs of each gifted child.

Chapter 14

WHAT IS A GOOD TEACHER?

As we ask this question, you no doubt begin to think of many things:
——What the teacher does in the classroom
——The teacher as a person
——How the teacher interacts with her students
——How he interacts with other teachers or other professional personnel
——How he represents the school or college in the community
——His background, training, knowledge, experience
——At the college level, his degrees, research, publications

The concept of good teaching has changed a great deal from different periods of history and in different cultures. Briefly, the concepts of a good teacher have seen the following changes:

The punitive teacher of writing in ancient Egypt.

The father-teacher of God's law among the Hebrews.

The male-nurse tutor of ancient Athens.

The "wild animal" trainer of the Middle Ages.

The sharpener of faculties in the eighteenth century.

The driver-out-of-devils of the late Reformation England and New England.

The authoritarian school master of the nineteenth and early twentieth centuries.

The overly permissive progressive educator of the 1930's and 1940's.

What Is a Good Teacher Today?

We are not as sure today about what takes place in good teaching as Comenius, Locke, or even John Dewey. There is no question that there is good teaching and there is poor teaching, and one can readily be distinguished from the other. There is no confusion or disagreement on this score. As a matter of fact, authorities are in remarkable agreement on this matter, and there is no dearth of definitive literature on the subject of what makes a good teacher or what makes a poor teacher.

For the purposes of this chapter, rather than confuse the issues with the repetitious opinions of literally hundreds of writers and researchers, we have chosen to use a few of the most representative writers and researchers in this field.

The single most comprehensive and definitive study of teacher characteristics and effectiveness was done a few years ago (1960) by the American Council on Education, using a huge grant, dozens of outstanding educators, plus the special testing services of the National Teachers Examination Center.

At the college level, some of the best writing in the area of teacher effectiveness is in a relatively new journal called *Improving College and University Teaching.* Other good professional journals on teaching which are recommended are *The Grade Teacher, The Instructor;* the various journals of specific subjects such as *The Science Teacher* and *The Math Teacher,* etc. For the teacher of exceptional children is the journal, *Teaching Exceptional Children,* published by the Council for Exceptional Children, Reston, Virginia 22091. These and other outstanding references are listed in the Bibliography and Additional Reading List.

We have chosen to present the summary of this material in a comparative chart form in order to simplify and categorize the wealth of material available and to make the material more readily understandable.

What Are the Bases for the Discrimination of Good or Poor Teaching?

Educational research devoted to teacher effectiveness accepts as the most valid and reasonable criteria of learning behavior, this: the various types of desirable behavior changes and achievement resulting from the difficult to observe learning process. This is an indirect approach, and the rationale for this method of evaluation of teacher effectiveness accepts the premise that the behavior of students and their accomplishments may be considered as the product of the teacher's efforts and reactions with her students.

As such, behavior, attitudes, and achievement are suitable measures of teacher behavior. These criteria should not be evaluated on the basis of a limited experience, but rather over a long period of time with various groups of students. These criteria are especially valid if most variables are controlled as in a laboratory-like investigation. Such factors, then, as amount or quality of training, specific classroom methods, and various media, become controlled relevant variables but are not the independent variables upon which the outcome depends.

Do Teachers at Various Levels Differ?

One essential concept which must be clarified before we go on: the factors which make a good elementary. teacher also are the factors which make a good secondary teacher and also are the factors which make a good college teacher. The literature on the subject makes no differentiation in this. The methods and the subject matter do differ, but the same skills, abilities, personal characteristics, and philosophy of education that make a good elementary teacher make a good college teacher.

You may have heard the appraisal of teachers which is bandied about rather jokingly to the effect the very best teachers are at the early elementary level, and the teachers get progressively worse as one goes up the educational ladder until we find the very worst teaching at the university graduate level.

To our knowledge no one has ever proven this either true or false. But there is some reason to believe it. This assumption is based upon the fact that the elementary teacher usually teaches because he loves children, while the college teacher often teaches because he loves his subject matter or discipline. To whatever degree this is the case, the teacher who primarily loves children will be a better teacher than one who loves primarily his subject matter. The methods, attitudes, philosophy of education, and relationship of teacher to students will be almost diametrically opposed in the two extremes. Obviously, there will be some blending and overlapping, but on the average one could probably plot a curve showing a positive trend from pupil centered teaching to subject matter centered teaching as one moves from the lower to higher education. As one does so, he will plot at the same time a deterioration of effective teaching. The good teacher adapts the lesson to his pupils, while the poor teacher adapts his pupils (or tries to) to the lesson. This is the basic difference between pupil centered teaching and subject matter centered teaching.

This is not to infer that a teacher who loves his children may not love his subject matter, or that a teacher who is deeply attached to his discipline may not be deeply attached to his students as well. Nevertheless, a good teacher is first of all a teacher who cares about his students and who secondly cares about his subject matter. To a child or person centered teacher the person comes first and the subject matter becomes merely the *means* to an end, not the end in itself. To put it another way, paraphasing a statement of the Great Teacher, man was not made for subject matter, but subject matter was made for man.

Essentials of Good Teaching

The first essential ingredient of effective teaching is a secure learning atmosphere. This has the highest priority, for without this basic and fundamental aspect of the learning environment, none of the others function properly, and even more importantly this lack may destroy all the other factors however good in themselves. The learning atmosphere is wholly within the control of the teacher.

Under this category are such essentials as fairness, warmth and affection, respect, trust, freedom to speak without fear of censure, success rather than failure reinforcement of learning, understanding, and acceptance. Furthermore, this warm and secure atmosphere *must be perceived by the students.*

It is sometimes assumed that this warm and secure learning environment is necessary at only the lower elementary levels. Recent studies, however, at the college level show conclusively that college students learn best, learn more, retain it longer, develop better understanding, and identify higher values — cheat far less — in an accepting, secure learning atmosphere in which they perceive the teacher first of all fair, then understanding and respectful.

Students will put up with poor specific methods of teaching at any level, lack of teacher interest, in fact almost anything, if they feel that they are treated fairly with accepting understanding; but let a teacher face a group with the attitude that he is going to show them how dumb they are, and how learned he is; let him act and behave as if they are never or rarely to be trusted; let them feel that he is testing or grading unfairly; then that teacher is through as an effective teacher even if some of the students continue by some miracle of sheer determination and manage to pass the grade or course. Yet these teachers wonder daily why students lie and cheat, lack interest, and attempt to avoid their classes. These teachers are asking for it.

Some teachers have the idea that no teacher is ever liked by students unless he is an easy mark — a softie — with nothing to offer but good grades. Research does not support this assumption. In fact, real learning cannot take place without communication, real communication is impossible without rapport between teacher and pupil, and effective rapport is impossible without acceptance and affection.

The Value of Love in Good Teaching

The most important thing you as a teacher will ever do is to make your pupils feel good about themselves, that they are persons of worth and value, that they are worthwhile individuals who are liked and who count for something valuable.

Every child born into this world has both a built-in conception of his own worth and a well-developed evaluation process. Unfortunately, as he begins to interact with other people, this optimum state of determining worth usually does not continue long. He begins to determine his own worth by how he perceives others evaluating him.

Yet, if he is to maintain a good self-concept and reasonable emotional health, he must continue to evaluate himself optimumly. It would indeed be fortunate if he could maintain some method of objective self-evaluation. This he does, perhaps, to some degree.

How he eventually learns to see himself and feel about himself develops as a result of how he thinks others see him and feel about him. If he is loved, he loves himself. If others feel he accomplishes something of worth, he feels the same way. Of course the opposite is true as well. If he sees other people who seem to dislike him, he tends to dislike himself; and if he is made to feel a failure most of the time, he feels bad in both senses of that word. Therefore, it is important, crucially important, how other people treat him.

If there is a mixture of feeling, confusion results. For instance, if his parents treat him as a person of worth but his teachers treat him as a failure, he will have mixed and confused feelings about himself. Both parents and teachers are important people in his life, and both affect him strongly. However, the one who affects his life most and whom he respects most determines to the greatest extent how he will feel about himself.

If we add the feelings of his peers to what the adults in his life feel, we bias the balance in favor of his peers. His peers reflect the feelings of the teacher for the most part.

The handicapped child needs acceptance and love even more than the average child inasmuch as his performance in the common classroom is usually below average, often far below average.

Self-concept Patterns Vary

One frequent pattern is the decreasing regard for his own worth in relationship to the worth of other people which he views as greater than his. Taken to its end result, the understanding of one's self, while overvaluing others, constitutes a neurotic state.

Not infrequently the offended child will react to further attack upon his person by a false regard for self. In this (usually unconscious) self-protection mechanism he will come to regard others as unacceptable and his performance as acceptable. In his own eyes he has greater worth than others and becomes an arrogant braggart and showoff.

A third outcome is to regard himself as unacceptable and others as even less acceptable than himself. A person who regards neither himself nor others frequently becomes a delinquent or criminal, an enemy of society as well as an enemy of himself.

A fourth outcome is possible. Suppose that the child who has been unloved, unaccepted, and failing suddenly begins to succeed. He learns how to do something that is acceptable. His usual conclusion: "I am a good person and liked when I accomplish something acceptable." He learns to feel he is not liked for himself but for what he is able to achieve.

A Different Outcome Is Possible

Suppose that the developing child is treated with respect, love, affection, and is *cherished for himself* rather than for what he can do. He will develop his own self-regard and, similarly, he comes to regard other people in a positive way, too.

The person who is treated with love loves other people. We cannot teach him to love; we must love him to love. Helping children to love themselves and others is a major task of the public schools, as well as that of the home. It is accomplished best when parents and teachers accept this as a part of teaching, that is as important, even more important than what is taught as the subject matter.

The Most Effective Teachers Are Warm and Loving

Teachers teach best when rapport has been established between themselves and their pupils. Rapport is best established when love and affection, understanding and acceptance are established.

Erect a wall of any sort between the teacher and the child and her effectiveness as a teacher ends.

Love builds no walls.

Love May Affect Intelligence

Robert Bills (1969) and others in increasing numbers are beginning to view intelligence in a new light. They view it as a *quality of behavior* rather than as a logical construct which varies in quantity among people.

Such educators observe that intelligent behavior is possible only when the person has had adequate opportunity for experience as needed to develop such behavior. That experience must be available to him as needed and must at the same time be undistorted and unwarped by unacceptance and lack of love. He must be in such a position as to be able to solve problems that come into his field of experience, unaffected by lack of love and understanding, so that he can work out his own solutions bringing all relevant past experiences into the problem-solving experience.

If this is true, then his *behavior is intelligent* and at that moment, at least, he is intelligent. Anything which limits or distorts his viewpoint or past experience will distort and limit his problem-solving experience. To that degree his behavior is less intelligent.

Lack of love in one's experience, present or past, limits and distorts the factors involved in the learning or in the problem-solving experience.

Students will remember and thank the teachers who were fair, understanding, interesting, and had high expectations; teachers who stimulated them and made them work, but who were fair and reasonable about it, and who had some flexibility in their stance with their classes.

Why should students ever thank the teacher in whose class they were bored or frightened or angered, and where they felt misunderstood and treated unfairly and made to fail because the teacher did not take time for their problems? Some of them, the fortunate ones, memorized enough to regurgitate on tests to pass the course, but they retain and remember very little for which to be grateful.

No educational psychologist today will agree that memorization of a list of facts, significant or trivial, constitutes learning. Learning has taken place if, and only if, one adds understanding, a change of behavior and attitudes, and is able to comprehend and use what he has learned when it is out of context. This takes place when facts are transposed into concepts, then principles and generalizations. Only then is transfer of learning possible. Only this can be called learning.

Good Teaching Spoiled by Bad Testing and Evaluation

There are a few teachers around who create a secure, warm, and interesting atmosphere in the classroom. They have excellent knowledge and present it well, but they destroy all of this by the kind of testing they do. It is an accepted fact in testing and measuring that a teacher can to a remarkable degree determine what the students will learn and how they will learn it.

For instance, if a teacher uses the very common completion, or fill-in-the-blanks, type of objective test or a multiple choice test, she will develop good memorizers. If, in addition, this teacher tests for many insignificant or trivial facts — trivial in fact or perceived as such from lack of importance imputed by good objectives — she compounds her memory course. It is a fact well-known in educational psychology that a student who memorizes for this sort of test forgets *in one hour* more than he remembers and has forgotten 75 to 80 percent in twenty-four hours.

If the teacher uses the rigid and rigorous horse-and-buggy technique of percentage grading — no matter how well she teaches or directs learning — the students will dislike her and call her unfair. It matters not in learning whether a teacher actually is unfair or not; it is how the students *perceive* her that counts.

Testing can enhance or destroy learning. Perhaps if we could forget grades as the primary purpose of testing and consider testing rather as a tool of learning, better and fairer tests would result. Remember, a teacher determines, by the kinds of tests she uses more than she may know, the kind of learning that takes place in her class. She can cause students to memorize or think, reason, think creatively, evaluate, synthesize, generalize, compare, and discriminate by the use of an effective testing program the primary effect of which is not grades, but learning of a particular kind.

What Research Has Found Characteristic of the Effective Teacher

High   *Low*

Shows warmth and affection,   Shows little warmth or

enjoys pupil relationships.

affection with little real enjoyment of pupil-teacher relationships.

Considers a warm and friendly manner with students more important than mastery of subject matter material. Child centered with subject matter to fit the child.

Considers subject matter mastery of greater importance than a warm friendly relationship with pupils; subject matter centered with the child to fit the subject matter.

Thinks well of students, believes that they usually will not:
  tax patience of teacher
  be disciplinary problems
  have obnoxious mannerisms
  try to cheat or
    lie.
But will, on the other hand:
  be considerate
  study reasonably well
  like and respect the
    teacher
  treat others fairly and
    kindly.

Thinks poorly of students, believes that they usually will:
  tax patience of teacher
  be discipline problems
  have obnoxious mannerisms
  try to cheat or lie
  not be considerate
  not study unless forced
  not like the
    teacher but may respect
    her if she is tough.
  not treat
    others fairly or kindly.

Believes parents accept their responsibilities well.

Believes that parents for the most part are shirking their responsibilities and obligations to children.

Enjoys the classroom situation.

Shows less enjoyment of the classroom.

Thinks her strongest traits are:

Thinks her strongest traits are:

Warmth and affection
for students, fairness
and understanding, inducing
student acceptance of her,
confidence in and respect
and acceptance for students,
good communication and
rapport, enthusiasm,
cheerfulness.

Common sense, practicality,
leadership ability, subject
matter proficiency, not
being a "soft" teacher, seeing
that students do not
get away with poor
learning in her class.

Believes that "getting off
the subject" is not
disruptive to class, has a
flexible approach to
learning.

Believes that too many
teachers allow students
to "get off the subject,"
and that most students
will try to "get off the
subject"; has a rigid
approach to learning.

Is extremely generous in
appraising the motives
and behavior of other
people, gives others the
benefit of the doubt. Has
good opinion of most students.

Is usually critical and
suspicious of motives and
behaviors of others. Has
poor opinion of most students
but may like a few of the
more able or more conforming students.

Values ideas of students
even if they are different,
or opposed to her own.

Usually insists on responses
and ideas that conform. No
matter what she *says* she will
allow, the students learn to
"parrot" her statements.

Has a strong interst in reading
and reads widely, rarely
makes excuses that she's
too busy to read.

Has little interest in reading
except in certain limited
fields, but also may say
she wishes she were not so
busy so she could read more.

Is also interested in music, painting and the arts in general.

Has little interest in these nonessentials.

Prefers nondirective, informal classroom procedures, likes free discussion of topics.

Feels more secure in a less permissive more directive classroom atmosphere, likes structured discussion, if any.

Has superior ability to express her thoughts clearly, uses many applicable and interesting illustrations. Is easy to understand.

Is hard to understand, finds it difficult to express thoughts clearly; illustrations may be stereotyped and boring, if used at all.

Shows superior emotional, adjustment, secure, at ease, informal, not easily upset.

Acts ill at ease and insecure, prefers a formal atmosphere, may be easily irritated or upset.

Teaching emphasis is upon conceptualizations, principles, generalizations, attitudes, and understandings which are reinforced by adequate tests of such types of learning.

Emphasis is upon mastery of facts and "content," which usually results in memorization which is reinforced by objective (factual) types of tests such as completion and listing being most common.

Tends to emphasize inquiry, exploration and discovery, and independent study. Leads students into the how? why? what-would-you-have-done- type of thinking. Encourages

Tends to rely on authority such as text, teacher, and other books. May not want dependence, but methods reinforce such attitudes.

autonomy and independence.

Is fair in testing and grading and students perceive her as such. Usually uses some variation of frequency distribution grading, or none at all.	Is often unfair in tests and grading and/or the students perceive her as such. Usually uses some absolute standard, often percentage grading.
Is unafraid to involve the emotional reactions of students.	Avoids emotional involvement or reactions of students.
Often gets students intellectually enthused and excited.	Rarely does so. May wonder why not, but usually unaware that this does not happen often.
Students consider the teacher as a "friend."	Teacher is more often the "enemy," or at best respected or feared.
Students rarely laugh at or make fun of the teacher.	Teacher often is the butt of off-color jokes.
Is always aware of the goals to be attained, and frequently states these objectives to the students.	May or may not be aware of the goals to be attained, but rarely states them to the students.
Students are obviously "with" the teacher; very few are loafing or inattentive.	Students obviously are not "with" the teacher; many are not paying attention or are wasting time.
Does not implicitly or explicitly continue to remind the students of the	Students are rarely able to forget that the teacher is the "teacher."

teacher role she is playing.
May often forget that she
is the "teacher."

| Compared to ability the achievement level is high; the teacher is usually pleased with the learning which is often reinforced with praise and rewards. | The achievement level is generally low; the teacher is usually not pleased with the learning. What reinforcement is used is usually negative. Praise is a rare thing. |

In conclusion let us quote from a report of the National Advisory Council on Education to President Johnson in 1966 made by Dr. O. Meridith Wilson, president of the University of Minnesota and Dr. John H. Fischer, president of Teachers' College, Columbia University:

> The difference between success and failure (in teaching) pivoted on the subtle aspects of mutual understanding, commoness of purpose, and warm human contact between teacher and pupil, which is referred to as *rapport*. This rapport is the cutting edge of the whole business. It is like a great machine tool. You have a tremendous structure providing the position, providing the power. But ultimately it comes down to an infinitesimally thin edge of metal that cuts right into another piece of metal. If that contact isn't right, you might as well forget the machinery.

Chapter 15

EXCELLENCE

No consideration of the whole spectrum of special-need children can overlook the end results of what we are trying to accomplish, the goals we set in order to produce a certain product, i.e. the kind of person who will make a genuine contribution to our society and who will enjoy life as he realizes his potential to the fullest.

There are many people, educators included, who believe that what we are after are excellent products, particularly as we get closer to the top of the educational ladder. Further, they believe that excellence can be obtained only by starting with that which is excellent and then polishing and developing that to a finely honed edge of excellence.

What kind of excellence are we discussing? Do we mean academic excellence (high test scores and good grades)? Are we talking about degrees and honors? The teacher with the kind of ability that enables her to earn a Ph.D. *summa cum laude* but who bores her students in the classroom and makes them forever hate her discipline with her unrealistic demands? Or are we talking about the teacher with the kind of ability that enables her, regardless of degrees and honors, to excite her students with her discipline so that they want to follow in her footsteps, but who cares very little about the scores on tests? Do we mean the excellence of an Einstein who changed the universe atomically but who had trouble with simple arithmetic? Or is it the excellence of Charles Shulz or Norman Ernest Borlaug or Henry Kissinger or Charles Kettering or Bob Hope or Truman Capote or Margaret Meade?

Is Excellence Produced?

Are we concerned about excellent input, great ability to start with? Or is it improvement, growth, development, and progress?

220

Or is excellence the ability to memorize and accumulate masses of facts? Does the learn*ed* person possess excellence? Or does the learn*ing* person have it? Is excellence doing superlatively (as it is defined by the teacher) what one is compelled (by tests and grades) to do? Or is it learning how to learn and liking to do so. Might it not be the ability to find as well as solve problems, the ability to achieve creatively in our culture? Does excellence imply that a person has what it takes to adapt optimally to and enjoy life? Is excellence self-actualized or is it other-actualized?

What Is Excellent Teaching?

Does excellent teaching consist of discovering those who are excellent test-takers and getters of high grades, and then pressurizing them through the academic mill by rigorous demands and tough tests? Or is excellence comprised of that which may be in some way deficient to start with and which is by skill and patience developed it to *its* fullest and finest potential?

Does excellent teaching consist of acting as a roadblock to all those who do not come up to arbitrarily set academic expectations? Or does excellent teaching consist of nurturing, encouraging potential so as to develop real interest and competence? In other words is the production of excellence a screening out process or is it the stimulation and development of potential? Must only the student be excellent? Or do we not need excellent teachers, produces or excellence, too?

One might be tempted to state that excellence is all of these things. But not so! We cannot have them all, for some commonly used attempts to foster excellence all too unfortunately destroy it. Some of what we label *excellence* is not excellence at all.

Many educators take the assumptive position that excellence in education consists of finding students with high IQ's, top grades, and high college entrance test scores, and then fostering excellence by means of grueling standards, tough tests, and restrictive grading. This may be an oversimplification, but it summarizes the idea.

It is interesting to note that these educators do not give one shred of research evidence to support this traditionalistic opinion. For good reason: such research evidence does not exist. On the contrary, research in education and psychology refutes every assumption presented.

Excellence in Education Today

Far, far too much of what is done in education today, at any level starting in kindergarten through graduate school, is based upon what has been done, what everyone is doing, or what one has had done to him. In other words, many educational practices hold to educational old wives tales and traditionalistic concepts, most of which have been exploded by relatively recent research. Many of the reasons for certain educational practices are not valid; stated objectives are not reached. Many commonly accepted processes used in education do not accomplish what most teachers and administrators think they do. They would be shocked and hurt could they but see the devastating effects of what they are doing. We believe all those who support such didactic views sincerely believe in what they are doing. All of which makes it even more tragic; think of how much good such devoted dedication could accomplish if it were to be used in more constructive educational practices.

Research Invalidates Many Popularly Held Educational Beliefs

In 1962 Getzels and Jackson published the results of their extensive research and exploded the notion that our most creatively productive people are those with the highest IQ's, test scores, and grades; instead these are conformists and low producers of productive ideas. The highly creative students are moderate grade getters with above average but not high IQ and college entrance test scores. (By creative people we do not mean only those in art or music, but creative teachers, salesmen, scientists, businessmen; creative people in *all* areas of human endeavor.)

The most creative and innovative adults that could be found, based upon actual performance in our culture, would not be accepted in our leading universities with excellence based on

IQ's, college entrance test scores, or high school grades. In other words, the policies of our best colleges, those which demand the highest sifting out, refuse admittance to the most creative students. True, Harvard and Yale and a few other colleges of the elite have begun in recent years (spurred by Getzels and Jackson and others) to make an occasional exception and admit moderate school achievers and score makers who have demonstrated some area of creative ability. Yet many educators still define excellence as the ability to take tests, make good grades, and please the teacher. The most creative students often do none of these things. As a matter of fact, some mentally retarded individuals are quite creative.

Many other studies support the research of Getzels and Jackson. (Some are Torrance, 1962, 1965, 1968; Guilford, 1967; Gallagher, 1964; Strang, 1968; Cole, 1969; Clark, 1969; Crutchfield, 1967; Holland, 1961, 1965; Machinnion, 1963.)

Ideas of Excellence Change

In the past there was almost total preoccupation with objectives and methods dealing with the knowledge and information peculiar to a discipline. There was relatively little emphasis placed upon objectives and methods dealing with assisting the learner in the discovery, acquisition, organization, and creative application of the information. Such an abortive approach is futile today for many reasons. For one, knowledge in most disciplines is rapidly changing and increasing so that information which may have been adequate yesterday may be insufficient, and even erroneous, today, and almost certainly by tomorrow. The student who has not learned how to learn and who does not like to discover and process information surely will not fit any standards of excellence, unless there is such a thing as anachronistic excellence.

One of the most important and overlooked factors in the progress and development of any valuable excellence is that one must like the pursuit of knowledge or like the activity involved in the practice of the skill being sought. Many studies have disclosed the great importance of liking and enjoying learning and creativity. In discovery learning and in creative thinking, we doubt that it is possible for anyone to do the enormous amount of thinking that it takes to be a learning and creative person unless he actually enjoys thinking. Most people will deny it, but the vast majority of mankind definitely does not enjoy thinking. Man is much more prone to use his mind simply to feel or to remember than he is to use it to think and create. Since it is easier, this is what teachers emphasize, both from the standpoint of the student and themselves.

Most, if not all, educational psychologists today define learning in terms of behavior modification. The student who has read a book or memorized certain facts, but who has no chance to demonstrate what he has learned, has not learned anything. Yet in most schools today the proof of learning is the examination, the recitation, even the mindless paper copied from one or more sources. The student who has digested his textbooks and his lecture notes and who presents a paper, notebook, or laboratory manual filled with correct answers and who is able to perform well on the tests, is presumed to have learned what the teacher wanted and is rewarded with a good grade.

The Student Has Not Learned What the Teacher Wanted Him to Learn

Unfortunately, too often what the student has learned is not science, history, or English, but a lesson in expediency. Consider science for a moment (but this could be any other subject.) Science, the student is led to believe, is concerned with the verification and memorization of accepted truths rather than the discovery of new truths and concepts. He learns that science (or history or psychology or any subject is drudgery, boredom, and skilled cheating. Experiments rarely work out the way they are supposed to, and if there should be a discrepancy between the textbook and his own data or if his reasoning comes to a different conclusion or he thinks of a new way to do it or say it, his ideas or discoveries are not often accepted. He learns that it does not pay to have ideas of his own.

This gratuitous lesson is not what his teachers intended to teach. Yet the proof of the perverted lesson is sadly demonstrated only when the disillusioned student turns his back on the dreary subject forever. By that time, however, his teachers are busy teaching the wrong lessons to new students, usually unaware of the nature of their spurious achievement; or if they could be aware of the negative attitude developed toward what they themselves love, the teachers will salve their consciences by the easy rationalization, "It was just too tough for them."

Real learning in the misguided viewpoint is hard and tough and onerous and is gotten only with blood, sweat, and tears. Such a viewpoint of what could (should!) be fun is taken straight out of the mouth of Jonathan Edwards. It should be a sobering thought to stop and consider that most of what we learn and remember as children and as adults is not learned in school and is fun! Have you noticed the look on a child's face when he takes his first short walk successfully, or later when he reads something which makes sense to him, or the boy who gets his bicycle to go where he wants it to, or finally connnects with a ball for a home run! Teachers of learning disabled children know the incredible joy of minute successes. You may be asking, "Is it joy in learning, or in the successes?" Can you have the first without the second? We think not.

George Dennison, in *The Loves of Children* (the result of extensive research), concludes that the ability to read well is the consequence of having a curious, challenged mind, the result of having learned that learning is essentially pleasureable. When you have a normal child who cannot (or will not) read, while it often is because of perceptual or reading problems, not infrequently the child hates books, schools, teachers, and anyone of a hundred other insufficiencies; all of this has a common cause — frustration of independent learning. Is this a reading problem?

Is Learning Fun?

As long as schools (college included) create, perpetuate, and reinforce a sense of failure by their repressive assembly lines, which very effectively condition negatively their clientele, we will continue to produce children who cannot or will not learn. What are we to say about excellence and the fostering of it as long as education is basically repressive? Is a youngster's education analogous to boot-camp? To industrial manufacturing? Are we to adhere to puritanism's ethic that anything that is fun is evil?

It may be an oversimplification to summarize the developing controversy in educational circles today by saying that we are developing basically two camps, but this is how we see it. One, the traditionalist's camp, believes that learning is arduous, even painful, and requires the discomfort of constant discipline, control, and pressure. The rewards of education are discovered at the end of the academic rainbow. This older camp believes that learning is for the future, but only for the future.

Yet education must be in and for the present as well. Each day is alive and exciting in its own right. Learning is an autonomous activity which in fact is very difficult to stop because the human being is basically a learning organism. One of the strongest drives innate in all animals is curiosity. It probably reaches its zenith in the human animal. Furthermore, the satisfaction of that drive produces intense pleasure. A child does not set out consciously to learn to walk or to talk or to find out how to understand and control his environment. He learns as a consequence of his direct exploration, and the rewards reinforcing his activities are intrinsic. *No student who learns in any normal, natural way needs extrinsic rewards.*

It must be some compliment to teachers today that they are able to inhibit curiosity, destroy the innate motivation to learn, and substitute grades and teacher praise or teacher blame for the real pleasure of learning. We are told that learning is the result of teaching. It never is and never was. Carl Rogers and others doubt that any person can teach any other person anything. *We can guide and facilitate learning, but we cannot, however we try, force it!* We can cause students (some of them) to go through the motions we want, but this is not learning. The only valid estimate of learning is that which happens *after* the teacher is no longer in control. He can force some students to memorize and regurgitate on command, but he cannot force them to like it, remember it, or make it a part of their lives.

Charles Silberman, after spending huge sums of money and years of research, has written *Crisis in the Classroom. Atlantic*

Monthly ran condensations in three issues — June, July and August, 1970 — and entitled them "Murder in the Classroom." His study reinforces emphatically what we have been saying, that the pressure of discipline, tests grades, and the frustration of poor teaching are destroying the minds and spirits of our children.

The Object of All Education Activity Is Children

What so many educators seem to forget is that the one true object of all educational activity is children, not the subject matter they are teaching. What we do to children, how we make them feel, the attitudes and behavior patterns we develop, will remain long after they have forgotten all the knowledge we think we have imparted. This is the real reason that in spite of the enormous amount of money we spend (and we want even more) and the effort expended, so little real progress toward excellence has been made in academia.

College teachers are the worst offenders. They are primarily subject oriented rather than student oriented, they have a biased view of excellence, and they tend to be aware only of the few children who somehow managed to survive the inept education of twelve years, and who even then need to be weeded out further. Can this be fostering excellence? What about those whose high ability and/or interest was successfully squelched? What about those wasted because they could not learn in the environment provided? Should not pursuit of excellence make some realistic attempts to reclaim these rather than do all that is possible to add to their number?

All the research of the past decade points to the inescapable conclusion that the most effective methods of learning follow the natural pattern, the innate drive of curiosity and the exploration to find out. A youngster will learn in spite of all a teacher can do, *if* there is present a highly stimulating verbal as well as nonverbal experimental involvement with the environment.

It is true that after surviving twelve years of an unnatural, pressurized and dependent learning environment, many college students find it difficult to make the transition to a more permissive learning atmosphere. They can make it if given a real opportunity. However, we doubt that every teacher has the ability to provide the freedom and stimulation necessary. This leads us to a question asked earlier in this chapter, what about excellence in teaching? Must only the student be excellent? If the teacher is not excellent, must we sacrifice many potentially excellent students on the altar of "excellence?"

Do Tough Tests and Strict Grading Practices Encourage Excellence?

Probably no aspect of formal education holds as affectionate a place in the hearts of teachers, is more widely used to motivate learning, is more overrated by teachers and detested by students than grades.

There are many aspects of the grading process, and recent empirical research has demonstrated that grades are worse than worthless (see chapter on grades).

For the purpose of this chapter, we will deal with only a few of these popular assumptions. First is the notion that strict and severe grading policies motivate students to study harder and learn more. In other words, low grades motivate learning. (Let us state that we agree that high grades do motivate the few good students who are able to earn them, but the motivation provided produces many undesirable kinds of learning.)

To understand the forces at work in the pressurized kind of motivation provided by unsatisfactory grades, we must examine its psychological aspects. Low grades, or grades less than what one desires, constitute a type of adversive reinforcement — punishment, if you please. The idea behind such motivation assumes that students will work (study) harder to escape or eliminate the undesirable marks. This may be true for the student who *usually* makes the kind of grades he aspires to; but for the student who has not been able to meet his and others' expectations, some devastating responses develop. Many studies support this conclusion, such as Sears (1964), Hurlock (1924), and Hilgard (1966).

Antedating most of these studies, Thorndike (1927, 1933) maintained that adversive reinforcement does not work to alter behavior or induce new learning. It only serves to suppress behavior temporarily as a physical restraint might do. When the adversive restraints are removed, the previous behavior is usually reestablished. Thorndike's hypothesis has been severely questioned and seemingly disproven until very recently.

In 1969 Bryon Campbell and Russell M. Church edited a book, *Punishment and Adversive Behavior,* in which their work and that of Howard Rachlin, R. J. Herrnstein, Frank Logan, Stephen Maier, Martin Seligman, Richard Soloman, and others strongly resupport Thorndike's law of effect. Adversive stimuli, negative reinforcement, does not induce or cause to develop new behavior patterns, if by behavior patterns we mean fundamental change in behavior and attitudes.

What actually happens, then, as a result of punishment is that the organism so pressured will do, or act as if he does, what the source of pain wants him to do. He only does so while that source of pressure is in control. For example, a dog can be trained to keep off the sofa by punishment, but just as soon as the trainer is out of sight and hearing, the dog gets right back on that sofa. The child who studies and can achieve acceptability because of the pressure of grades, will do so only so long as the teacher is in control. Once that control or pressure is removed, the student finishes the course or drops out, doing only what he wishes; this usually does not coincide with what the teacher wants (wanted). The child who cannot achieve acceptability, no matter what pressure, learns not to learn, and if this failure and frustration continue long enough, the student's self-concept is destroyed; he may never learn to learn again. Exceptional children are even more susceptible.

All of this explains why teachers try to motivate with the pressure of grades to get some apparent but deceiving positive responses; but were they to reduce or remove the pressure, they would get a minimum of response. It also explains why some teachers who motivate by positive reinforcement manage to do so without the pressure of grades. There are many better and more effective motivators (see the chapter on motivation).

Concerning the qualities (excellence) of learning induced by strict grading practices, let us review them in this context very briefly:

1. Grades usually become the ends, the "what," the goals of students rather than meaningful learning. Ask any student what he wants most to know after a test or at the end of a course.

2. Grades usually cause students to study only that which will be tested or which will receive rewards from the teacher. Learning is hereby reduced and narrowed. Hardly the pursuit of excellence.

3. Creative activities and reflective thinking, excellent goals by any criteria, are seldom encouraged; they cannot be tested and graded objectively. Therefore memorizing, the lowest intellectual function, is emphasized to the detriment of higher and more excellent intellectual functions.

4. Of all our considerations of excellence and its cultivation, none merits graver attention than the discoveries of Holland (1965-1969) and his associates of the Research and Development Division of the American College Testing Program. Dozens of their research studies strongly support the finding that there is little (or no) correlation between college grades and subsequent competency and success in any vocation or avocation. (Many other researchers have supported the conclusions of Holland, et al. (see the various *ACT Research Reports* 1965 through 1969). If the implications of these findings do nothing else, they put into serious question the popular, current criteria for academic excellence, i.e. high test scores and good grades.

Several explanations for this disturbing paradox are possible. Holland and his associates propose that creative ability and talent figure little, if at all, in most educational teaching and testing, but do figure largely in nonacademic (vocational) success. Another possibility suggests that student evaluation (testing and grading) has low validity and reliability coefficients compared to actual learning and course work retention. Still a third possibility: academic learning has little correlation with vocational competency. In other words, schooling has little relevancy to adult pursuits, or it could be a combination of all three causes. In any case, our usual definition of academic excellence either needs drastic revision or academic learning is an end in itself without significant meaning for life outside of school.

What Is Excellence in Learning?

There are as many definitions of excellence as there are those concerned about it. John W. Gardner in his book, *Excellence,* describes it as the development of everyone to his fullest potential as we conserve his individuality and enhance his ability to think and express himself creatively. Carl Rogers wants the "fully functioning person." E. Paul Torrance emphasizes creative thinking, while Jerome Bruner wants to stimulate the inquiring problem solver. Louis and Helen Geiger (1970) seem to want to find the most able students and to enhance their academic achievement with a rigorous program of testing and grading. Doubtless Billy Graham's idea of excellence would differ from Nelson Rockefeller's, Leonard Bernstein's, or Jackie Onassis'. The late Albert Einstein would define excellence differently than would the late Charles De Gaulle or the defecting football hero, Dave Meggyesy. The producers of "Sesame Street" doubtless conceptualize educational excellence far differently than most teachers.

Excellence Is Multifaceted

Surely there is a place in our society for excellence of all kinds and varieties. To be sure, we want academic excellence (whatever that may be), and we also want the excellence of those who work with their hands and eyes and ears and feet. Not all young people ought to go to college; some could never make it even if standards were lowered significantly. Others would rather work with their hands than with their brains; they would rather shape a piece of metal than philosophize about an idea. Even for the "academically excellent," other characteristics are as important as the ability to memorize and think. What about excellence in drive, leadership, dependability, tact, values, social graces, imagination, management, or compassion? There are many other qualities valued by individuals and society, all of which are essential.

What about the excellence of a teacher who has the ability to stimulate and inspire students to learn far more than they may have done before? Can she not do this with her warm acceptance and challenging enthusiasm as compared to the excellence of a teacher who is skilled in weeding out the less able and poorly motivated students? Other teachers may excel in their research and publishing, being renowned for their contributions to the general fund of knowledge. Still others stand out as lecturers holding their listeners spellbound, while there are those who are unexcelled as administrators.

A Comparison of Two Kinds of Excellence

Atkinson and Feather (1966) summarize a wealth of research on motivation and achievement with two pictures of individuals differing widely in their personality characteristics. One is the achievement oriented personality and the other is the failure oriented personality. One is motivated by optimistic anticipation of success; the other is motivated by fear of failure.

The success oriented personality is generally attracted to activities which require the successful exercise of skill. He is a moderate risk taker who finds unplanned events challenging and interesting. He possesses high self-esteem and confidence. He is realistic; if he succeeds he raises his sights, and if he fails he lowers his sights in moderation. He has a strongly developed positive approach to failure which he uses to enhance his achievement. Whatever the level of his challenge to achieve, he will strive more persistently than others even when confronted with an opportunity to quit gracefully. He is not only persistent, but ingeniously so, as long as he believes he has a chance to succeed. He likes the challenge of new and different tasks. However, he does not waste time in pursuit of impossible goals nor rest content with continual mastery of old familiar tasks when there are new realistic possibilities for accomplishment open to him.

He may be a maverick, but more frequently he is a moderate nonconformist. He is not afraid to stick his neck out with innovative ideas and hypotheses. His approaches to learning and replies to teacher's questions may be unusual. He will stand up for what he believes even if he is alone. He will champion the cause of the underdog if he believes it is right. Being right is more important to him than being popular. He has such ego strength that, while he likes praise and approbation, his ego will not suffer without it. He is highly self-motivated and self-disciplined. He may not do what others (teachers) want him to do unless it makes sense to him.

He can endure great ambiguity as he attempts to figure things out. Although he takes pride in accomplishment, he is not a perfectionist. He may be a getter of excellent grades, but more frequently he is satisfied with good moderate achievement; there are more important things to do than get hung-up on high marks which for the most part mean very little.

More often than not he is quite versatile, attempting many things and being able to do them well. His realistic approaches to challenges in the past, his enthusiasm, imagination, and persistence have made him more successful than others. Therefore, many tasks viewed by others as risky or very difficult are likely to be viewed as challenges or calculated risks to him. He is rarely bored because he is surrounded by so much to learn and to do, so many ambiguous possibilities, that he can construct for himself a world of interesting challenges. Although he values learning of all sorts, he prizes that which has most practical meaning for himself. Many of his peers consider him possessed of what they call horse-sense, but he can theorize, too.

He finds the didactic and dictatorial teaching boring and uninteresting and may do (usually does) a less than acceptable amount of study for that teacher. The teacher who allows him a good deal of freedom to learn and engage in independent projects, however, will discover an unusually interested and interesting student. Even for this teacher, though, he may not strike for the highest grades; he establishes his own standards of excellence. This is the type of personality that becomes the enterpreneur, the innovative achiever. He may not win the accolades in school that the overachieving, fear-oriented student will, but he will enjoy living, and his world will usually be immeasurably better for his having lived in it. There must be some kind of excellence in this.

In the failure oriented personality who strives for excellence, we have the person in whom the motive to avoid failure greatly exceeds the motive to risk uncertain achievement. He is dominated by the threat of failure and therefore resists activities in which he perceives himself a possible failure. He further is strongly motivated by social pressures and peer approval; he is the ultimate conformist. His fear of failure will usually take one of two directions: he probably will either be an underachiever or an overachiever. He lacks self-confidence and has a poor self-concept; he may have adopted a contrary view of himself with little real insight.

The underachiever will take few chances; he has to be assured of success in any venture before he will attempt to do it. Thus he spends an inordinate amount of time and energy trying to assess the probability of failure, looking for all possible failure producing angles. He is indecisive but calls it carefulness. He believes that anyone can avoid failure if he looks carefully enough before he leaps. He is most threatened by what the success oriented person considers the greatest challenge. Usually he attempts very little, taking refuge in the rationalization that he could do it if he tried, but no one can blame him for failure if he does not try. In some instances he is absolutely convinced that he does not have the ability his teachers think he has. He may score high on IQ or other ability tests, but he knows someone made a mistake; he is just not that bright. He has a long persistent history of failure, and the prognosis for achievement in the future is dismal.

The overachiever, on the other hand, while failure-escape oriented has discovered something that he can do well. He therefore exerts every effort in that direction. He often is a perfectionist meticulously performing his success producing tasks. If he has true intellectual ability, he will be among the highest achievers and grade getters in school. He may be a gambler, taking inordinate risks for which no failure could be imputed should he not achieve his goal. In most cases he plays it safe. He has found a meritorious avenue by which to escape failure, and he plays it for all he is worth.

He conforms carefully to the standards and wishes of his teachers and says and does and learns the right things. As a result he reaps the reward of good grades and academic approbation. If he ever has a divergent creative thought, he carefully puts it aside in favor of what is safe and acceptable. He prefers teachers who assume most of the responsibility for the structuring of his learning activities. He finds a real measure of security in being carefully told what he is to do. He does not find rigorous testing and grading threatening because he has learned how to succeed in this environment. However, when he runs into an occasional teacher who provides real emphasis upon intellectual and creative independent learning, he feels insecure and threatened and usually gets lower grades; the threat is multiplied. He will avoid such teachers if he can.

Upon finishing school he becomes the correct cog in the machine of business or industry or in academia. He is often known as safe, dependable, plodding; and he will achieve some measure of success. If he becomes a teacher, and he may, he tends to teach as if all his students learn and feel as he does. As a result mediocrity is perpetuated in the name of excellence (however much fear produced).

The manner of didactic teaching tough testing and rigorous grading which most frequently is practiced in schools and colleges tends to produce the fear-escape-motivated student. Surely this cannot be excellence!

Would excellence not be produced, rather, when a student learns in a manner that challenges his ability whatever that ability is, while capturing his interest and enhancing his personality so that he continuously enjoys living and learning and creating because he sincerely believes he can achieve at least in his own estimation? Does anyone have any real problem in deciding which of these two kinds of excellence is truly excellent?

BIBLIOGRAPHY

ACT Research Report No. 31: Iowa City, Research and Development Division, American College Testing Service, 1969.

Association For Supervision And Curriculum Development. *Evaluation As Feedbacks And Guide, 1967 Yearbook.* Washington, National Education Association, 1967.

Atkinson, S. W.: *A Theory of Achievement Motivation.* New York, John Wiley, 1966.

Axelrod, Joseph: The creative student and the grading system. In Heist, Paul (Ed.): *The Creative College Student: An Unmet Challenge.* San Francisco, Vossei-Bass, 1968.

Banfield, Edward C.: *The Unheavenly City.* Boston, Little and Brown, 1970.

Barry, H.: Classes for aphasics. In Frampton, M. E., and Gall, E. D. (Ed.): *The Physically Handicapped and Special Health Problems.* Boston, Sargent, 1955, vol. II.

Beatty, Walcott H., and Clark, Rooney A.: A self-concept theory of learning. In Lendgren, Henry C. (Ed.): *Readings in Educational Psychology.* New York, Wiley, 1968.

Berry, Mildred F.: *Language Disorder of Children: The Bases and Diagnosis.* New York, Appleton, 1969.

Bills, Robert E.: Love me to love thee. *Theory into Practice, 8:*79, April, 1969.

Blank, Marion, and Klig, Sally: Individual teaching for disadvantaged children: A comparison of two methods. *Special Education, 6:*207, Fall, 1972.

Bowers, William J.: *Student Dishonesty and its Control in College.* New York, Columbia U, 1964.

Christensen, C. M.: Relationship between pupil achievement, pupil affect-need, teacher warmth, and teacher permissiveness. *J Educ Psychol, 51:*169, June, 1960.

Cruickshank, William M., et al.: *A Teaching Method for Brain Injured and Hyperactive Children.* Syracuse, Syracuse Pr, 1961.

De Haan, R. F., and Havinghurst, R. V.: *Educating Gifted Children.* Chicago, U of Chicago Pr, 1957.

Deutsch, Morton: The effects of cooperation and competition in group process. In Cartwright, D., and Zander, A., *Group Dynamics: Research and Theory,* Evanston, Row and Peterson, 1960.

Doman, G. J., Delacato, C. H., and Doman, R.: *The Doman-Delacato Developmental Profile.* Philadelphia, Institute for the Achievement of

Human Potential, 1964.

Education For The Gifted. Fifty Seventh Yearbook of the National Society for the Study of Education. Part II. Chicago, U of Chicago Pr, 1958.

Education of the Gifted and Talented: Report Congress of the United States by the U. S. Commissioners of Education and Background papers submitted to the U. S. Office of Education. Washington, U. S. Government Printing Office, 1972.

Fernald, Grace M.: *Remedial Techniques in Basic School Subjects.* New York, McGraw, 1943.

Fitzgerald, E.: *Straight Language for the Deaf.* Washington, The Volta Bureau, 1966.

Gallagher, James J.: *Teaching the Gifted Child.* Boston, Allyn, 1964.

Gartner, Alan, et al.: *Children Teach Children Learning by Teaching.* New York, Har-Row, 1971.

Getzels, J. W., and Jackson, P. W.: *Creativity and Intelligence.* New York, Wiley, 1962.

Gillingham, A.: *Remedial Training for Children with Specific Disability in Reading, Spelling, and Penmanship,* 7th ed: Cambridge, Educators Publishing Service, 1965.

Glasser, William: *Schools Without Failure.* New York, Har-Row, 1969.

Goldberg, Lewis: Grades as motivants. *Psychology in the Schools, 2:*17, 1965.

Good, Thomas L., and Brophy, Jere E.: *Looking In Classrooms.* New York, Har-Row, 1973.

Goertzel, Victor, and Goertzel, Mildred: *Cradles of Eminence.* Boston, Little, 1962.

Hazen Foundation, Committee On The Student In Higher Education: *The Student in Higher Education.* New Haven, The Hazen Foundation, 1968.

Hewett, Frank M.: *The Emotionally Disturbed Child in the Classroom.* Boston, Allyn, 1968.

Holland, J. L., and Austin, A. W.: The prediction of the academic, artistic, scientific, and social achievement of undergraduates of superior scholastic aptitude. *J Educ Psychol, 53:*132, 1962.

Holland, J. L., and Richards, J. M.: Academic and nonacademic accomplishment: Correlated or uncorrelated? *Journal of Educational Psychology, 56:*165, 1965.

Holland, J. L., and Richards, J. M.: Academic and nonacademic accomplishments in representative sample of students taking the american college tests. *College and University, 43:*60, 1967.

Hollingworth, Lita: *Children Above 180 I.Q.* New York, Har-Brace J, 1942.

Hoyt, D. P.: The relationship between college grades and adult achievement: A review of the literature. *The Educational Record, 18:*70, Winter, 1966.

Hurlock, E. B.: An evaluation of certain incentives used in school work. *J of Educ Psychol, 16:*145, 1925.

Hutt, Max L., and Gibby, R. G.: *The Mentally Retarded Child.* Boston, Allyn, 1958.

Jackson, Charles D.: Students Grade Themselves. *Today's Education, 59*:24, Oct., 1970.

Kephart, Newell: Perceptual-motor aspects of learning disabilities. *Except Child, 31*:201, Dec., 1964.

Kirk, David L.: The great sorting machine. *Phi Delta Kappan, 55*:921, April, 1974.

Koch, Robert: The teacher and nonverbal communication. *Theory Into Practice, 10*,(4):231, Oct., 1971.

La Benne, W. D., and Greene, B. I.: *Educational Implications of the Self-Concept Theory.* Pacific Palisades, Goodyear, 1969.

McCarthy, James J., and McCarthy, Joan F.: *Learning Disabilities.* Boston, Allyn, 1969.

McGinnis, M. A.: *Aphasic Children.* Washington, Volta Bureau, 1963.

Maier, S. F., Seligman, M. E. P., and Solomon, R. L.: Pavolovian fear conditioning and learned helplessness. In Campbell, B. A., and Church, R. M. (Eds.): *Punishment and Adversive Control.* New York, Appleton, 1970.

Media and Methods: School is Boring, 5:3(entire issue), April, 1969.

Morse, William C., and Wingo, G. Max: *Psychology and Teaching.* Chicago, Scott, 1962.

Morton, J. (Ed.): *Slate, Supplement to the General Catalogue, Spring 1967.* Berkeley, Associated Students, University of California, 1967.

Mouley, George J.: *Psychology for Effective Teaching.* New York, HR & W, 1968.

Myklebust, H. R.: Learning disabilities: Definition and overview. In *Progress in Learning Disabilities.* New York, Grune, 1968, vol. I.

Neill, George: Washington Report: Right to read, ingredients for successful program. *Phi Delta Kappan, 55*:718, June, 1974.

Olson, Willard C.: *Child Development,* 2nd ed. Boston, Heath, 1969.

Orton, S.: *Reading, Writing, and Speech Problems in Children.* New York, Norton, 1937.

Passow, A. Harry (Ed.): *Education of the Disadvantage.* New York, HR & W, 1967.

Pegnato, W., and Birch, J. W.: Locating Gifted Children in Junior High School. *Except Child, 26*:304, March 1959.

Peterson, R. E.: *The Scope of Student Protest in 1964-65.* Princeton, Educational Testing Service, 1966.

Price, L. (Ed.): *Dialogues of Alfred North Whitehead.* Boston, Little, 1954.

Price, P. B., et al.: Measurement of physician performance. *Journal of Med Educ, 39*:203, 1964.

Reed, H. B.: Effects of teacher warmth. *Journal of Teacher Education, 12*:330, 1961.

Reese, Frederick D.: School age suicide and the educational environment.*Theory Into Practice, 7*:10, Feb., 1968.

Reisman, D.: *Foreward in R. Heath: The Reasonable Adventurer.* Pittsburgh,

University of Pittsburgh Pr, 1964.

Reisman, Frank: *Helping the Disadvantaged Pupil to Learn More Easily.* Englewood Cliffs, Prentice-Hall, 1966.

Rogers, Carl: *Freedom to Learn.* Columbus, Merrill, 1969.

Rosenthal, Robert: The pygmalion effect lives. *Psychology Today,* 7:56, September, 1973.

Rosenthal, Robert, and Jacobson, Lenore: *Pygmalion in the Classroom.* New York, HR & W, 1968.

Ryans, David G.: *Characteristics of Teachers: A Research Study.* Washington, Amerikn Council on Education, 1960.

Sears, Pauline S., and Hilgard, Ernest R.: Theories of Learning and Instruction. National Society for the Study of Education. *Sixty-Third Yearbook.* 1964.

Sears, Pauline: Levels of aspiration in academically successful and unsuccessful children. *J of Abnormal and Social Psychology, 35*:498, 1940.

Simon, Sidney B.: Grades must go! *School Review, 78*:397, May, 1970.

Skinner, B. F.: *The Technology of Teaching.* New York, Appleton, 1968.

Smith, James O., and Arkans, Joan R.: Now more than ever: A case for the special class. *Except Child, 40*:497, April, 1974.

Spalding, R. B., and Spalding, W. T.:*The Writing Road to Reading.* New York, Morrow, 1957.

Stallings, W. M., and Leslie, E. K.: Student attitudes towards grades and grading. *Improving College and University Teaching, 18*:66, Winter, 1970.

Sumption, Merle R., and Lueeking, Evelyn M.: *Education of the Gifted.* New York, Ronald, 1960.

Terman, L. M.: *Genetic Studies of Genius.* Stanford, Stanford U Pr, 1925-1959, vols I-V.

Torrance, E. Paul: Curiosity of gifted children and performance on timed and untimed tests of creativity. *Gifted Child Quarterly,13*:155, Autumn, 1969.

Torrance, E. Paul: *Guarding Creative Talents.* Englewood Cliffs, Prentice-Hall, 1962.

Torrance E. Paul, and Storm, Robert (Eds.): *Mental Health And Achievement.* New York, Wiley, 1965.

Travers, Robert M. W.: *Essentials of Learning,* 3rd ed. New York, McMillan, 1972.

Waetzen, Walter B.: The Teacher and Motivation. *Theory Into Practice, 9*:10, Feb., 1970.

Wallace, Gerald, et al.: *Teaching Children with Learning Problems.* Columbus, Merrill, 1973.

Weller, Jack: *Yesterdays' People.* Lexington, U of Kentucky Pr, 1965.

Werts, C. E.: The Many Faces of Intelligence. *J Educ Psychol, 58*:198, 1967.

Witty, Paul (Ed.): *The Gifted Child.* Boston, Heath, 1951.

Wrinkle, William: *Improving Marking and Reporting Practices in Elementary and Secondary Schools.* New York, HR & W, 1947.

ADDITIONAL READING LIST

Abraham, Willard: *Common Sense About Gifted Children.* New York, Har-Row, 1958.

Alanishah, William H.: Blockings to creativity. *The Journal of Creative Behavior.* 6:105, 1972.

Arena, J. E.: Instrument for individualizing instruction. *Educational Leader,* 27:775, May, 1970.

Aylesworth, Thomas G., and Reagan, Gerald M.: *Teaching for Thinking.* Garden City, Doubleday, 1969.

Badley, Betty Hunt, et al.: *Teaching Moderately and Severely Retarded Children: A Diagnostic Approach.* Springfield, Thomas, 1971.

Bannatyne, Alexander: *Language, Reading and Learning Disabilities.* Springfield, Thomas, 1971.

Bannatyne, Alexander, et al.: One-to-one process analysis of learning disability tutorial sessions, part II. *Journal of Learning Disabilities, 3*:509, October, 1970.

Barbe, Walter F. (Ed.): *Psychology and Education of the Gifted.* New York, Appleton, 1965.

Barker, Roger C.: Success and failure in the classroom. *Progressive Education, 19*:221, 1942.

Barr, A. S.: *Wisconsin Studies of the Measurement and Prediction of Teacher Effectiveness.* Madison, Dunbar Publications, 1961.

Baymur, Feriha B., and Patterson, C. H.: A comparison of three methods of assisting underachieving high school students. In Gallagher, James J. (Ed.): *Teaching Gifted Students.* Boston, Allyn, 1965.

Beatty, Walcot H.: Emotions: The missing link in education. *Theory Into Practice, 8*:86, April, 1969.

Beck, I. L., and Bolvin, J. O.: Model for nongradedness: The reading program for individually prescribed instruction. *Elementary English, 46*:130, Feb., 1969.

Becker, Wesley C., et al.: *Teaching: A Course in Applied Psychology.* Chicago, Science Research Associates, 1971.

Beez, W. Victor: Influence of psychological reports on teacher behavior and pupil performance. *Proceedings of the American Psychological Association Convention,* 1968, p. 605.

Berg, D. W.: Independent study; transfusion for anemic english programs. *English Journal, 59*:254, Feb., 1970.

241

Boder, Elena: Developmental dyslexia: Diagnostic screening patterns based on three characteristic patterns of reading and spelling. Claremont, Calif. Claremont Reading Conference, 1968.

Borg, Walter F.: *Ability Grouping in the Public Schools.* Madison, Dembar Educational Research Services, 1966.

Bowley, Agatha H., and Gardner, Leslie: *The Young Handicapped Child.* London, E. and S. Livingstone, Ltd., 1969.

Broome, Elizabeth: *Educating for the Future.* Raliegh, Dept. of Public Instruction of N. C., 1973.

Brown, Frank B.: *The Appropriate Placement School.* West Nyack, Parker, 1965.

Brown, Frank B.: *Education by Appointment.* West Nyack, Parker, 1968.

Buckland, Pearl, and Balow, Bruce: Effect of visual perceptual training in reading achievement. *Except Child, 39*:299, Jan., 1973.

Budoff, Milton: Providing special education without special classes. *Journal of School Psychology, 10*:199, 1972.

Bush, Clifford L., and Huebner, Mildren H.: *Strategies for Reading in the Elementary School.* New York, MacMillan, 1970.

Butler, L.: Performance objectives for individual instruction. *AV Instruction, 15*:45, May, 1970.

Carin, Arthur A., and Suno, Robert B.: *Teaching Science Through Discovery,* 2nd ed. Columbus, Merrill, 1970.

Christoplos, Florence: Keeping exceptional children in regular classes. *Except Child, 39*:569, April, 1973.

Clark, Donald H., and Kades, Asya L.: *Humanistic Teaching.* Columbus, Merrill, 1971.

Cook, Desmond L.: The Hawthorn Effect in education research. *Phi Delta Kappan, 44*:116, Dec., 1962.

College and University Bulletin. Conference on Student Suicide. December, 15, 1968.

Combs, Arthur W.: The myth of competition. *Childhood Education, 23*:264, 1957.

Commissioner of Education, U. S. Dept. H.E.W.: *Education of the Gifted and Talented.* Washington, U. S. Government Printing Office, 1972.

Coopersmith, Stanley: *The Antecedents for Self-Esteem.* San Francisco, Freeman, 1967.

Cortines, R. C.: Reaching the underachiever through media. *A. V. Instruction, 13*:952, Nov., 1968.

Cowen, Emory L., and Lorion, Raymond P.: Which kids are helped? *Journal of Special Education, 8*:187, Summer, 1974.

Cratty, Bryant J.: *Active Learning.* Englewood Cliffs, P-H, 1971.

Cruickshank, William M., et al.: *Misfits in the Public Schools.* Syracuse, Syracuse Pr, 1969.

Dallmann, Martha, et al.: *The Teaching of Reading,* 4th ed. New York, HR & W, 1974.

Davidson, H. H., and Lang, G.: Children's perceptions of their teachers' feelings towards them related to self-perception, school achievement and behavior. *J Exper Psychol, 29*:107, 1926.

De Cecco, John P.: *The Psychology of Learning and Instruction.* Englewood Cliffs, P-H, 1968.

Delaney, A. A.: When students rate their teachers. *Peabody Journal of Education, 37*:222, Jan., 1960.

Dinkmeyer, D., and Dreikus, R.: *Encouraging Children to Learn.* Englewood Cliffs, P-H, 1963.

Dreikurs, Rudolph, et al.: *Maintaining Sanity in the Classroom: Illustrated Teaching Techniques.* New York, Har-Row, 1971.

Drowne, F.: Individualizing instruction through the use of tapes. *AV Instruction, 14*:41, May 1969.

Dugan, R. R.: Personality and the effective teacher. *Journal of Teacher Education, 25*:345, 1974.

Dunn, Lloyd M.: *Exceptional Children in the Schools,* 2nd ed. New York, HR & W, 1973.

Dunn, Lloyd M.: Special education for the mildly retarded — Is much of it justifiable? *Except Child, 35*:5, Sept., 1968.

Dunn, Rita, and Dunn, Kenneth: *Practical Approaches to Individualizing Instruction.* West Nyack, Parker, Peabody, 1972.

Durrell, D. D.: *Durrell Analysis of Reading Difficulty.* New York, HarBrace J, 1955.

Eaves, Linda C., and Kendall, D. C., and Crichton, M. B.: The early detection of minimal brain dysfunction. *Journal of Learning Disabilities, 5*:454, Oct., 1972.

Engle, Kenneth B., et al.: Interpersonal effects on underachievers. *Journal of Educational Research, 61*:208, January, 1968.

Esbensen, Thorwald: *Working with Individualized Instruction: The Duluth Experience.* Palo Alto, Fearon, 1968.

Feature Editorial. Special education: A major event in 1973. *Phi Delta Kappan, 50*:513, April, 1974.

Fliegler, Louis A.: Factors which affect motivation and achievement of the culturally different. *Gifted Child Newsletter, 11*:40, March, 1962.

Forness, Steven R., and MacMillan, D. L.: The origins of behavior modification with exceptional children. *Except Child, 37*:93, Oct., 1970.

Frazier, Alexander (Ed.): *Freeing Capacity to Learn.* Papers and Reports from Fourth ASCD Research Institute. Washington, Association for Supervision and Curriculum Development, NEA, 1960.

Frazier, A.: Individualized instruction. *Educational Leader, 25*:616, April, 1968.

French, Lois: How does it feel to fail? In Torrance, E. P., et al. (Eds.): *Mental Health and Achievement.* New York, Wiley, 1965.

French, Joseph, L. (Ed.): *Educating the Gifted: A Book of Readings.* New York, HR & W, 1960.

Freymeir, Jack R.: Learning and life: Some answers must be questioned. *Theory into Practice, 8*:36, Feb., 1969.

Freymeir, J. R. (Ed.): Pressures on children. *Theory Into Practice, 7*:4 Feb., 1968 (Editorial).

Frostig, Marianne, and Maslow, Phyllis: *Learning Problems in the Classroom: Prevention and Remediation.* New York, Grune, 1973.

Fuller, Renee: Breaking down the I.Q. wall "severely retarded people can learn to read." *Psychology Today, 8*:96, Oct., 1974.

Gallagher, James (Ed.): *Talent Delayed - Talent Denied - The Culturally Different Gifted Child.* Reston, Va., The Foundation for Exceptional Children, 1974.

Gallagher, James: Phenomenal growth and new problems characterize special education. *Phi Delta Kappan, 55*:516, April, 1974.

Galloway, Charles, et al.: Body languages. *Today's Education, 61*:32, Dec., 1972.

Galloway, Charles: Nonverbal communication. *Theory Into Practice, 9*:172, Dec., 1968.

Garrett, Harry E.: *The Art of Good Teaching.* New York, McKay, 1964.

Gates, A. I., and McKillap, A. S.: Gates-McKillap Reading Diagnostic Tests. New York, Teachers' College, 1962.

Garton, Malinda, Dean: *Teaching the Educable Mentally Retarded.* Springfield, Thomas, 1970.

Garvey, J. F.: Possible over emphasis on large group instruction. *Education, 89*:213, Feb., 1969.

Gillespie, Patricia H., and Johnson Lowell E.: *Teaching Reading to the Mildly Retarded Child.* Columbus, Merrill, 1974.

Ginsburg, Herbert: *The Myth of the Deprived Child: Poor Children's Intellect and Education.* Englewood Cliffs, P-H, 1972.

Glavach, Matt, and Stoner, Donnovan: Breaking the failure pattern. *Journal of Learning Disabilities, 3*:106, Feb., 1970.

Gowan, John Curtis, and Torrance E. Paul (Eds.): *Educating the Ablest: A Book of Readings on the Education of Gifted Children.* Itaska, Peacock, 1971.

Gozali, Joav, and Meyen, Edward L.: The influence of the teacher expectancy phenomenon on the academic performance of EMR pupils in special classes. *Journal of Special Education, 4*:417, Fall-Winter, 1970.

Greene, David et al.: Intrinsic motication: How to turn play into work. *Psychology Today, 8*:49, Sept., 1974.

Grimes, Jesse W., and Allinsmith, Wesley: Compulsivity, anxiety and school achievement. *Merrill-Palmer Quarterly, 7*:247, 1961.

Grzynkowicz, Wineva M.: *Teaching Inefficient Learners.* Springfield, Thomas, 1971.

Hallahan, Daniel, and Cruickshank, William: *Psychoeducational Foundation of Learning Disabilities.* Englewood Cliffs, P-H, 1973.

Hammill, Donald: The resource room model in special education. *Journal of Special Education, 6*:354, Winter, 1972.

Hammill, Donald P., and Partel, Nettie R.: *Educational Perspectives in Learning Disabilities.* New York, Wiley, 1972.

Heath, Douglas H.: Student alienation and school. *School Review, 78:*515, August, 1970.

Heller, Harold W.: The resource room: A mere change of real opportunity for the handicapped. *Journal of Special Education, 6:*369, Winter, 1972.

Heil, C. M.: Characteristics of teachers related to children's progress. *Journal of Teacher Education, 12:*401, 1961.

Hewett, Frank M., and Forness, Steven R.: *Education of Exceptional Learners.* Boston, Allyn, 1974.

Hilbard, E. R., et al.: Levels of aspiration as affected by relative standing in an experimental social group. *J Exper Psychol, 27:*411, 1924.

Holt, John: *How Children Fail.* New York, Pitman, 1964.

Holt, John: *The Underachieving School.* New York, Pitman, 1969.

Hoppe, F.: Erfolg and Misserfolg. *Psychol Forsch, 14:*1, 1930.

Hunter, M.: Tailor your teaching to individualized instruction. *Instructor, 79:*53, March, 1970.

Iano, Richard P.: Shall we disband special classes? *Journal of Special Education, 6:*167, Summer, 1972.

Illich, Ivan: *Deschooling Society.* New York, Har-Row, 1971.

Jacobs, John F., and DeGraaf, Carl A.: Expectancy and race: Their influences on intelligence test scores. *Except Child, 40:*108, Oct., 1973.

Jacobson, J.: Learning is a highly personalized matter. *Social Education, 32:*707, Nov., 1968.

Jansky, Jeanette, and DeHirsch, Katrina: *Preventing Reading Failure: Prediction, Diagnosis, Intervention.* New York, Har-Row, 1972.

Jones, Charles J.: *Learning.* New York, HarBrace J, 1967.

Jones, R. L., et al.: Modifying perceptions of trainable mental retardates. *Except Child, 34:*309, Jan., 1968.

Josik, M.: Breaking barriers by individualizing. *Childhood Education, 45:*65, Oct., 1968.

Kaplan, A.: Individualization without nongradedness. *Instructor, 79:*66, Feb., 1970.

Kaplan, Louis: *Education and Mental Health.* New York, Har-Row, 1971.

Kegel, C. H.: The distinguished teacher. *Improving College and University Teaching, 12:*102, Spring, 1964.

Keogh, Barbara, and Becker, Lawrence: Early detection of learning problems: Questions, cautions, and guidelines. *Except Child, 40:*5, Sept., 1973.

Kirk, Samuel: *Educating Exceptional Children,* 2nd ed. Boston, HM, 1972.

Kozal, J.: *Death at an Early Age.* Boston, HM, 1967.

Krauch, Velma: Hyperactive engineering. *American Education, 7:*12, June, 1971.

Krippner, Stanley: The use of hypnosis and the improvement of academic achievement. *Journal of Special Education, 4:*451, Fall-Winter, 1970.

Lee, D. M.: Do we group in an individualized program? *Childhood Education, 45:*197, Dec., 1968.

Lembo, John M.: *Why Teachers Fail.* Columbus, Merrill, 1971.

Leonard, George B.: *Education and Ecstacy.* New York, Delacorte, 1968.

Lerner, Janet W.: *Children with Learning Disabilities, Theories, Diagnosis, and Teaching Strategies.* Boston, HM, 1971.

Lewis, James, Jr.: *A Contemporary Approach to Nongraded Education.* West Nyack, Parker, 1969.

Lewis, James, Jr.: *Administering the Individualized Instruction Program.* West Nyack, Parker, 1971.

Lewis, Wilbert W.: From project re-ed to ecological planning. *Phi Delta Kappan, 55*:538, April, 1974.

Lifton, Walter M. (Ed.): *Educating For Tomorrow.* New York, Wiley, 1970.

Logan, Frank A.: *Learning and Motivation.* Fundamentals of Psychology Series. Dubuque, Brown, 1970.

Lovitt, Thomas: behavior modification: The current scene. *Except Child, 37*:85, Oct., 1970.

Lundstedt, Suen: Criteria for effective teaching. *Improving College and University Teaching, 15*:27, Winter, 1967.

Lyon, Harold C.: Talent down the drain. *Am Educ, 8*:12, Oct. 1972.

MacKinnon, P. W.: What do we mean by talent, and how do we test for it? *The Search for Talent.* New York, College Entrance Examination Board, 1960.

Mager, Robert F., and Pipe, Peter: *Analyzing Performance Problems.* Belmont, Liegler, 1970.

Mager, Robert F.: *Developing Attitude Toward Learning.* Palo Alto, Fearon, 1970.

Mann, Philip, and Suiter, Patricia: *Handbook in Diagnosis Teaching, A Learning Disabilities Approach.* Boston, Allyn, 1974.

Manning, Duane: *A Humanistic Curriculum.* New York, Har-Row, 1971.

Martin, Edwin W.: Individualism and behaviorism as future trends in educating handicapped children. *Except Child, 38*:317, March, 1972.

Medlley, D. M.: Teacher personality and teacher-pupil rapport. *Journal of Teacher Education, 12*:152, 1961.

Mellen, M. E.: Individualizing: To stimulate the slow reader. *Grade Teachers, 85*:109, March, 1968.

Michaelis, John V.: *Social Studies for Children in a Democracy.* Englewood Cliffs, P-H, 1972.

Meyers, Patricia I., and Hammill, Donald O.: *Methods for Learning Disorders.* New York, Wiley, 1969.

Mill, C. R.: Attitudes affect pupil's learning. *Educational Leadership, 17*:212, January, 1960.

Miller, Richard I.: *The Non-Graded School.* New York, Har-Row, 1967.

Miller, S.: *Measure, Number and Weight: A Polemeical Statement of the College Grading Policy.* Knoxville, Learning Resources Center, University of Tennessee, 1967.

Moustakes, Clark: *Creativity and Conformity.* Princeton, D. Van Nostrand Company, 1967.

Muscatine, C.: *Education at Berkeley*, Berkeley; University of California, 1966.

Myres, Patricia I., and Hammill, Donald: *Methods For Learning Disorders*. New York, Wiley, 1969.

National Advisory Committee On Dyslexia and Related Reading Disorders: *Reading Disorders in the United States*. Washington, Department of Health, Education and Welfare, 1969.

National Institute of Mental Health: Delinquency decreases when students drop out. *Psychology Today, 9:*22, June, 1970.

NEA Reporter: Are you more accountable than you think. *NEA Reporter, 13:*5, May, 1974.

Newsnotes: New York finds schools count on reading achievement. *Phi Delta Kappan, 55:*721, June, 1974.

Novack, Harry S., et al.: A scale for early detection of children with learning disabilities. *Except Child, 40:*98, Oct., 1973.

Ogston, T. J.: Individualized instruction: Changing the role of the teacher. *AV Instruction, 13:*243, Mar., 1968.

Opulente, B. J.: The great teacher is a creative individual. *Improving College and University Teaching, 13:*89, Spring, 1965.

Oho, Wayne, et al.: *Corrective and Remedial Teaching*. Boston, H-M, 1973.

Passow, A. Harry: *Intellectual Development: Another Look*. Washington, Association for Supervision and Curriculum Development, 1964.

Payne, James S., et al.: *Exceptional Children in Focus*. Columbus, Merrill, 1974.

Pines, Maya: *Revolution in Learning*. New York, Har-Row, 1966.

Powell, Robert S.: Participation is learning. *Saturday Review, 56:*53, January 10, 1970.

Preston, R. Wilcox: Teachers' attitudes and student achievement. *Teacher's College Record, 68:*371, Feb., 1967.

Rafferty, Max: *Suffer, Little Children*. New York, Signal, 1962.

Raths, Louis E.: Security among one's peers. *Teaching For Learning*. Columbus, Merrill, 1969.

Raths, Louis E.: What is a good teacher? *Childhood Education, 40:*56, May, 1964.

Rice, Joseph P.: *The Gifted: Developing Total Talent*. Springfield, Thomas, 1970.

Reissman, Frank: *Helping the Disadvantaged Pupil to Learn More Easily*. Englewood Cliffs, P-H, 1966.

Richards, J. M., et al.: The prediction of student accomplishment in college. *J Educ Psychol, 58:*343, 1967.

Ripple, R. E.: Affective factors influence classroom learning. *Educational Leadership, 22:*476, April, 1965.

Rivlin, Harry N.: Teaching and teacher education for urban disadvantaged schools. *Journal of Teacher Education, 16:*136, June, 1965.

Rogow, Sally, and David, Charlotte: Special education: Perspectives, trends, issues. *Phi Delta Kappan, 50:*514, April, 1974.

Rosenthal, Robert, et al.: Body talk and tone of voice; The language without words. *Psychology Today, 8*:64, Sept., 1974.

Rosenthal, Robert: Self-fulfilling prophecy. *Psychology Today, 24*:44, Sept., 1968.

Roswell, Florence, and Natchez, Gladys: *Reading Disability: Diagnosis and Treatment.* New York, Basic, 1964.

Rubin, Louis J. (Ed.): *Life Skills in School and Society. ASCD 1969 Yearbook.* Washington, Association for Supervision and Curriculum Development, NEA, 1969.

Ruch, Lloyd L.: *Psychology and Life,* 7th ed. New York, Scott F, 1967.

Sabatino, David A.: Resource rooms: The renaissance in special education. *The Journal of Special Education, 6*:335, Winter, 1972.

Sanders, Norris M.: *Classroom Questions: What Kinds?* New York, Har-Row, 1966.

Sanford, Nevitt: Ego process in learning. In Lambert, Nadine et al. (Eds.): *The Protection and Promotion of Mental Health in Schools.* Public Health Service Publication Number 1226. Washington, Department of Health, Education and Welfare, 1964.

Schueler, Herbert, and Lesser, Gerald: *Teacher Education and the New Media.* Washington, The American Association of Colleges for Teachers, 1967.

Scoby, M. M., and Graham, Grace (Eds.): *To Nurture Humaneness.* 1970 Yearbook ASCD. Washington, Association for Supervision and Curriculum Development, NEA, 1970.

Sexton, Michael J.: Which students are yours? The turned off? The turned on? *Today's Education, 62*:20, Mar., 1973.

Siegel, Ernest: *Special Education in the Regular Classroom.* New York, Day, 1969.

Silberman, Charles: *Crisis in the Classroom.* New York, Random, 1970.

Skinner, B. F.: Reinforcement today. *Am Psychol, 13*:94, March, 1958.

Smith, Robert M.: *Clinical Teaching: Methods of Instruction for the Retarded,* 2nd ed. New York, McGraw, 1974.

Smith, Robert M.: *Teacher Diagnosis of Educational Difficulties.* Columbus, Merrill, 1969.

Solomon, R. L., and Wynne, L. C.: Traumatic Avoidance Learning. *Psychol Rev, 51*:353, 1965.

Spache, G. D.: *Diagnostic Reading Scales.* Monterey, McGraw-Hill, 1963.

Spodek, Bernard: Pressures on young children. *Theory into Practice, 9*:14, February, 1968.

Spong, H., et al.: Selective attentiveness and cortical evoked responses to visual and auditory stimuli. *Science, 48*:397, April 17, 1965.

Stabler, E.: What is this thing called love? *Peabody Journal of Education, 37*:338, May, 1960.

Stahl, Dona Kofod, and Anzalone, Patricia: *Individualized Teaching in Elementary School.* West Nyack, Parker, 1970.

Steinberg, Ira S.: *Education Myths and Realities.* Reading, Addison-Wesley, 1968.

Stephens, John M.: *The Psychology of Classroom Learning.* New York, HR & W, 1965.

Stephens, Thomas M.: *Directed Teaching of Children With Learning and Behavioral Handicaps.* Columbus, Merrill, 1970.

Storm, Robert D.: School evaluation and mental health. *The High School Journal.* October, 1964.

Tanner, Laurel N., and Lindgren, H. C.: *Classroom Teaching and Learning: A Mental Health Approach.* New York, HR & W, 1971.

Thomas, George I., and Crescimbeni, Joseph: *Individualizing Instruction in the Elementary School.* New York, Random, 1967.

Tinbergen, Nikolaas: Ethology and stress diseases. *Science, 185*:145, July 5, 1974.

Turner, T. N.: Individualization through inquiry. *Social Education, 34*:72, Jan., 1970.

Vallett, Robert E.: *Effective Teaching, A Guide to Diagnostic - Prescriptive Task Analysis.* Belmont, Fearon, 1970.

Vallett, Robert E.: *Prescriptions for Learning — A Parent's Guide to Remedial Home Training.* Belmont, Fearon, 1970.

Waetjen, Walter B., and Leeper, Robert R. (Eds.): *Learning and Mental Health in the School.* Washington, NEA, Association for Supervision and Curriculum Development, 1966.

Wallach, M. E., and Wing, C. W.: *The Talented Student.* New York, HR & W, 1969.

Wayne, Otto, et al.: *Corrective and Remedial Teaching,* 2nd ed. Boston, HM, 1973.

Webster, H., et al.: Personality changes in college students. In Sanford, N. (Ed.): *The American College.* New York, Wiley, 1962.

White House Conference on Children and Youth: A healthy personality for every child. Washington, Midcentury Whitehouse Conference on Children and Youth, 1951.

Wilson, John A. R. (Ed.): *Diagnosis of Learning Difficulties.* New York, McGraw, 1971.

Wilson, Robert M.: *Diagnostic and Remedial Reading for Classroom and Clinic.* Columbus, Merrill, 1972.

Wilson, S. R., and Tosti, D. T.: *Learning Is Getting Easier.* San Raefael, Calif. Individual Learning Systems, Inc. 1972.

Wolfson, B., and Wolfson, J.: Pupil and teacher roles in individualized instruction. *Elementary School Journal, 68*:357, April, 1968.

Wright, D.: Try a quest. *English Journal, 59*:131, Jan., 1970.

Yates, James R.: Model for preparing regular classroom teachers of 'mainstreaming.' *Except Child, 39*:471, March 1973.

Zeller, Robert: *Lowering the Odds on Student Dropouts.* Englewood Cliffs, P-H, 1966.

APPENDIX

Boehm Test of Basic Concepts
  Psychological Corporation
  304 East 45th St.
  New York, New York 10017
Detroit Tests of Learning Aptitude (1967)
  Bobbs-Merrill Co., Inc.
  Test Division
  4300 West 62nd St.
  Indianapolis, Indiana 46206
The Marianne Frostig Developmental Test
  of Visual perception (1966)
  Consulting Psychologists Press
  Palo Alto, California
Gates-MacGinitie Reading Tests
  Bobbs-Merrill Col, Inc.
  Test Division
  4300 West 62nd St.
  Indianapolis, Indiana 46206
Gilmore Oral Reading Test (1968)
  Harcourt, Brace & World, Inc.
  Atlanta, Georgia
Goldman - Fristoe - Woocock Test of
  Auditory Discrimination
  American Guidance Service, Inc.
  Publishers' Building
  Circle Pines, Minnesota 55014
Key Math Diagnostic Arithmetic Test
  American Guidance Service, Inc.
  Publishers' Building
  Circle Pines, Minnesota 55014
Peabody Picture Vocabulary Test

American Guidance Service, Inc.
Publishers' Building
Circle Pines, Minnesota 55014
Peabody Individual Achievement Test
American Guidance Service, Inc.
Publishers' Buildilng
Circle Pines, Minnesota 55014
Slingerland Screening Tests for Identifying
Children with Specific Language Disability
Educators Publishing Service, Inc.
Cambridge, Massachusetts 02138
Spache Diagnostic Reading Scales
Belmonte Research Park
Monterey, California 93940
Auditory Discrimination Test
Joseph M. Wepman, Ph.D.
Special Education Materials, Inc.
484 So. Broadway
Yonders, New York 10705
A Basic Screening and Referral Form
for Children with Suspected Learning
and Behavioral Disabilities
Robert E. Valett, Ed. D.
Lear Sieglar, Inc.
Fearon Publishers
Belmont, California

INDEX